Page	Section	Title	Author
1	Front	Datacatcher	Interaction Research Studio

Datacatcher
Interaction Research Studio
www.gold.ac.uk/interaction

Edited by Andy Boucher, Dave Cameron, Bill Gaver and Sarah Pennington
Design by Hyperkit
Printed by Lecturis, Eindhoven

ISBN 978-1-906897-35-2

First published in Great Britain in 2015 by Goldsmiths, University of London, New Cross, London SE14 6NW

Additional copies of this publication are available from Interaction Research Studio, Department of Design, Goldsmiths, University of London, New Cross, London SE14 6NW.

This publication has been supported by the European Research Council's Advanced Investigator Award no. 226528.

About the Interaction Research Studio

The Interaction Research Studio in the Design Department at Goldsmiths explores the design of computational systems for everyday life. Our practice-based research integrates design-led research methods with work on embedded and ubiquitous technologies to produce prototype products embodying new concepts for interaction. We don't pursue design as problem solving, but instead design products to create situations that encourage playfulness, exploration and insight.

Because our prototypes are evocative and open ended, a crucial part of our process involves asking volunteers to live with our designs to see how their experiences evolve. The outcomes of our work include articles and exhibitions that expose our philosophies, methods and empirical work to academic, industrial and general publics.

The Datacatcher studio team: Andy Boucher, Dave Cameron, Bill Gaver, Mark Hauenstein, Nadine Jarvis, Jen Molinera, Liliana Ovalle, Sarah Pennington.

Acknowledgements

This research has been supported by the European Research Council.

With extra special thanks to James Pike and Robin Beitra for all their data wrangling.

Thanks also to Paul Basford, Matias Bjorndahl, Kirsten Boehner, John Bowers, Alan Boyles, Richard Cook, Chaka Films, Michael Guggenheim, Marine Guichard, Nia Hughes, Robin Hunter, Tobie Kerridge, Doh Lee, Ros Lerner, Jamahl Lindsay, Eleanor Margolies, Kitty McMahon, Mary Mead, Sebastian Melo, Lee Murray, Belén Palacios, Veronika Papadopoulou, Cristina Picchi, Matthew Plummer-Fernandez, Jonathan Rowley, Jared Schiller, Kate Sclater, Charles Staples, Alex Taylor, UsCreates, Nicolas Villar, Alex Wilkie, Justin Wilson.

Contributors

Robin Beitra is a creative programmer working in London.

Kirsten Boehner is a researcher in the Public Design Workshop group at the Georgia Institute of Technology, USA.

John Bowers is Professor of Creative Digital Practice at Culture Lab, Newcastle University.

Richard Cook is a charity worker and writer living in London.

Michael Guggenheim is a Senior Lecturer and Senior Research Fellow in the Department of Sociology, Goldsmiths, University of London.

Mark Hauenstein is a creative programmer now working at Apple.

Robin Hunter is studying for a BA in Computing at Goldsmiths.

Lee Murray is a Senior Design Technologist at Microsoft.

Belén Palacios is a freelance designer.

James Pike is a creative programmer working in London.

Jonathan Rowley is Design Director of Digits2Widgets, a 3D printing studio in London.

This book is about the Datacatcher

Author

Interaction Research Studio

The Datacatcher is a mobile device with a screen on one end and a large control dial set in a recess underneath. Short sentences appear on the screen every few seconds, providing facts about the surrounding area. Topics include average house prices, typical income, the number of pubs or of GP surgeries. Turning the dial one way scrolls through all the messages that have appeared on the device; turning it the other way accesses a set of poll questions that can be answered using the dial to select among alternatives.

The Datacatcher was designed to support multiple orientations. Its primary use is to give a sense of the sociopolitical texture of the neighbourhoods where it is used. The messages are derived from public and private datasets, such as the census and credit agency data. As we will explain, our initial motivation was to support an expanded view of environmental issues by linking them to related concerns. The Datacatchers are also relevant to current activities aimed at making data more transparent and empowering — indeed, during a test of an early version of the Datacatcher, one participant said that it presented 'Big Data for little people'.

To understand the multiple engagements the Datacatcher would afford, we manufactured 130 prototypes and distributed them to people in the Greater London area, who used them for up to two months. Before this project, our usual studio practice was to build one-off prototypes to be loaned to one or a few participants at a time. Integral to our funding bid — accepted for 5-year-funding by the European Research Council — was the goal of batch producing prototypes to lend to many participants simultaneously. This project is the last phase of that programme and represents a massive expansion in our capability, as we moved from building tens to hundreds of research prototypes. It was also the riskiest tranche of the research as we invested in developing a device more technically advanced than anything we had built before.

Designing, developing, and managing the deployment of so many research devices meant that, at various times, the studio had to expand significantly. This publication reflects that growth by incorporating viewpoints and descriptions of practices from the many people involved with the project, even if their involvement was brief, or tangential. Their diverse voices tell the story of how the Datacatcher developed from early conceptual ideas, though development dramas and hurdles to its deployment to people in and around London.

The sections of this book — Politikos, Something about, Develop, Manufacture, Participants, And then, Voices — show the trajectory of the project with dozens of images and short texts, but this is still only a small selection of the vast number of ideas and proposals generated by the project. Though the contents are an edited selection, we have tried to include a fair number of red herrings — design paths not taken because of technical challenges or time restrictions — because these may be of interest in their own right.

Although this publication predominantly focuses on the processes around the design of the Datacatcher as a device, perhaps the true outcome of this project — of any of our projects — are the participants' experiences during its deployment. We hired two documentary filmmaking teams to capture these experiences, and a selection from the transcripts of their videos can be found in the final section of this book. It is the participants' voices that tell us what it is we have made. This is not a simple and unitary narrative, however; each one has their own version to tell, and the experiences they describe vary so widely they might be describing different devices. Rather than producing a clear account then, the voices mingle and weave to create a kind of polyphonic, fragmentary story of the Datacatcher — one that will resonate through our future research and practice.

Contents

Politikos

Politikos

Research through design can seem like the most difficult thing in the world: there's so much to be done.

Each project involves a string of challenges: to find a fertile area for exploration, investigate it empirically and conceptually, explore possible design directions, choose a particular one to develop, and then design, produce and field test a device that works technically, aesthetically, and socially, and so on.

The start of a new project is particularly daunting. Design-led research does not have clients in the traditional sense. The only brief is a funding proposal we have written ourselves, usually about a year earlier — and we purposely avoid saying exactly what we'll do in our proposals. That way we can follow our interests as the project develops. But the result is that, even at the best of times, starting a project is like sitting down in front of a blank page of paper.

This project was even more fraught than usual.

This project was tricky to begin because of its history.

The original proposal was more than four years old by the time we started. During the intervening time, we had produced another set of prototypes. These established a course of development that was successful in many ways, but less so in others.

The easy thing to do would have been to build on our earlier work. But we didn't want to do the easy thing. We wanted to do something new. We wanted to do more.

So the opening phase of this project involved finding a new direction for our designs. We needed to weave the broad aims of the original proposal with the lessons we had learned from the work just finished. More than that, we wanted to reflect new thinking about the environment, both our own and that of colleagues in our field. And even more than that, we wanted to reflect larger trends in society. We wanted to make our work political.

And so the project began.

In this section we describe how our thinking evolved from this beginning to the first brief for the Datacatchers. Starting with our earlier designs, we explain the thinking that led us to — and ultimately beyond — a political view of environmental issues. Then we show images from an exhibition of political art that we curated, as a way of exposing ourselves to work by fellow travellers. The section culminates in a brief, produced in a moment of inspiration that was to guide the project to its end.

Title

Where the beginning was

Author

Bill Gaver

We started the Datacatcher project as the third phase of a programme of work funded by the European Research Council. The overall aim of the research was to investigate batch producing and deploying dozens of devices that took a playful, non-prescriptive approach to environmental issues.

In the project before the Datacatcher, we had developed about 22 sets of 'Indoor Weather Stations' for people to try in their homes. These were small domestic appliances that we intended to draw attention to the microclimate of the home, both as an indirect way of pointing to the ways energy is used and as a kind of conceptual rhyme to the planet's climate.

There are three Indoor Weather Stations in each set. The Wind Tunnel has a sensor mounted on its 'chimney' which picks up tiny gusts of air; these are magnified by a fan in its canopy to visibly buffet a forest of laser-cut 'trees'. The Temperature Tape has two 2.5m-long ribbon cables with temperature sensors in a hook and eye on either end; a dial on the device's body shows the temperature difference between the two ends. The Light Collector adds a pixel-deep strip of colour to the top of its display every 10 minutes, building a profile of the ambient light colour surrounding the device.

The Weather Stations were designed as an alternative to the energy monitors frequently deployed as a way of reducing energy consumption. Monitors tend not to be very effective, and are implicitly disciplinarian, admonishing their users to cut energy consumption even in circumstances where that is difficult or impossible. We wanted to explore a less didactic, gentler approach to environmental reflection.

We gave the Weather Stations to 20 volunteer households to try for about half a year. The results were good — most people were positive about the devices, even if they didn't engage with them for long. Some described the devices as 'like curious visitors' in their homes, quietly reminding them about activities and patterns in their homes, seasonal changes, and the continuities and discontinuities between inside and outside environments.

The Weather Stations point to an interesting trajectory for devices meant to support reflection about the environment. Rather than nagging us about our responsibilities, they balance data and aesthetics, reminding us in subtler ways of the environments we construct.

In taking the work on further, however, we wanted to go beyond the home, and indeed beyond 'the environment' as an understood topic for research. The Weather Stations served well to soften the stridency of environmental monitors, but perhaps at the expense of drawing too far into the aesthetics of the home, and away from a confrontation with the global realities of environmental change.

Rather than building directly on the Weather Stations project then, we started to explore other possibilities.

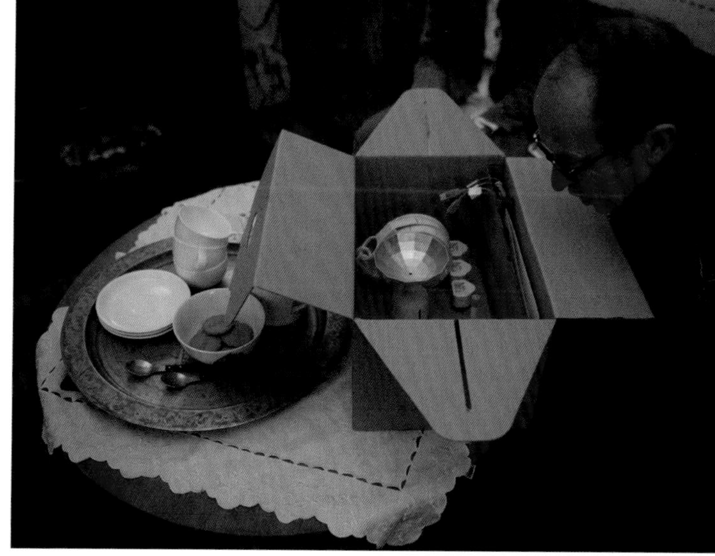

The Indoor Weather Stations, developed in a previous phase of the project, highlighted the domestic microclimate as a way to open thinking about environmental issues.

Title

The environment in a larger context

Author

Bill Gaver

In addition to the trajectory of our own work, there were a number of developments around us that were pointing us in new directions.

In the field of Human-Computer Interaction (HCI), researchers interested in developing 'environmental HCI' were also starting to think beyond energy models, in a number of ways. Yolanda Strengers and Elizabeth Shove have pointed out that people don't simply 'use energy', but pursue practices that use energy — and those practices are embedded in and motivated by their sociocultural context. From this point of view, rather than targeting energy use per se, it makes more sense to reconfigure practices and the norms behind them, as, for example, Lenneke Kuijer has done by designing a system for washing that uses far less water than showering or bathing.

Others link approaches to solving environmental problems to broader political themes. For instance, Paul Dourish points out that thinking narrowly about individual or household energy use diverts attention from the larger scale economic and political responses that are needed. Hrön Brynjarsdóttir and her colleagues link many environmental HCI projects to 'persuasive computing', an approach to interaction which seeks to influence people's behaviour, and to modernist approaches that are both totalising and apt to lead to unintended consequences.

We began to see that environmental issues shouldn't be viewed in isolation, but as a manifestation of broader socio-political-cultural-technical arrangements.

This chimed with other concerns of the time — the inequality that cocoons the rich and exposes the rest, the lack of responsibility and sense of entitlement fuelled by an imbalanced access to resources, the surveillance and deprivation excused by invocations of terrorism and austerity, and the consumerist envy and egocentric thinking that go hand in hand. From this perspective, our impact on the environment, and our seeming inability to ameliorate or even focus on it, is a 'natural' outcome of the sociopolitical patterns of our time.

Thus we started to explore a broader view of how to support reflection about this context for environmental problems. We wanted to maintain the sense of open-endedness, if not play, that characterises most of our designs — though we might have strong feelings about these issues, we don't want to force our opinions on others. Instead, we started to explore ways to draw attention to the sociopolitical realities of our surroundings, without insisting on how these should be addressed.

The Social Insurgents, Deptford Town Hall, September 2012. We curated this exhibition to help us to engage with a more overtly political agenda.

× ×

THE SOCIAL INSURGENTS

STAPLE

How can one be insurgent when overt protest is stifled or ignored? How does one rebel against a culture dominated by a totalising market logic without looking quaint or unfavorabable?

This exhibition suggests the possibility of quietly disengaging from the large systems of media, commerce and government that overhang our lives. The collection may be small, but the work makes big statements: One media mogul shouldn't control our news. One Internet company shouldn't supply all our maps. There can't be just one version of the Iraq war.

But these social insurgents are neither heroic individuals nor isolated cranks. Many of the pieces shown here enhance and distill work done by larger publics. For example, Bridle's books are publishing 'our' shifting views of the Iraq war. Arunachalam Muruganantham's low cost sanitary napkin machines not only provide hygienic female sanitary products at an affordable price to those below the poverty line, but also provide jobs for women. The Balloon Toolkit forms part of a larger network of grassroots mapping available online. The Prayer Companion re-presents social news as a potential resource for prayer.

We like to think that this exhibition echos some of the themes and tactics of our exhibitors. In occupying the Deptford Town Hall, the baroque headquarters of a former council, it follows a number of high profile protests that took place here in the recent past. Moreover, in choosing a site that is off the well-established design trail (for the London Design Festival these days, that means the affluent West Brompton quarter) we want to emphasise the disparity in these recessionary times between design for the elite and the more grassroots efforts shown here, and to suggest that real change is as likely to come from below as above. Finally, in gathering work that, in some cases, is years old, we mean to question the tendency for LDF to value novelty, and suggest instead that what is new here is the way that these pieces come together to suggest a new landscape for design.

This exhibition is not a polemic, however. In fact, it is a methodological experiment, an exploration in our ongoing research on the sociocultural possibilities of new technologies. We are trying to open a space and ask questions, not create a definitive manifesto. Our catalogue reflects this: inspired by the Society of Independent Artists, we are allowing visitors to collect individual pages and collect them together as they see fit, thus allowing each of us to curate our own version of the exhibition. We hope your version will be thought-provoking, inspiring and optimistic.

INTERACTION RESEARCH STUDIO, SEPTEMBER 2012

STAPLE

TWO OF TEN

The foreword from the catalogue for *The Social Insurgents* exhibition.

Mobile Political Intelligence

A mobile device which provides politically relevant information (in some sense) in response to the device's location (in some sense)

Web scraped, 'pre-made information', algorithmically generated/selected material

Not necessarily literal GPS

A little like the original proposal but with something like 'psychogeopolitical' replacing 'psychogeographical'

The brief we set ourselves. The ‘original proposal’ mentioned in the brief refers to the funding application written three years before which suggested a psychogeographical mobile device.

Something about

Section

Something about

The 'Mobile Political Intelligence' brief set us in a direction, and The Social Insurgents exhibition helped us find some fellow travellers. What followed was a period of intense and slightly chaotic exploration, as we all imagined what we might produce, exploring and pushing against the edges of the brief we had set ourselves.

Most of this work took the form of sketches, notes and conversations. To draw it all together, we produced a workbook that captured the ideas in a more systematic and considered way.

Design workbooks are a form that we have used regularly in our previous projects. Comprising dozens of proposals, they create a design space for a given project and implicitly suggest its major issues as well as ways these might be addressed, defining an open-ended interest in doing 'something about...'. Proposals are typically quite spare, often consisting of little more than an image or diagram accompanied by short indicative captions, but they point to avenues for design that can be developed because they are (usually) reasonably specific and technically and socially plausible.

Workbooks function well within our core design team because they externalise proposals and separate them from their original authors — on this project, Andy, Bill, Dave, Mark, Nadine and Sarah. They can be ordered and reordered to discover emerging themes and similarities, providing a basis for discussions about directions we would like to take.

We reproduce here a few pages of the workbook we developed at the outset of this phase, annotated to indicate some of the concerns or implications of the proposals. It should be evident that we were just beginning to understand what a 'mobile political intelligence' might be, at a phase of the project when the possibilities were wide open.

There are a number of pages that highlight key areas. 'Contested Boundaries' draws attention to the issue that public bodies have conflicting methods for defining borders, making an accurate description of place problematic. 'App vs Device' raises the subject that interactive experiences are now commonly expected to be delivered though smart phones and tablets. 'What Colour is it?' is a sketch for a simple system that allows multiple users to tag places with a CMYK value. This can be infinitely overwritten, building a timeline of opinions about a place from many different people. As trivial as this may seem at first, the ideas for a system that could deliver this proposal defined a framework for the Datacatcher's final system architecture.

(MOBILE) POLITICAL ORIENTATOR

A mobile device that tells you you the political orientation of the area you are in, or heading towards.

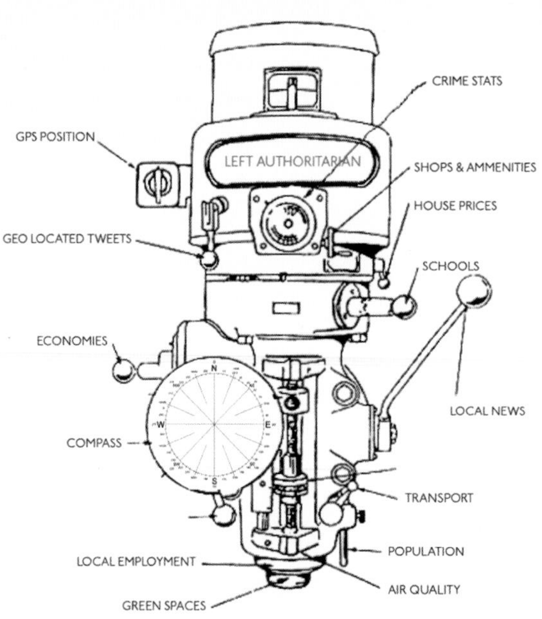

This foreshadowed many of the data sources we used to realise a "mobile political intelligence"...

... but narrowing a rich set of information to a single label seemed thin.

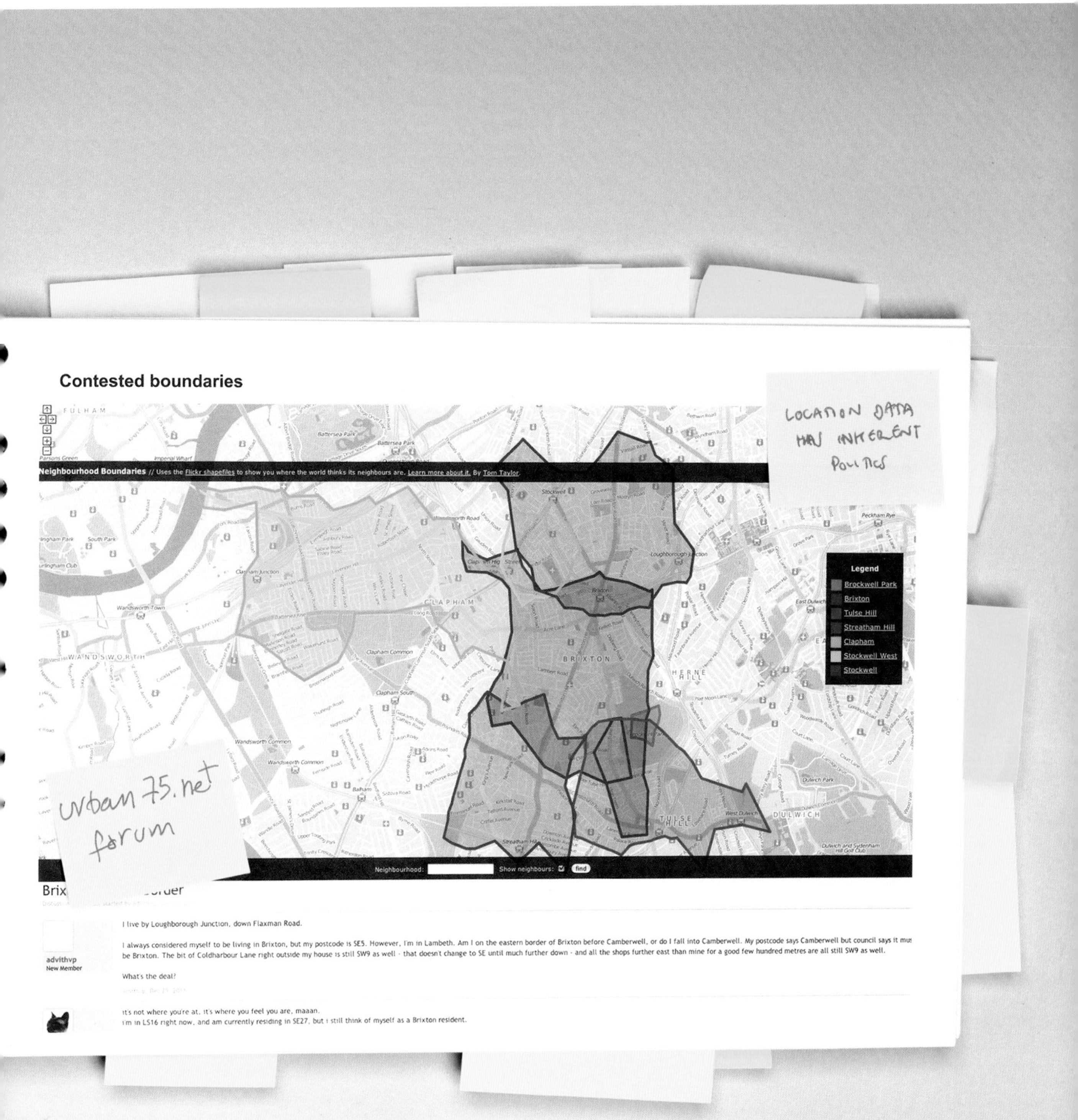

Contested boundaries
LOCATION DATA HAS INHERENT POLITICS
Neighbourhood Boundaries // Uses the Flickr shapefiles to show you where the world thinks its neighbours are. Learn more about it. By Tom Taylor.
Legend
Brockwell Park
Brixton
Tulse Hill
Streatham Hill
Clapham
Stockwell West
Stockwell
urban 75.net forum
Neighbourhood:
Show neighbours:
find
Brix
order
advithvp
New Member
I live by Loughborough Junction, down Flaxman Road.
I always considered myself to be living in Brixton, but my postcode is SE5. However, I'm in Lambeth. Am I on the eastern border of Brixton before Camberwell, or do I fall into Camberwell. My postcode says Camberwell but council says it mus
be Brixton. The bit of Coldharbour Lane right outside my house is still SW9 as well - that doesn't change to SE until much further down - and all the shops further east than mine for a good few hundred metres are all still SW9 as well.
What's the deal?
it's not where you're at, it's where you feel you are, maaan.
i'm in LS16 right now, and am currently residing in SE27, but i still think of myself as a Brixton resident.

[TWITTER] POLITICAL PARTY GENERATOR

Getting to the *real* concerns of Britain today

THE POLITICAL LANDSCAPE OF BRITAIN BASED ON THE VALUES OF THE TWITTERATI?

29/11/2013

HEAD OF PARTY:
Jeremy Kyle

IMPORTANT FIGUREHEADS:
Luiz Felipe Scolari
Serena Williams

ISSUES OF IMPORTANCE:
Christmas
Jobs
FIA

VIEWS ON EDUCATION:
Every teacher is not a parent but every parent is a teacher

VIEWS ON EMPLOYMENT:
Now Hiring: Ghost writer for blog on web-marketing 2.0

#PMQs
#ThoughtsDuringSchool
Christmas
#WantedWednesday
Jeremy Kyle
MSG
London
Champions League
Xmas
Glad

The [Twitter] Political Party Generator

To get a real sense of the political landscape in Britain, you need to get beyond the activists, beyond even the voting public (just 65.1% of Britons in 2010).

Forget the two party state, the political party generator - generates new political parties based on the (banal) values from the Twitterati. Some people mistake being non-party with being apathetic, but everything that one does or says is political, and a political orientation can be inferred.

The Landscape of Political Engagement

The people of Renfrewshire East are the most politically engaged.

The people of Manchester Central are the most politically apathetic.

More men than women exercise their right to vote.

The older you are, the more you care about politics.

GENERAL ELECTION TURNOUT HAS DECLINED SINCE 1940S

In 2010, Renfrewshire East had the greatest turnout of voters at the general election.
Manchester central were had the least.
Data from http://www.ukpolitical.info/Turnout10.htm

Apps vs Device

We have concerns about building a prototype that will do what an app can do, but there are several categories of single purpose mobile device that perform better than an app on a smartphone or tablet. Such devices are:

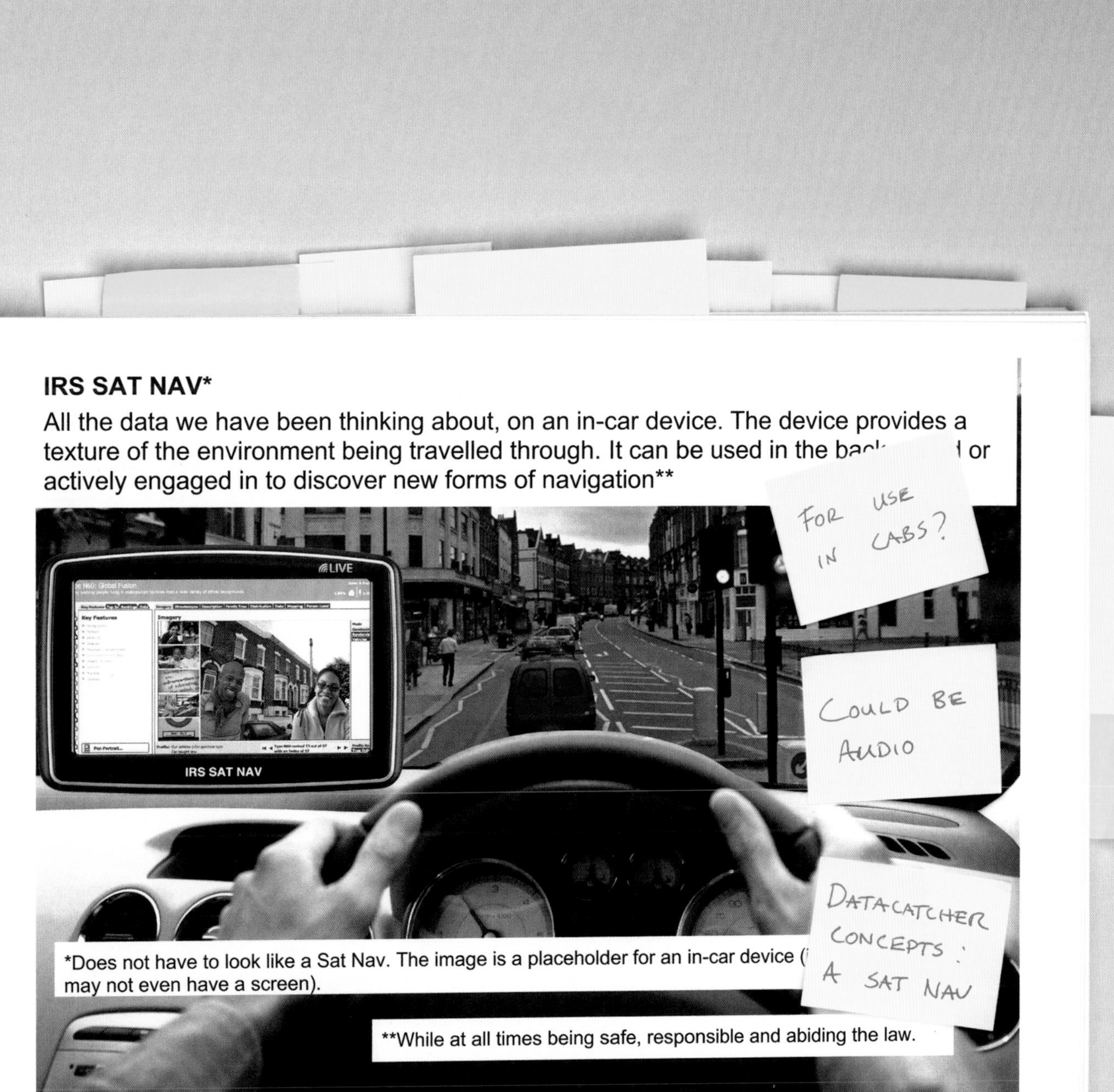
IRS SAT NAV*
All the data we have been thinking about, on an in-car device. The device provides a texture of the environment being travelled through. It can be used in the bac[…] or actively engaged in to discover new forms of navigation**
LIVE
IRS SAT NAV
*Does not have to look like a Sat Nav. The image is a placeholder for an in-car device (
may not even have a screen).
**While at all times being safe, responsible and abiding the law.
FOR USE IN CABS?
COULD BE AUDIO
DATACATCHER CONCEPTS: A SAT NAV

Mobile Prayer Companion-like device
Exploring the texture of the city with geo-tagged social media
DATACATCHER AS HANDHELD TEXT DISPLAY
REFERENCING PREVIOUS STUDIO PROJECTS

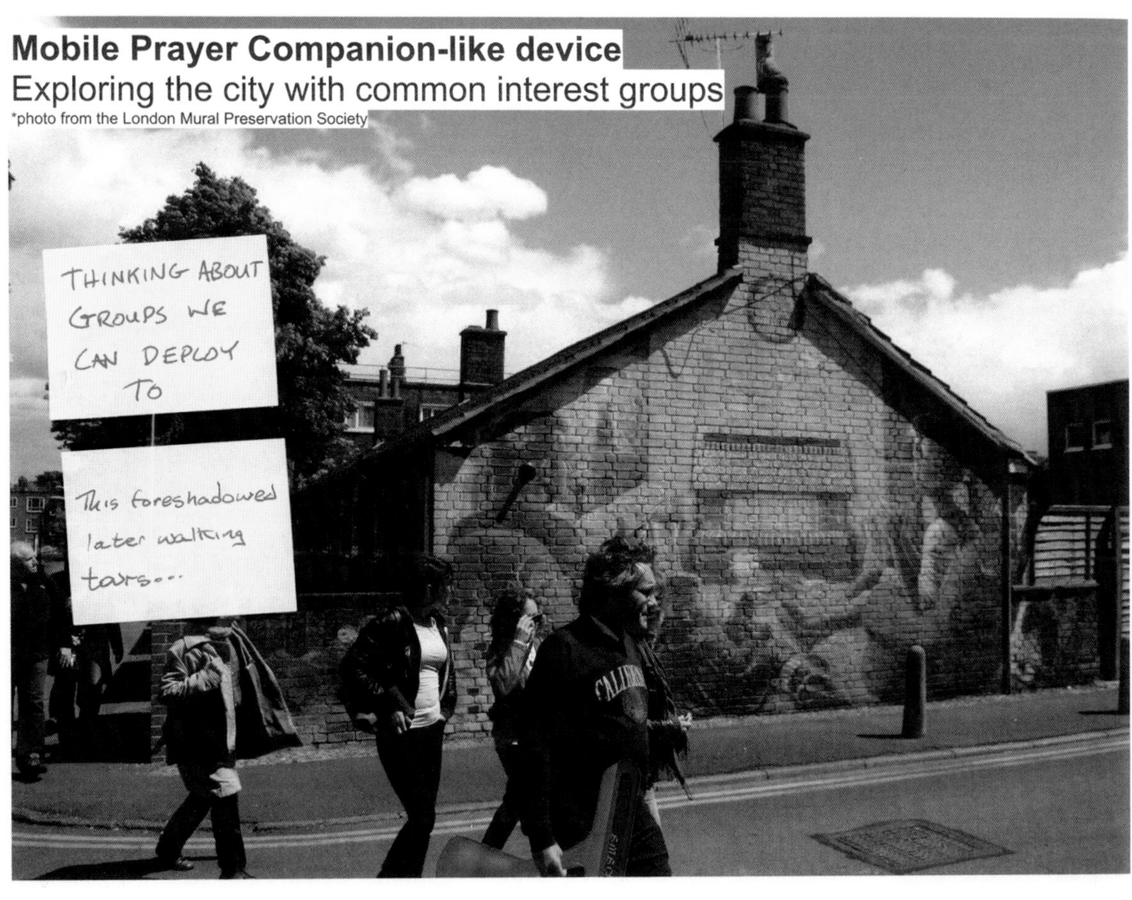
Mobile Prayer Companion-like device
Exploring the city with common interest groups
*photo from the London Mural Preservation Society
THINKING ABOUT GROUPS WE CAN DEPLOY TO
This foreshadowed later walking tours...

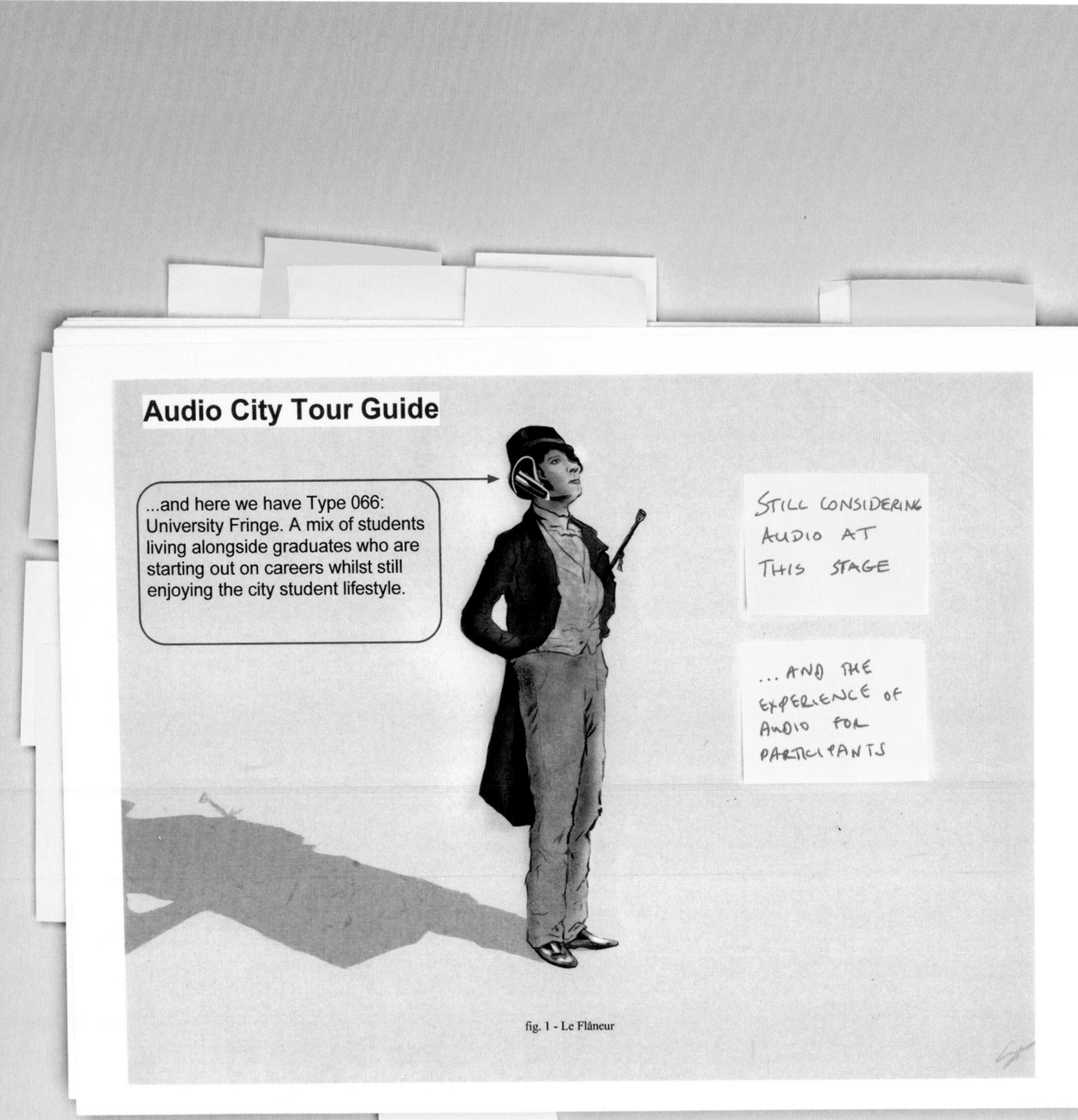
Audio City Tour Guide
...and here we have Type 066: University Fringe. A mix of students living alongside graduates who are starting out on careers whilst still enjoying the city student lifestyle.
STILL CONSIDERING AUDIO AT THIS STAGE
...AND THE EXPERIENCE OF AUDIO FOR PARTICIPANTS
fig. 1 - Le Flâneur

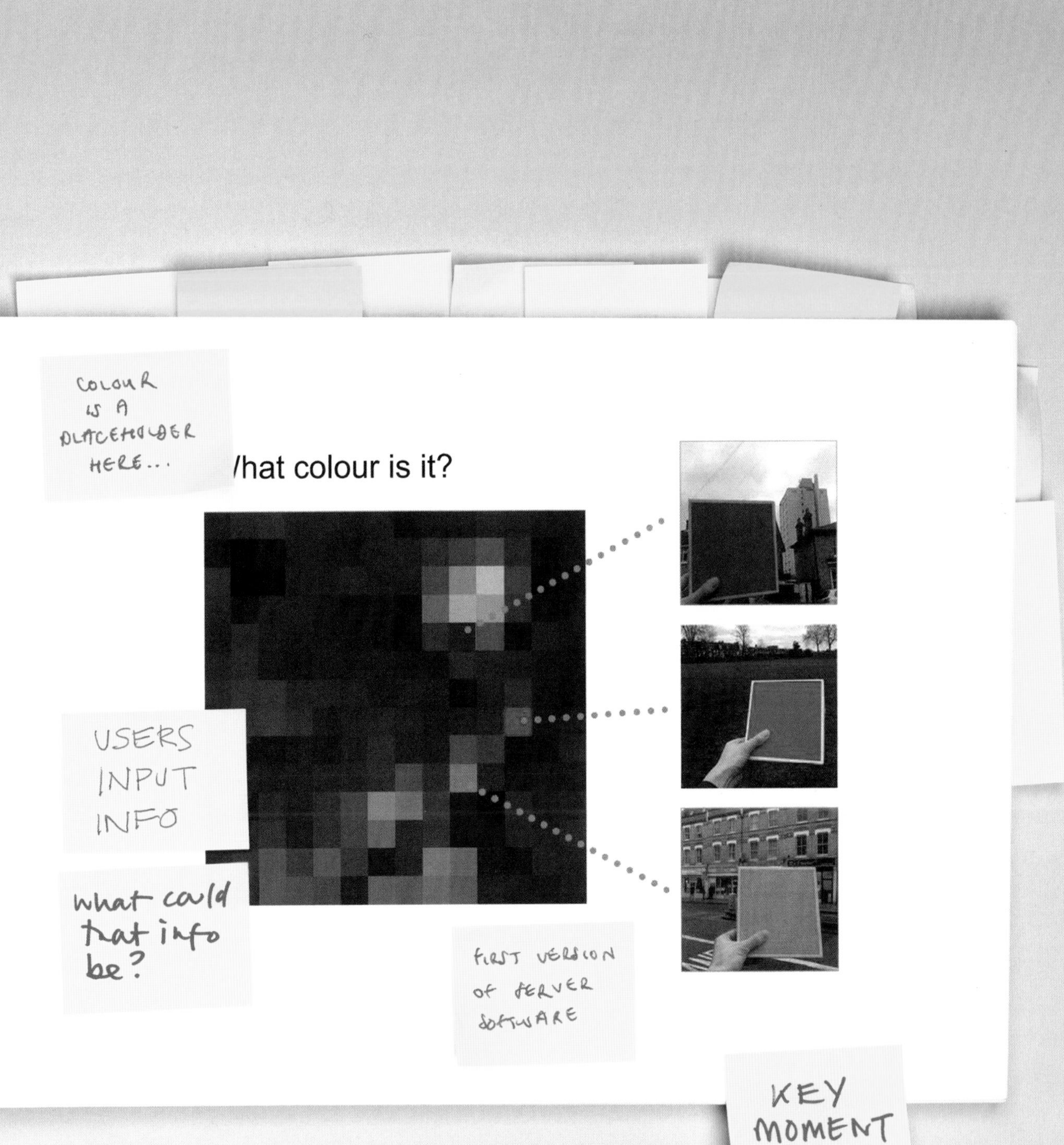
COLOUR IS A PLACEHOLDER HERE...
/hat colour is it?
USERS INPUT INFO
what could that info be?
FIRST VERSION OF SERVER SOFTWARE
KEY MOMENT

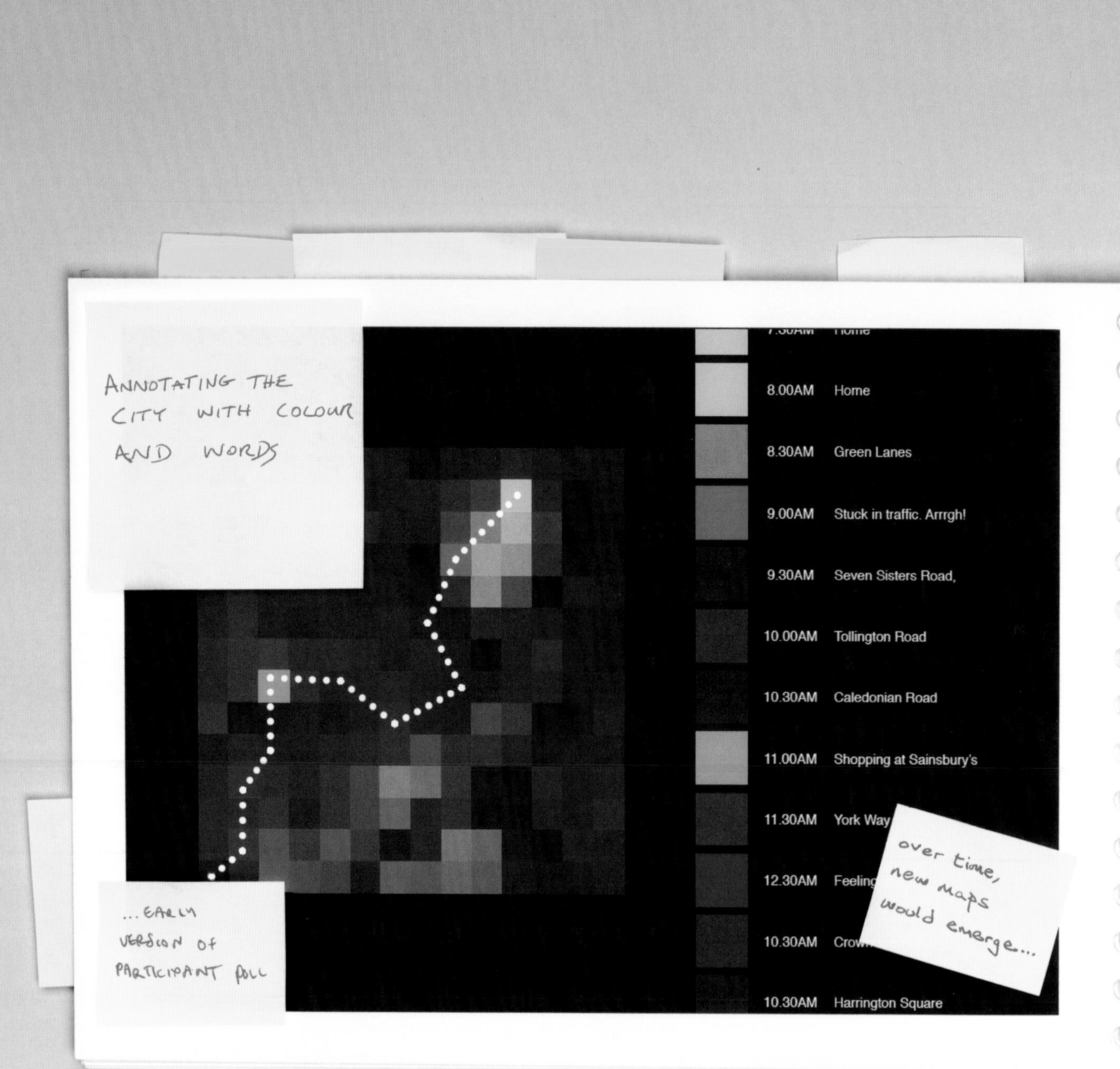
ANNOTATING THE CITY WITH COLOUR AND WORDS
8.00AM Home
8.30AM Green Lanes
9.00AM Stuck in traffic. Arrrgh!
9.30AM Seven Sisters Road,
10.00AM Tollington Road
10.30AM Caledonian Road
11.00AM Shopping at Sainsbury's
11.30AM York Way
12.30AM Feeling
10.30AM Crow
10.30AM Harrington Square
over time, new maps would emerge...
...EARLY VERSION OF PARTICIPANT POLL

PILGRIMAGE SAT NAV

Organised religion may be in decline, but the credit crunch has prompted a renewed spiritual hunger. The Pilgrimage Sat Nav can provide spiritual guidance in a busy world. With 'Spiritual Resonance' turned on you will be alerted to places of spiritual comfort or signifiance during your daily commute. Or for times when you are just seeking sancturary, consider going for a drive and switching to 'Pilgrimage' mode to be guided on a journey of a length set by you. Sometimes the journey is as important as the destination.

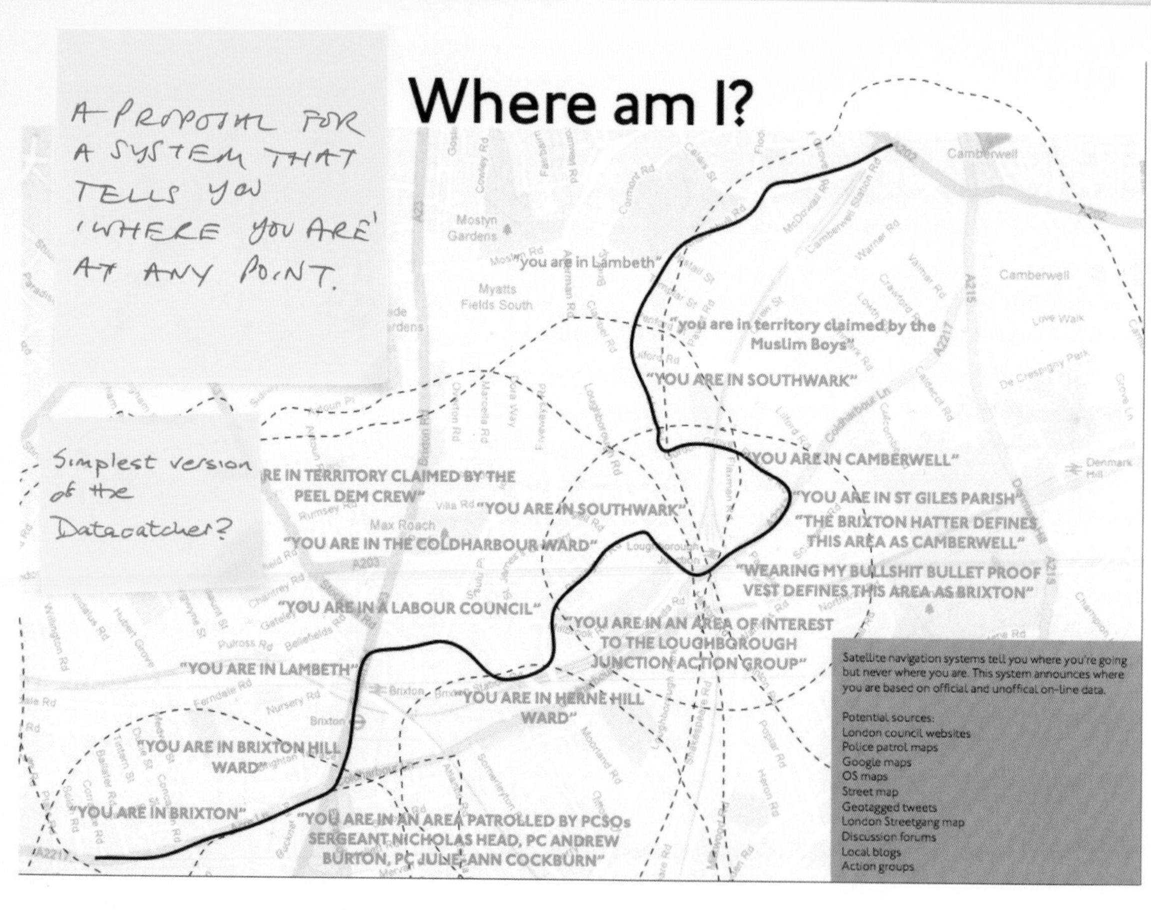
A PROPOSAL FOR A SYSTEM THAT TELLS YOU 'WHERE YOU ARE' AT ANY POINT.
Simplest version of the Datacatcher?
Where am I?
"you are in Lambeth"
"you are in territory claimed by the Muslim Boys"
"YOU ARE IN SOUTHWARK"
"YOU ARE IN CAMBERWELL"
"YOU ARE IN ST GILES PARISH"
"THE BRIXTON HATTER DEFINES THIS AREA AS CAMBERWELL"
"WEARING MY BULLSHIT BULLET PROOF VEST DEFINES THIS AREA AS BRIXTON"
RE IN TERRITORY CLAIMED BY THE PEEL DEM CREW"
"YOU ARE IN SOUTHWARK"
"YOU ARE IN THE COLDHARBOUR WARD"
"YOU ARE IN A LABOUR COUNCIL"
"YOU ARE IN AN AREA OF INTEREST TO THE LOUGHBOROUGH JUNCTION ACTION GROUP"
"YOU ARE IN LAMBETH"
"YOU ARE IN HERNE HILL WARD"
"YOU ARE IN BRIXTON HILL WARD"
"YOU ARE IN BRIXTON"
"YOU ARE IN AN AREA PATROLLED BY PCSOs SERGEANT NICHOLAS HEAD, PC ANDREW BURTON, PC JULIE-ANN COCKBURN"
Satellite navigation systems tell you where you're going but never where you are. This system announces where you are based on official and unoffical on-line data.
Potential sources:
London council websites
Police patrol maps
Google maps
OS maps
Street map
Geotagged tweets
London Streetgang map
Discussion forums
Local blogs
Action groups

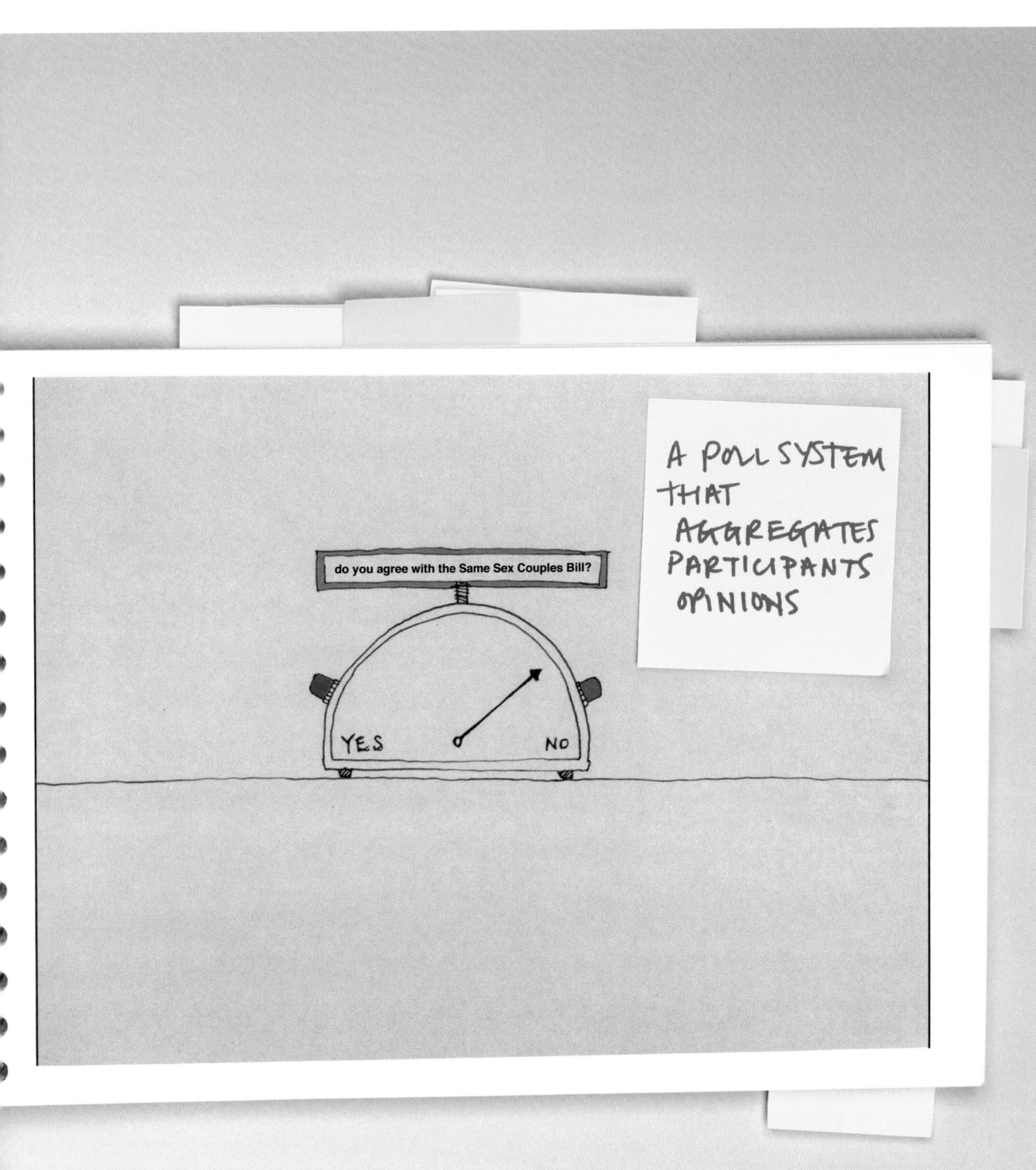
do you agree with the Same Sex Couples Bill?
YES
NO
A POLL SYSTEM THAT AGGREGATES PARTICIPANTS OPINIONS

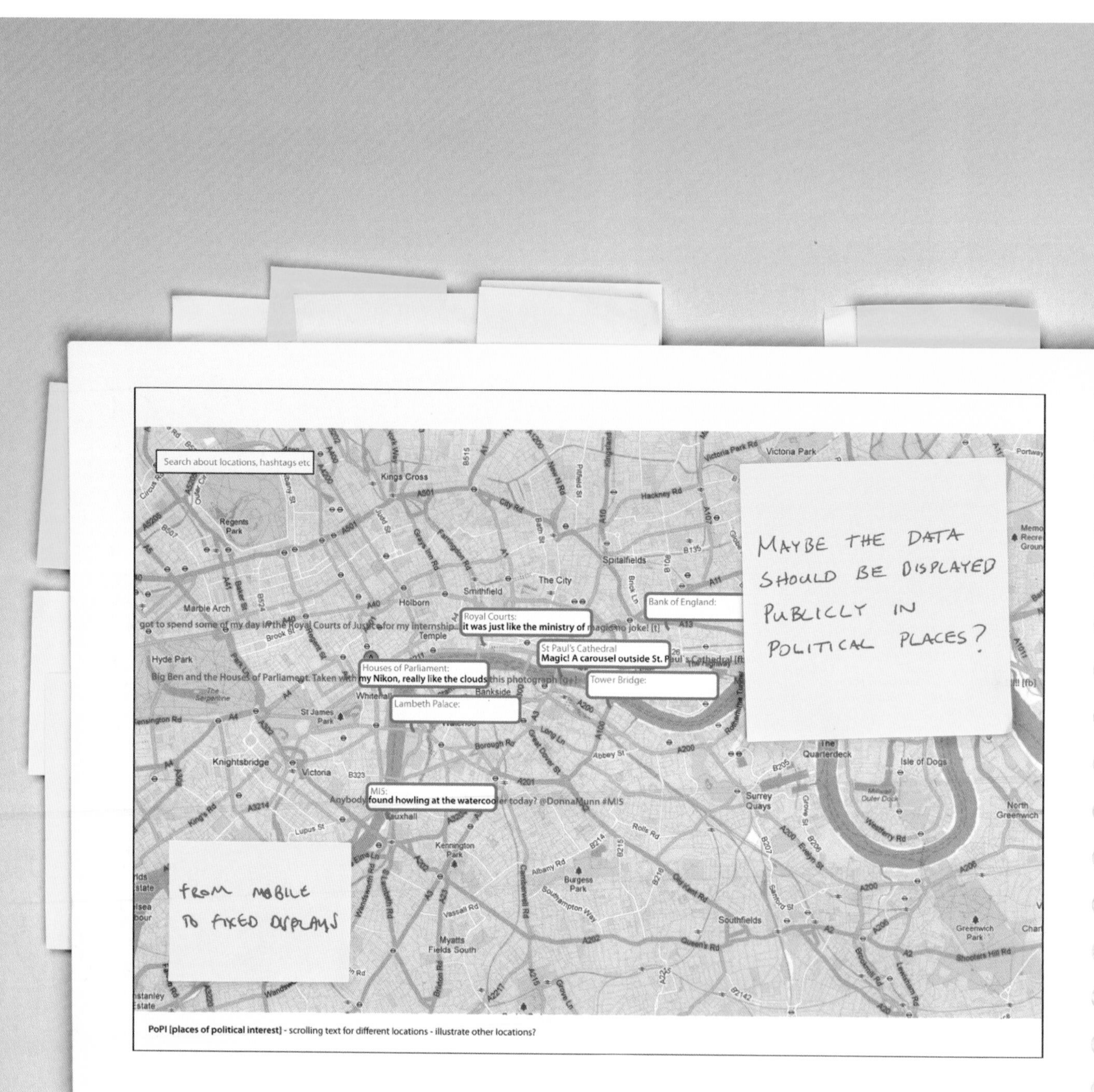
Search about locations, hashtags etc
Royal Courts:
it was just like the ministry of
St Paul's Cathedral
Magic! A carousel outside St. Paul's Cathedral
Houses of Parliament:
my Nikon, really like the clouds
Bank of England:
Tower Bridge:
Lambeth Palace:
MI5:
found howling at the watercooler today? @DonnaMunn #MI5
MAYBE THE DATA SHOULD BE DISPLAYED PUBLICLY IN POLITICAL PLACES?
FROM MOBILE TO FIXED DISPLAYS
PoPI [places of political interest] - scrolling text for different locations - illustrate other locations?

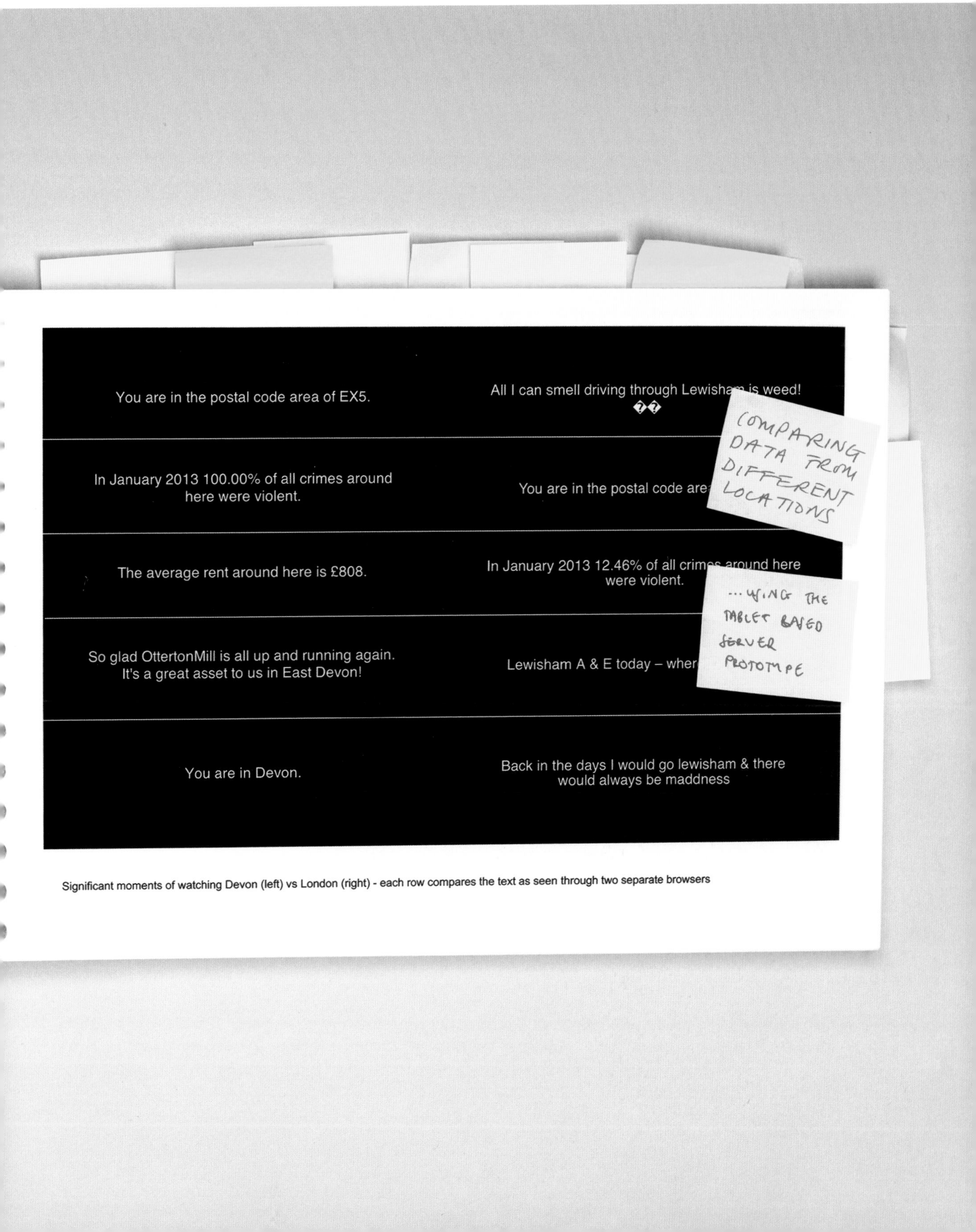
You are in the postal code area of EX5.
All I can smell driving through Lewisha
is weed!
In January 2013 100.00% of all crimes around here were violent.
You are in the postal code are
The average rent around here is £808.
In January 2013 12.46% of all crim
around here were violent.
So glad OttertonMill is all up and running again. It's a great asset to us in East Devon!
Lewisham A & E today – wher
You are in Devon.
Back in the days I would go lewisham & there would always be maddness
COMPARING DATA FROM DIFFERENT LOCATIONS
...USING THE TABLET BASED SERVER PROTOTYPE
Significant moments of watching Devon (left) vs London (right) - each row compares the text as seen through two separate browsers

Develop

Working on — and with — the design workbook left us with a strong sense that what we wanted to make was a portable, location-aware device that would stream politically- and environmentally-relevant information about its immediate environment. This, in other words, is what a 'mobile political intelligence' came to mean for us.

In seeking to detail this notion, however, we blew it all up again. What does it mean to be mobile? How, and for whom? Should the device be handheld, or perhaps mounted on a bike, or automobile? Or should it be left behind, chained to a lamp post, for later collection or the benefit of passers by?

And what sort of information should it present? Where would that information come from? Perhaps it should only talk about where you are, exposing the multiple overlapping and sometimes contentious identities of a given area. Or perhaps it should reflect the ways that marketers see us, as 'bright young things' or 'affluent homeowners'. Maybe it should show a stream of tweets, or talk about local problems, or expose environmental statistics, or...?

Meanwhile, what should the device's 'voice' be? Dry and factual, critical or sardonic? Perhaps it should be an actual voice, coming from an audio-only interface. How could we construct readable messages from database entries anyway? For that matter, could the contents be 'curated', for instance to link local information to national trends in the news, or the economy?

Questions such as these led to investigations, and to experiments. We explored forms and built models. We uncovered sources of information and began to understand their workings. We constructed fragmentary experience prototypes and tested the experiences they offered. Over the course of these months, the design slowly coalesced from a myriad of small considerations and decisions — an achievement brought to life when we finally decided on its name: the Datacatcher.

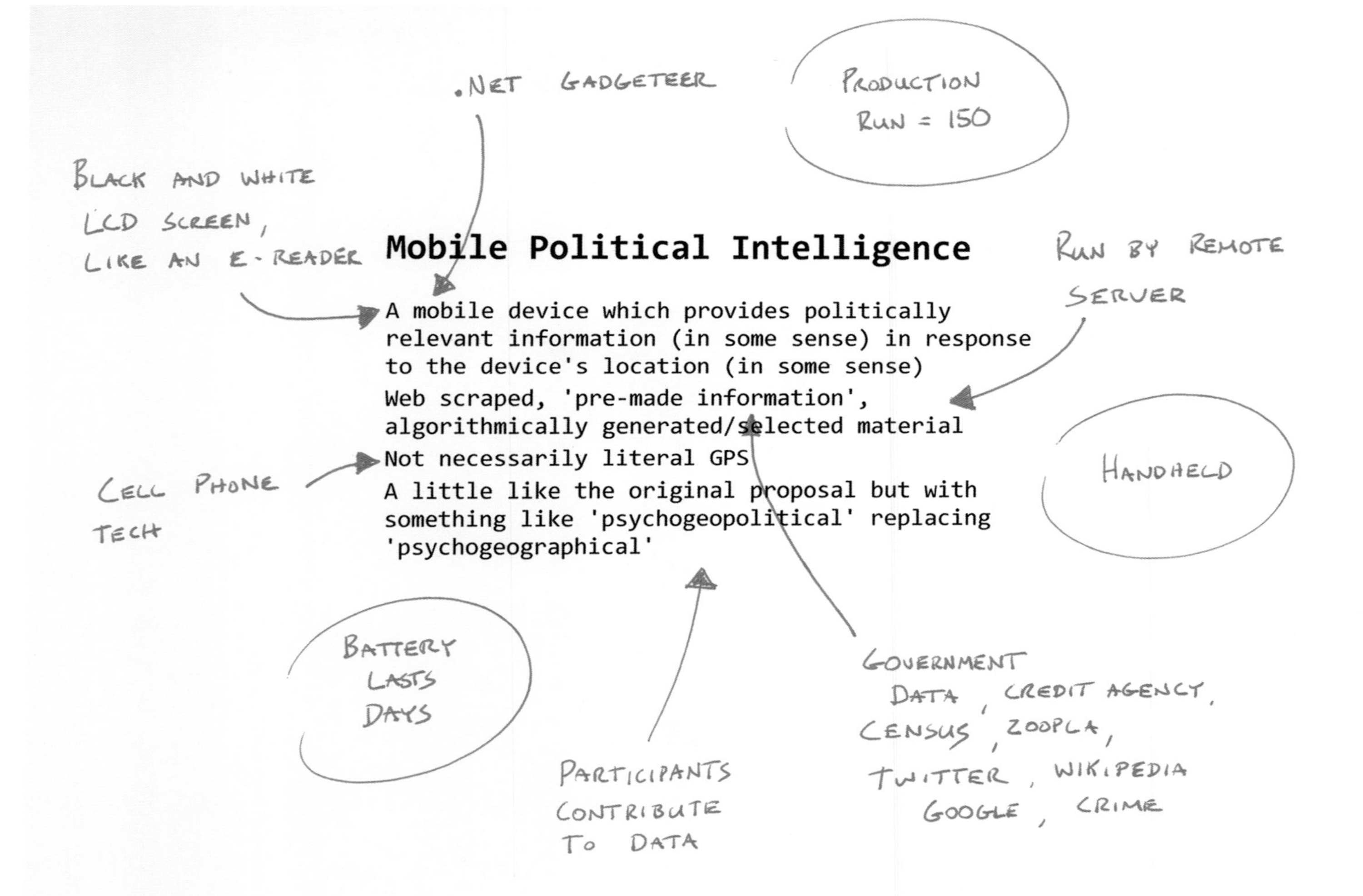

.NET GADGETEER
PRODUCTION RUN = 150
BLACK AND WHITE LCD SCREEN, LIKE AN E-READER
Mobile Political Intelligence
A mobile device which provides politically relevant information (in some sense) in response to the device's location (in some sense)
Web scraped, 'pre-made information', algorithmically generated/selected material
Not necessarily literal GPS
A little like the original proposal but with something like 'psychogeopolitical' replacing 'psychogeographical'
RUN BY REMOTE SERVER
HANDHELD
CELL PHONE TECH
BATTERY LASTS DAYS
PARTICIPANTS CONTRIBUTE TO DATA
GOVERNMENT DATA, CREDIT AGENCY, CENSUS, ZOOPLA, TWITTER, WIKIPEDIA GOOGLE, CRIME

After our initial explorations, we revised the brief with more specific ideas about how the system could be developed.

Title
How can a small team do this?

Author
Mark Hauenstein

When I joined the project, the team was facing an ambitious technical challenge. This was to build a set of devices to a standard that would usually involve a whole company, including designers, engineers, technicians and managers. I was curious to discover if the tools and know-how available to produce an object had developed to the point that a small group of non-specialists could batch produce a technological object that would rival a commercially manufactured product.

This question was in some sense inspired by a common reading of how the emergence of the internet has democratised and transformed the act of publishing. Everything has been pointing towards a parallel in the world of physical objects:

— 3D printers and laser cutters to rapid prototype objects
— Web-based services to manufacture small batches of printed circuit boards (PCBs) and device enclosures
— Open source programming frameworks to create software for micro controllers, servers and mobile devices
— Public data APIs [Application Programming Interfaces] to access a vast set of information about the world we live in
— A thriving DIY and open source community, acting as a dynamic knowledge repository for anything you want to make

The batch production of connected devices to collect and display various sets of data from the everyday world seemed to be an experiment with calculated risk. The batch deployment of the devices, on the other hand, generated a set of unknowns. These included questions such as: what do you do with the data that the devices collect 24/7 in multiple households? How do you cross-reference the collected data with significant moments in the everyday experience of people living with the objects?

It soon became clear that a linear approach — developing and building an object, deploying the objects, collecting and then dissecting the data — was neither practical nor manageable for a small team. Nor did it resonate with the idea of wanting something unexpected to emerge out of the interaction between the participants and the devices in their daily life.

A different approach was needed. A more distributed production and deployment model that would take into account the fallibility of the designer, the recurring necessity to adapt a design based on practical limitations and a means to allow participants to shape and affect the manifestation of something new.

The resulting strategy was to go beyond the design of an individual object to the design of a network of devices that would become a platform for an evolving eco-system. The designers would become participants themselves and each participant's experience of living with the object would feed back into how people would make use of the eco-system.

When I left the project it was clear to me that a small group of broadly skilled and technically minded designers can develop and batch produce a set of connected devices to a very high standard. The challenge had shifted towards the sustained deployment of a network of devices and the establishment and maintenance of a community of participants using the devices. And all of this has to be done in a manner that leaves as much space as possible for unforeseen things to happen.

Prototype hardware for a mobile device that can send and receive data, built with Microsoft's Gadgeteer platform. This was the first generation of the Datacatcher's hardware (v1.0).

We decided to use the Sharp LS027B7DH01 memory LCD screen. It has low power consumption, similar to e-ink displays, can be read in sunlight and has densely packed pixels, making it particularly suitable for displaying text. Its compact size also makes it perfect for a handheld, mobile device.

this is a screen test with helvetica 11pt

this is a screen test with courier 11pt

this is a screen test with Johnston 11pt

this is a screen test with helvetica 11pt, with no anti aliasing

this is a screen test with courier 11pt, with no anti aliasing

this is a screen test with Johnston 10pt, with no anti aliasing

Testing different fonts on the screen.

Testing message length on the screen.
The screen would fit most tweets.

this is a screen test with calibri 10pt

This is a screen test with calibri 10pt. You can fit around forty to forty four characters in one line when fully left justified.

This is a screen test with calibri 10pt. You can fit around forty characters across the screen when left justified.

This is a screen test with calibri 10pt. You can fit around forty to forty four characters in one line when fully left justified. With automatic leading and hyphenation on, you can fit eight lines of text, around fifty seven words and a total of three hundred and twenty seven characters (including spaces) in a paragraph. Lorem

This is a screen test with calibri 10pt. This has a 5mm border. You can fit around thirty-eight characters in one line when fully left justified. With automatic leading and hyphenation on,

Hardware footprint - rechargeable battery version
Consider access to:
Wheel switch
On/off switch
SIM card
USB power socket
Reset button

Considering the hardware footprint of possible components and battery type and size. All of the components were scaled 1:1 in the original document, enabling it to be used as a reference when modelling early prototypes.

A show about boatbuilding and the small matter of building a few hundred Datacatchers

Author Andy Boucher

In the 1980s, the BBC produced a television series to rival US sagas such as *Dallas and Dynasty*. The working title of the programme was *The Boatbuilders* and the storylines centred on the personal and professional lives of wealthy families living in the fictional town of Tarrant on the south coast of England. This was a place that had a thriving local economy based on the ostensibly lucrative leisure industry of yachting, and all the characters in the show were somehow connected to this sector. The stories described a community that encapsulated Thatcherite values of aspiration, enterprise and conspicuous consumption. There were no poor characters in the show whatsoever, though a kind of class struggle was represented by tensions between the *nouveau riche* and those who were from old money. The programme did not just present a community living in a wealthy bubble — it depicted a world where the concept of poverty simply did not exist.

The show had an escapist appeal that endures; tales of glamour and excess among the rich and famous have always provided inspiration for fiction. Even contemporary reality television shows about wealthy families offer a vicarious transport to a universe far removed from everyday life. Television fiction often creates places like Tarrant for the wealthy to frolic, as any reference to the poor could shatter the narrative illusion. But in a megacity like London, wealth isn't contained in bubbles, it bleeds through and contrasts starkly with poverty. In the real world, the rich employ *hostile architecture* such as *poor doors* or *anti-homeless spikes* to create a physical separation from inequality. In the world of data, it is much harder to hide inequality or compel it to move on, and data is increasingly being used to represent place.

When we embarked on the Datacatcher project we faced several challenges in how we would scale our practice to make visible the macrocosm of Big Data. Our goal was to build hundreds of devices that people could take out into the world to engage with the invisible layer of data that is used to describe the people, issues and environment of a place. These devices would be able to read and translate the — often anarchic — data into meaningful sentences that would expose a different kind of reality from the way the physical world presents itself.

Bringing together every geo-tagged dataset available to construct a stream of legible and pertinent messages about a place was an onerous task, which we cover in some detail later on in this publication. But this was also risky as the Datacatcher marked a shift in the conceptual direction of our work. Our research devices often shape content in playful ways; we create explorative spaces that contain issues and themes that have pliable connections to reality. In this project we were creating rigid connections to immobile data points, unyielding facts that were often harsh and uncomfortable about the here and now. Our designs often encouraged daydreaming, but the Datacatcher was grounded in the reality of its surroundings. Drawing together data for the device also required a considerable investment of time and resources before we could judge whether the experience was likely to pay off. At the same time, we also needed to take a leap of faith regarding the manufacturing of the devices.

The challenges we faced in manufacturing resonated with the fictional world of boatbuilding. Behind all the melodrama of the 80s television programme, there was a background story about craft and the transition to manufacturing. This is the reason I still remember the programme today. When we were approaching this project, I was frequently reminded of Jack Rolfe, one of the older characters, with values from a different era; he was a traditional craftsperson who made luxury wooden yachts. He owned the local boat-building yard but his resistance to change (in this Thatcherite utopia) meant his business was facing financial disaster. A solution comes in the shape of the show's lead protagonist and recently redundant aircraft designer, Tom Howard. He invests his redundancy money into the business and uses his aeronautical experience to design fast new yachts for the boatyard — yachts made from fibreglass for series production.

The two characters repeatedly clash about manufacturing technique and the plan to volume produce yachts. Jack has a particular hatred of fibreglass. To appease him, Tom has the first prototype, a complex form designed specifically for fibreglass production, built from wood. This decision would have made very little sense in the real world, but this is a fiction and so the finished prototype breaks several speed records and attracts the attention of a volume boat builder. They strike a deal to license the design to this manufacturer to build fibreglass copies in a factory, producing a huge income for them both — a happy ending. Despite the absurdity of this storyline, I remember fondly the impassioned arguments between the two characters about manufacturing processes, something which is not often represented in television drama.

There are parallels with our own approach to the transition from one-off to volume production. The Datacatcher was the second phase of a five-year project that was to exploit batch production as method to produce many research prototypes for distribution to multiple participants during field trials. This was radically different from our usual practice of making highly finished, robust one-off devices and this new approach presented a significant challenge to the project team. During the first phase, we had produced 22 sets of three digital devices called the Indoor Weather Stations. This was our first foray into batch production and we should have made fundamental changes to our methodology to rationalise the production of prototypes. Instead, I believe the approach we took made the devices more complex to make than usual.

The project was ambitious and afforded the purchase of an industrial 3D printer. We started to use this machine to print housings for our devices, but we feared that the devices would look too machine-made, too easy and impersonal. The housings looked unfinished, and they had an unusual ridged texture, which is an artefact of the layered printing process. They lacked the highly finished aesthetic that our research devices normally had and we worried that our participants would not take these artefacts seriously. We decided not to sand and paint each device, as we had with previous 3D printed housings, both because of the time we calculated this might take and because we wanted to create a new finish. To add value to these printed parts, we adopted a strategy of applying highly crafted elements to each of the three pieces in a set. The Light Collector had a component that was covered in copper leaf. The Wind Tunnel had a lasercut miniature paper forest, hand-inserted with tweezers into a miniature typographic landscape. The Temperature Tape featured a complex silkscreen print of layered thermochromic inks on a hand-made fabric tape, which enclosed the electrical ribbon cable that connected the temperature sensors to the main body. These handcrafted elements became extremely labour intensive over the quantity we were building.

The complexity of the exteriors of these devices was matched, if not exceeded, by the complexities on the inside. The Weather Stations used a new kind of embedded technology platform from Microsoft, named Gadgeteer. This allows devices to be built from a kit of different modules or printed circuit boards (PCBs) that each have specialist functions. This technology works extremely well, but it was so new at the time we were unable to consider rationalising the number of PCBs in each device. So each unit had up to ten PCBs crammed into its diminutive housing. This made them very fiddly and time consuming to assemble, especially as we used tried and tested techniques from our one-off production rather than developing new practices for volume production. For instance, we secured these numerous PCBs with machine screws, bolted into threaded inserts that had to be melted into bosses inside the 3D printed housings. We always used this technique with one-offs as it made it easier to remove or replace parts during servicing without damaging the housing. For the Weather Stations, this meant heat welding 2,500 inserts by hand.

In almost every area of the production we were using our traditional techniques to produce the devices. To satisfy our own standards of what we thought a quality research prototype should be, we had done exactly what Tom Howard had done for Jack Rolfe and had built our new prototypes using the skills we knew and had, rather than developing new ones — we were making the equivalent of wooden versions of fibreglass boats.

When we started work on the Datacatcher, we knew we had to fundamentally change our practice. In this phase we planned a production run of hundreds and so we wouldn't be able to afford to embellish each unit with handcrafted details. We needed to choose a material for the housing that we would be happy to use straight off the production line and we would need to seriously rationalise the internal architecture. We had to learn from our mistakes in the previous phase of the project and design the Datacatcher to be assembled in minutes rather than hours; we needed to think far more in terms of volume than before. At this stage we were unsure of how many Datacatchers we would finally produce, so we took the view that we should design the device so that it would be as easy to produce a thousand units as a hundred.

The first step was to realise that wouldn't be able to produce all the housings ourselves and that we would need to subcontract the production to a third party. The second was to understand that we had to design our own PCB. Again based on the Gadgeteer platform, it would incorporate all the functions of several off-the-shelf modules in a single board. This would also have to be manufactured and populated with the electronic components by a specialist. With these two steps, we had shifted our core practice — from being a studio of craftspeople producing one-off research devices to becoming a low-volume manufacturer of a telecoms device. This transition brought many new challenges, especially in how we would have to work with external suppliers to achieve quality on a par with our one-off devices. Lessons from this steep learning curve are detailed later in this publication.

As exciting as this challenge was, the craftsperson in me mourns the loss of the connection that I enjoyed when we were building our one-off devices. Much as Jack Rolfe hated the thought of fibreglass yachts produced on a production line, untouched by the hand of craft, I missed the contact time building the devices. I know every nook, cranny and flaw of our previous pieces through the labour required to make each one, which makes them somehow precious. I have to admit that I could not care less about any particular Datacatcher. The assembly procedure was so quick with each unit that passed through my hands, that I feel little of that connection that I enjoyed with our previous work. However this is unimportant, as our research devices are not built for me. One of the unfortunate features of one-off pieces is so few people get to experience them. Our ambition with this project was to produce as many research prototypes as possible so we could capture the views of the many instead of the few. We had to change our practice to do this, but as will be clear later, we think it was worth it.

Sketches exploring how a mobile device might be used, different screen and battery arrangements, and possibilities for attaching the Datacatchers to other objects.

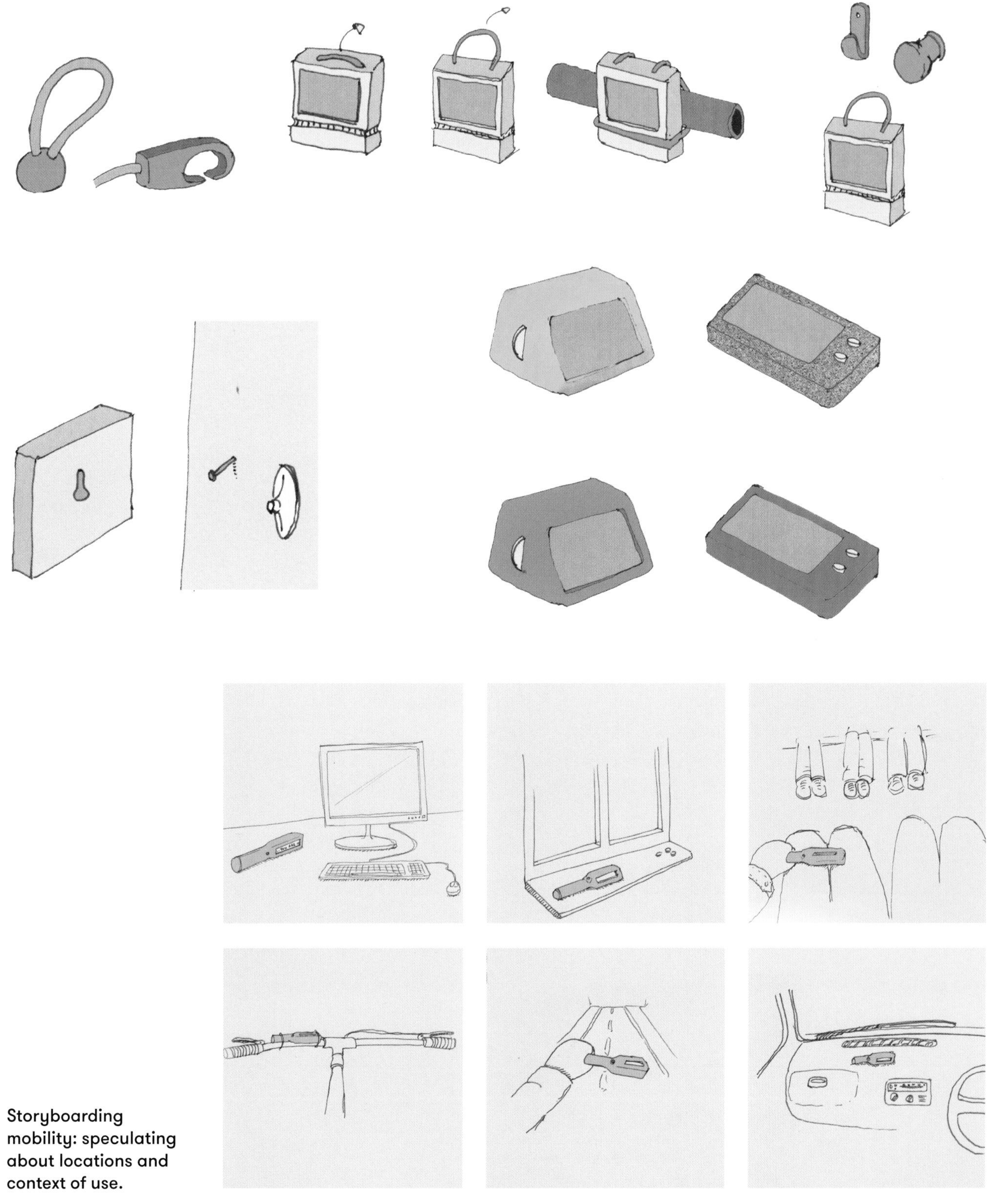

Storyboarding mobility: speculating about locations and context of use.

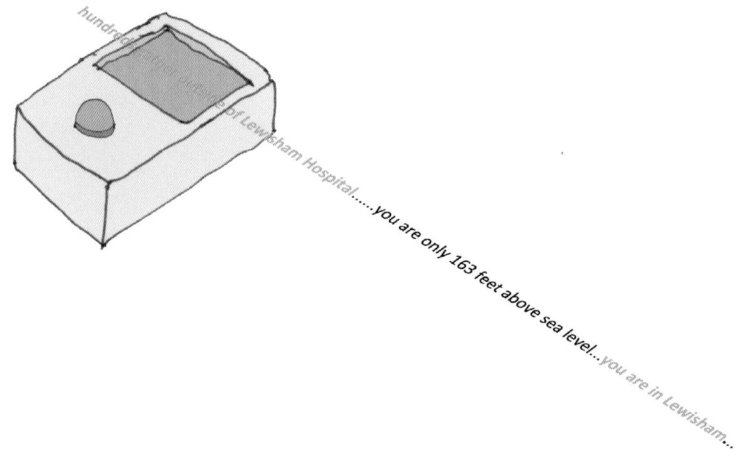

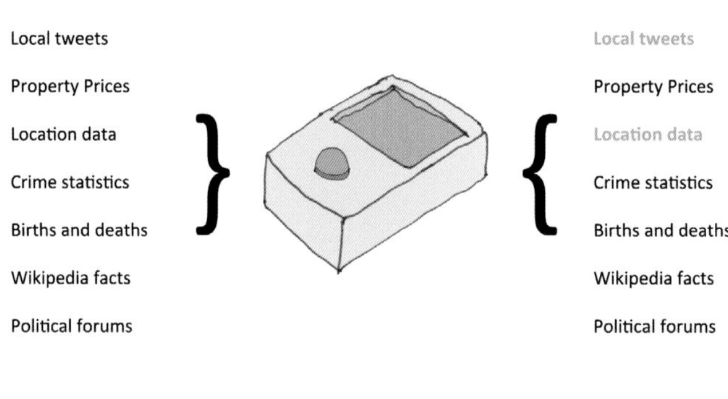

Sketching interactions for collecting 'significant moments', using a button to tag messages. We also added the feature of scrolling the history of the data. Other interactions considered were digging into data, and editing data using 'less' and 'more' feedback buttons.

(POLITICAL PLACEHOLDER)

ANTI-APATHY DEVICE

Making you very present, very aware of socio-political texture of place

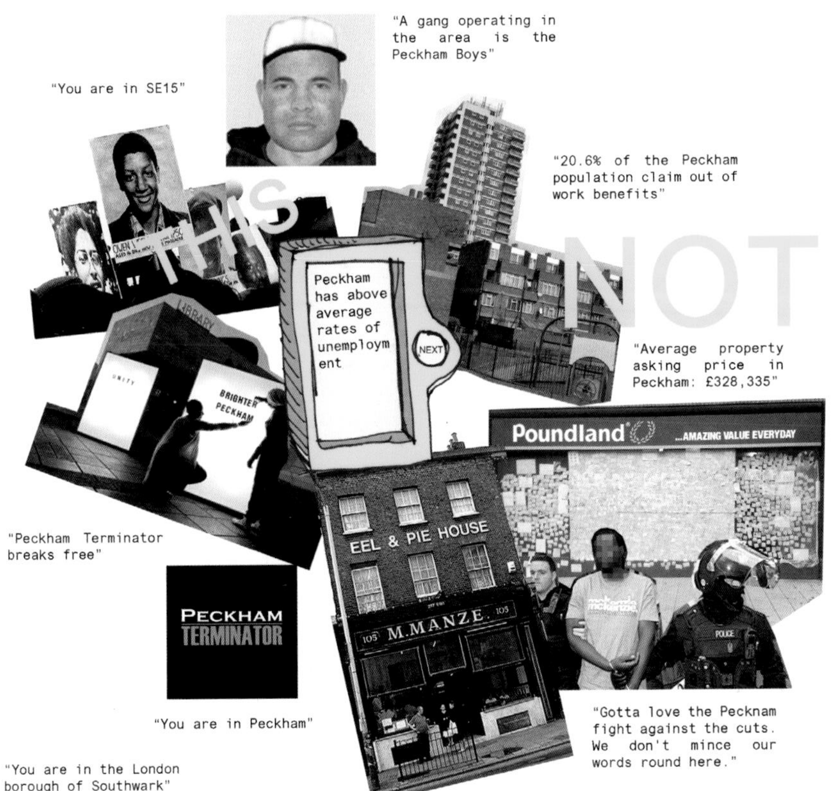

"A gang operating in the area is the Peckham Boys"
"You are in SE15"
"20.6% of the Peckham population claim out of work benefits"
THIS
NOT
Peckham has above average rates of unemploym ent
NEXT
"Average property asking price in Peckham: £328,335"
Poundland ...AMAZING VALUE EVERYDAY
EEL & PIE HOUSE
M.MANZE
"Peckham Terminator breaks free"
PECKHAM TERMINATOR
"You are in Peckham"
"Gotta love the Pecknam fight against the cuts. We don't mince our words round here."
"You are in the London borough of Southwark"

Mimi drifts away as she reads her Facebook feed on her smart phone

More a manifesto than a proposal, we wanted to draw attention to a place, not distract from it.

We considered designing the Datacatchers to be left in public spaces as a kind of electronic graffiti, or sending them on journeys apart from their owners.

"Jeremy Hunt's Lewisham hospital cuts plan quashed at High Court"

"Yesterday, this area had a low level of happiness"

"recording"

"recording"

PLACEHOLDER FOR
A CONSIDERED VOICE

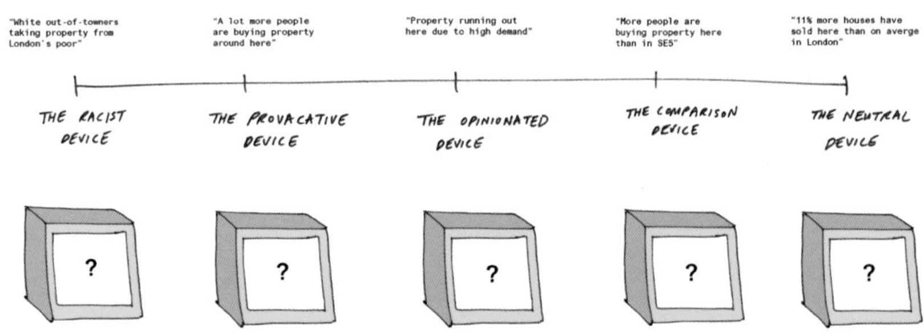
"White out-of-towners taking property from London's poor"
"A lot more people are buying property around here"
"Property running out here due to high demand"
"More people are buying property here than in SE5"
"11% more houses have sold here than on averge in London"
THE RACIST DEVICE
THE PROVACATIVE DEVICE
THE OPINIONATED DEVICE
THE COMPARISON DEVICE
THE NEUTRAL DEVICE
?
?
?
?
?

Exploring the potential tones of voice for delivering data.

THE OPINIONATED DEVICE AS PROVOCATEUR FOR ANTI-APATHY

(though I don't think we need to design 'opinion', with enough social news sources it WILL inevitably embody this)

Loughborough
Junction is
what is known
in the trade
as a complete
hole!! #Dive

belowtheriver @belowtheriver 17m
Guess which London borough has one of the country's highest ratios of fast-food takeaways to people? http://ow.ly/k45fd

Alex Lee @AlexGeLee 11 Apr
Loughborough Junction is what is known in the trade as a complete hole!! #Dive

belowtheriver @belowtheriver 6h
How many chicken shops is too many chicken shops? http://ow.ly/k44Wu

Joe Simpson @JoeSimpsonArt 14 Apr
Someone was shot outside my studio in Loughborough Junction last night. Pretty grim.

mike @urban75 12 Apr
The inquisitive hoarding, Wanless Road, Loughborough Junction - http://tinyurl.com/c4kc8my

A$AP Jonny @SoShanz 12 Apr
Someone go Loughborough junction tesco n rob them now please

Data from a portable server running on a location-aware tablet — one of many simple 'experience prototypes' we made to experience the system while travelling.

I took the tablet prototype on a train journey between London and Devon, documenting snippets of data and moments of significance. I've listed a few notes about some of the messages I found interesting...

East Devon 5 mins drive from the sea :)
This tweet gives context to an area. A place name would only provide insight into the geographical location, whereas this message reveals the nearby physical landscape, and a flavour of what it's like to live there.

Colyton return to the top of the East Devon Short Mat Bowls League
Although this local news headline doesn't present the most interesting fact about a place, I find it more honest than some of the more summative data, such as Mosaic, that attempt to characterise a place. This headline references a real, current community activity.

I'm in south Somerset my daffodils have snow on them
This tweet resonates with some of our concepts of 'people as sensors', supporting the idea that people can provide more information about a place than technology. It tells me more information than a temperature sensor, or weather report.

Severe weather warning for snow issued for Somerset
A lot of the messages I've read tell me about current, or very recent data about a place — for example, house prices. This message (which I think is from a local news headline) stood out as it presents data about the future condition of a place.

Even more of this place Weeke Barton in Devon is not just any bit of East London but Hackney. When will see it the other way round?
I enjoyed this individual's tweet comparing two locations. Our tablet prototype compares a few data sets, such as house prices. But this was more interesting to me, as it questions influences between rural and urban locations.

Dave Cameron

You are in the district of Islington Borough Council

- The Saturday Shake Up, The Hideaway, 114 Junction Road, Archway, N19 | 9 minutes from N19 5NR. Local guest DJs Decadence, Jonny Silcock, Sunshineman, Michael Dodds and Liam Devall spin a mix of pop, hip hop, rock, funk, Motown, club classics and commercial ...
- Open Mic, The Hideaway, 114 Junction Road, Archway, N19 | 9 minutes from N19 5NR
- An average domestic property in this area, who has not transferred energy supplier would be paying 357.86 per annum for their gas and electricity.
- In 2008, Islington Local Education Authority had 38.90% of students achieving at least five GCSEs at grades A*-C — including English and Maths
- Average house prices in N19 5NR over the past 6 months: Property Type Sales Terraced: 739,000
- In the latest Index of Multiple Deprivation (IMD) this area was ranked 4,855 out of 32,482 in England, where 1 was the most deprived and 32,482 the least

Population

Total number of people: 175,797
Males: 84,229 / Females: 91,568 / Aged 0 to 15: 32,241 / Aged 16 to 74: 135,661 / Aged 75 and over: 7,895

Closest businesses

[source: 118.com]

- SMS UK Construction Ltd, 37 Despard Road, Archway, Greater London, N19 5NP
- Lambo (African-Caribbean) Centre, 48 Despard Road, Upper Holloway, Archway, Greater London, N19 5NW
- Retina Images Limited, 36 Despard Road, Archway, Greater London, N19 5NW
- Undugu African Swahiliphone Refugee Project 1b Waterlow Road, Upper Holloway, Archway, Greater London, N19 5NJ
- Conscience Taxes for Peace Not War, 1b Waterlow Road, Archway, Greater London, N19 5NJ
- Everyman Project, 1a Waterlow Road, Archway, Greater London, N19 5NJ
- IANSA, 1a Waterlow Road, Archway, Greater London, N19 5NJ
- Stop the War Co, 1b Waterlow Road, Archway, Greater London, N19 5NJ
- Zimbabwe Human Rights NGO Forum, 1b Waterlow Road, Archway, Greater London, N19 5NJ
- Peace Brigades International UK Section, Waterlow Road, Archway, Greater London, N19 5NJ
- Archway Design & Build, 22 Highgate Hill, Archway, Greater London, N19 5NL

Blue plaques within one mile

- Vinayak Damodar Savarkar 1883–1966 Indian Patriot and Philosopher lived here
- Mary Kingsley 1862–1900 Traveller and ethnologist lived here as a child
- Arthur Waley 1889–1966 Poet, Translator and Orientalist lived and died here
- A.E. Housman 1859–1936 Poet and Scholar wrote "A Shropshire Lad" while living here
- J.B. Priestley 1894–1984 Novelist, playwright and essayist lived here
- Frank Matcham 1854–1920 Theatre Architect lived here 1895–1904
- Sir John Betjeman 1906–1984 Poet lived here 1908–1917
- Sir Geoffrey Jellicoe 1900–1996 Landscape Architect lived here 1936–1984
- Kwame Nkrumah 1909–1972 First President of Ghana lived here 1945–1947
- Ford Madox Brown 1821–1893 Painter lived here

Tweets

[source: Twitter with Archway as search term]

- So whacking my head on the archway wasn't the best start to the day
- free tonight? How about a free stage combat taster class with in Archway? Contact lyndall@rc-annie.com to attend
- 40mins of police sirens in archway going toward central
- Y have a life, if you are not willing 2 live it
- Lets live life yo!!! FRIDAY NIGHT SLAMM, THIS FRIDAY @ LATIN GROOVE, 1 ARCHWAY CLOSE, N19
- EXCLUSIVE AND BRAND NEWLY REFURBISHED TO A VERY HIGH STANDARD. A TWO DOUBLE BEDROOM, TWO BATHROOM: Archway, ...
- Beautiful Archway RedGage leading to a shop love the light arch shop lamps light photo

We collected all the data we could find for an N19 postcode using basic web tools to get a feel for the content the Datacatchers would find in a particular location.

Obituary
Professor Jon Driver, who has died aged 49, was Professor of Cognitive Neuroscience at University College, London, and one of the world's leading experts on the workings of the brain

Altitude
You are 75 meters above sea level

MP activity
[source: http://www.theyworkforyou.com]
- Jeremy Corbyn is your local MP and has discussed Iraq, Western Sahara, British Indian Ocean Territory, London Metropolitan University, Colombia in Parliament
- Your MP Voted strongly for a smoking ban
- Your MP Voted strongly for an investigation into the Iraq war
- Your MP Voted a mixture of for and against a wholly elected House of Lords
- Your MP Voted a mixture of for and against automatic enrolment in occupational pensions
- Your MP Voted moderately for a transparent Parliament
- Your MP Voted strongly for equal gay rights
- Your MP Voted very strongly against introducing foundation hospitals
- Your MP Voted very strongly against university tuition fees
- Your MP Voted moderately against allowing ministers to intervene in inquests

Meetup
[source: http://www.meetup.com]
- People are meeting for Osho Active meditations – North London
- People are meeting for HeartBeat – Dark Moon Shemanic Drumming

Local blogs
[source: local blogs found via openlylocal.com]
- The local community is talking about Stroud Green Beautification
- The local community is talking about Leaving Stroud Green
- The local community is talking about On no telling on Jack the Ripper
- The local community is talking about Blushing unseen and all that
- The local community is talking about Or you could buy flowers for yourself
- The local community is talking about Professionally presented Pop Music Quiz every Thursday Night plus...
- The local community is talking about Letting agents in London stand to get more work
- The local community is talking about Services that let you operate your business from the cloud

Local news
[sources http://www.islingtontribune.com search terms are local landmarks: Whittington, Archway, Islington North + http://www.archwaytowncentre.co.uk/news]
- The council is working to prevent aggressive behaviour and discourage people from giving to beggars around Archway tube station
- Whittington Hospital doctors criticised after woman dies following knee operation
- An Archway novelist whose thriller was turned down by seven book agents is hoping to shake up the literary world by establishing her own publishing company for new writers
- Islington North MP Jeremy Corbyn has condemned the cost of Margaret Thatcher's funeral and the expense of recalling Parliament for Wednesday's debate on the former Prime Minister

Street Gangs
[source: http://www.londonstreetgang.com]
- Bemerton Mandem street gang are in this area
- Busy Blocks Archway Mandem street gang are in this area
- Crouch Hall Court C–Blocks street gang are in this area
- EC1 Easy Cash street gang are in this area
- Essex Road Gang street gang are in this area

Several songs namecheck the area
[source: http://www.wikipedia.com]
- The Boo Radleys' cult song *Blue Room in Archway*
- Saint Etienne's *Archway People*
- New Model Army's *Archway Towers*
- Zoe Heller's novel *Notes on a Scandal* was filmed around Archway, as were some scenes in *Shaun of the Dead*
- The novel *The Diary of a Nobody*, by Weedon Grossmith and George Grossmith was set in and around Archway and Holloway.
- Writer Iain Sinclair's epic poem *Suicide Bridge* takes its title from a local nickname for the Archway Bridge

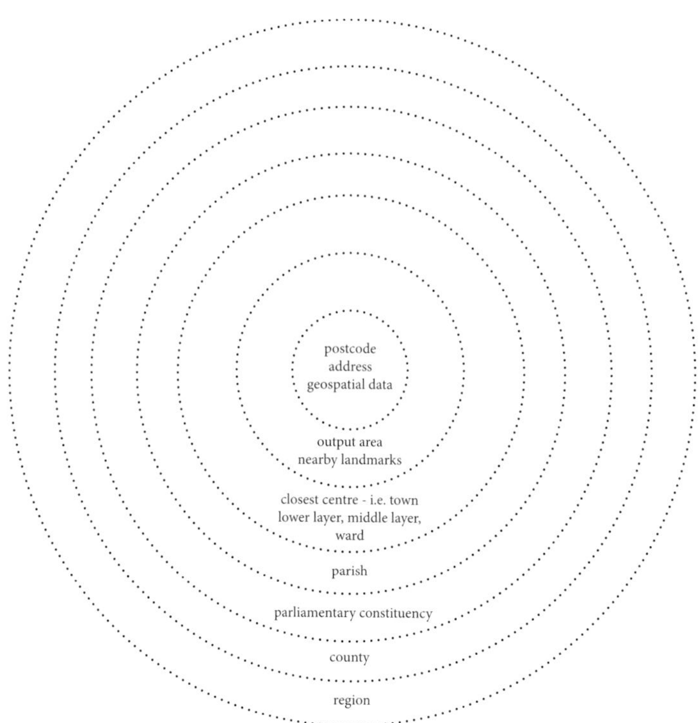

http://www.neighbourhood.statistics.gov.uk
Enter the name of an area OR full postcode: SE23 3XJ

local authority: Lewisham
middle layer super output: Lewisham 028
lower layer super output: Lewisham 028
ward: Forest Hill
output area: E00016459
primary care organisation: Lewisham
health authority: London
education authority: Lewisham
westminster parliamentary constituency: Lewisham West and Penge
parish: not found

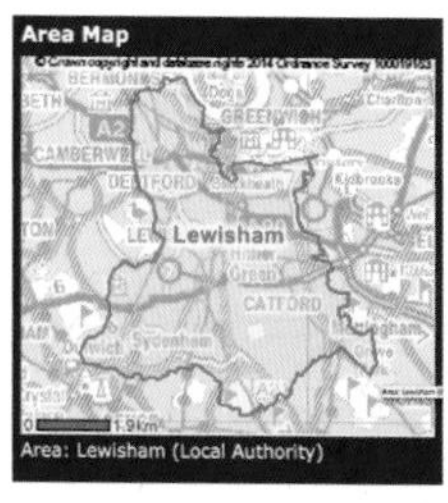

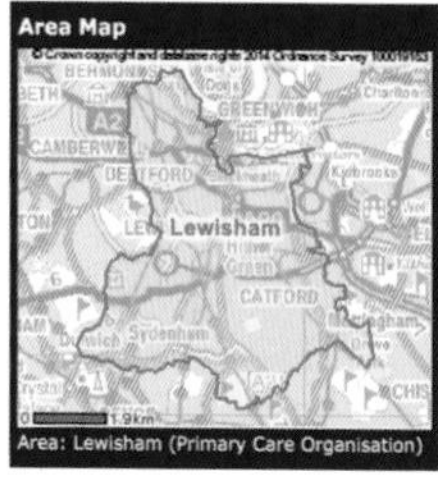

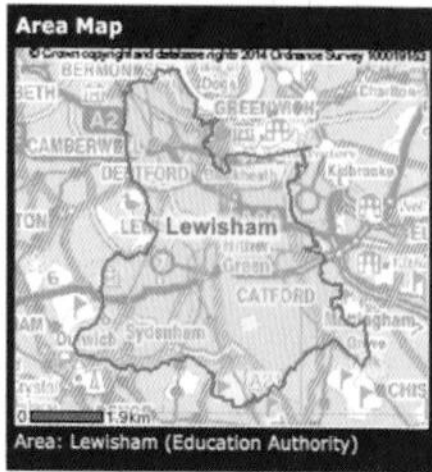

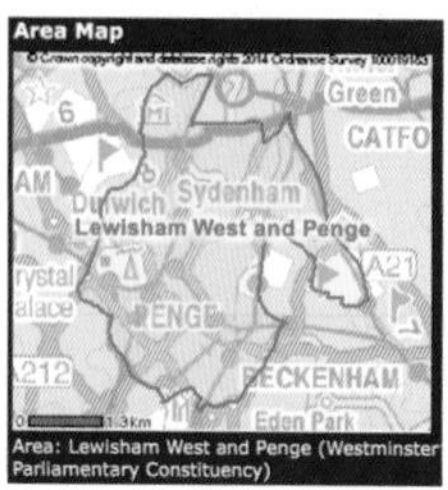

Location is a complicated notion when accessing data, as databases use various scales and definitions, often producing areas with overlapping boundaries.

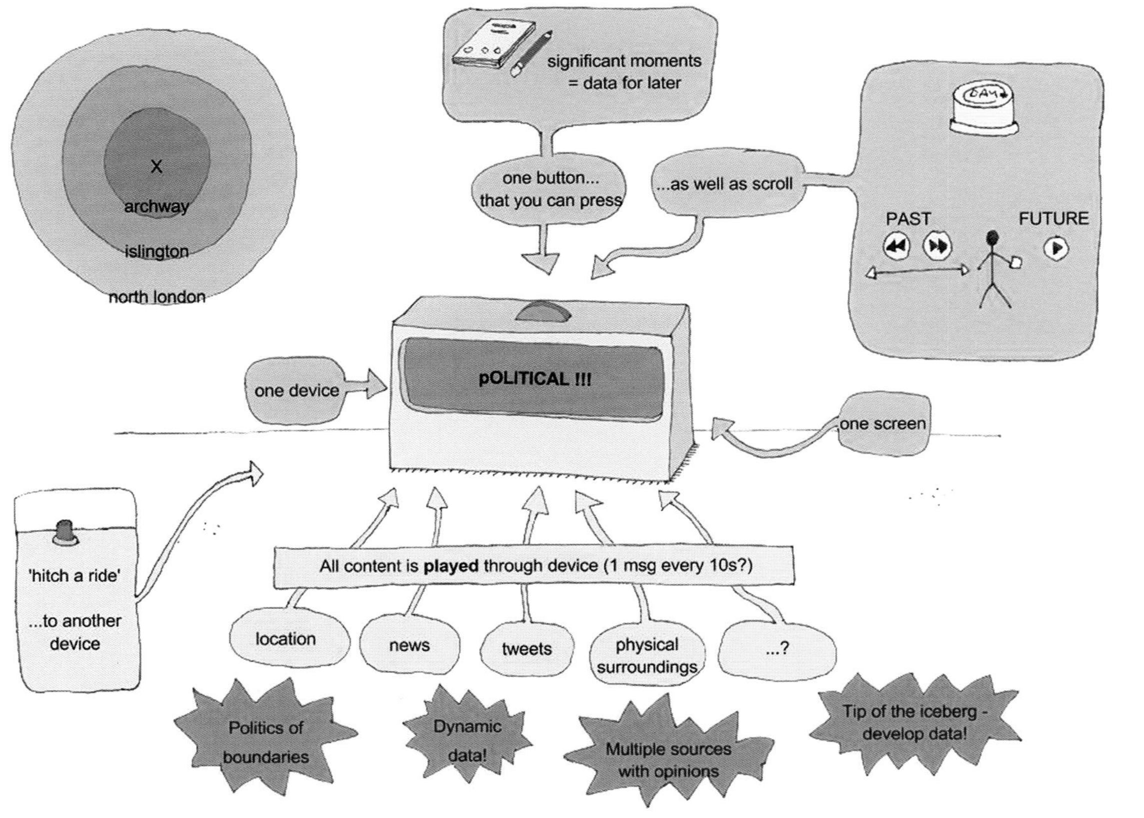

A pivotal moment, when we could finally summarise how the final Datacatcher should work in a single sketch and a simulated stream of messages (see overleaf). However, this was by no means a final specification.

Choreography of a desired feed

You are in Lambeth

The local government is Tory

The area itself deteriorated over the years, due partly to planning blight related to transport schemes that were never realised and to the neglect of its housing stock by both private and council landlords

Drug and gang related problems resulted in the closure of several pubs in the area

Ouch, unemployment is high here

Property prices have gone up by 6% locally
which is the same as the rise of Gas prices in England

Pollution round here is moderately bad
compared with the UK average which is low

Gosh people here are not very healthy

67% of people round here don't eat enough fruit and veg

Government says, we are fatter today than we were 10 years ago

Councillors approved all the Tesco plans for George IV pub in Brixton Hill tonight

Nearby there are 9 people who are in very bad health whilst 28% of people round here smoke

Locally, Mandy M says "*I love ghetto places but Loughborough Junction is NOT. THE. ONE!*"

People here are fatter but happier than where you were yesterday

Nadine's proposal for a desired feed was the first time we imagined how data might be turned into sentences, and a benchmark for what we hoped to achieve.

It is much more affluent in the neighbouring Herne Hill, oh how the other half live

Most people round here read the daily mail and don't own cars

The property in the area is a mixture of Victorian and Georgian mansion blocks and town houses, and local authority housing estates

The main estates are the Loughborough Estate, the Angell Town Estate, and the Moorlands Estate

but it will cost you £291,000 to buy a property round these streets

Did you know the average household income is just £35,000

it's no wonder people can't own cars

Over 10% of people compared with just over 1% where you were yesterday

795 people around here have been declared homeless
but the average property value on this street is £306,920

There are 4,251 households with no central heating
but local emissions are going up

Notes
- local average with uk average
- random census juxtapositions (within category?)
- nonsense correlations
- generational comparisons
- comparisons with where you have been (timeframe?)
- comparison with neighbouring or drift locations (for those who don't travel far)
- no punctuation so that sentences can be joined
- local news can be effectively found via Twitter
- transparency of data - announce source?
- real figures, percentages and rounding up

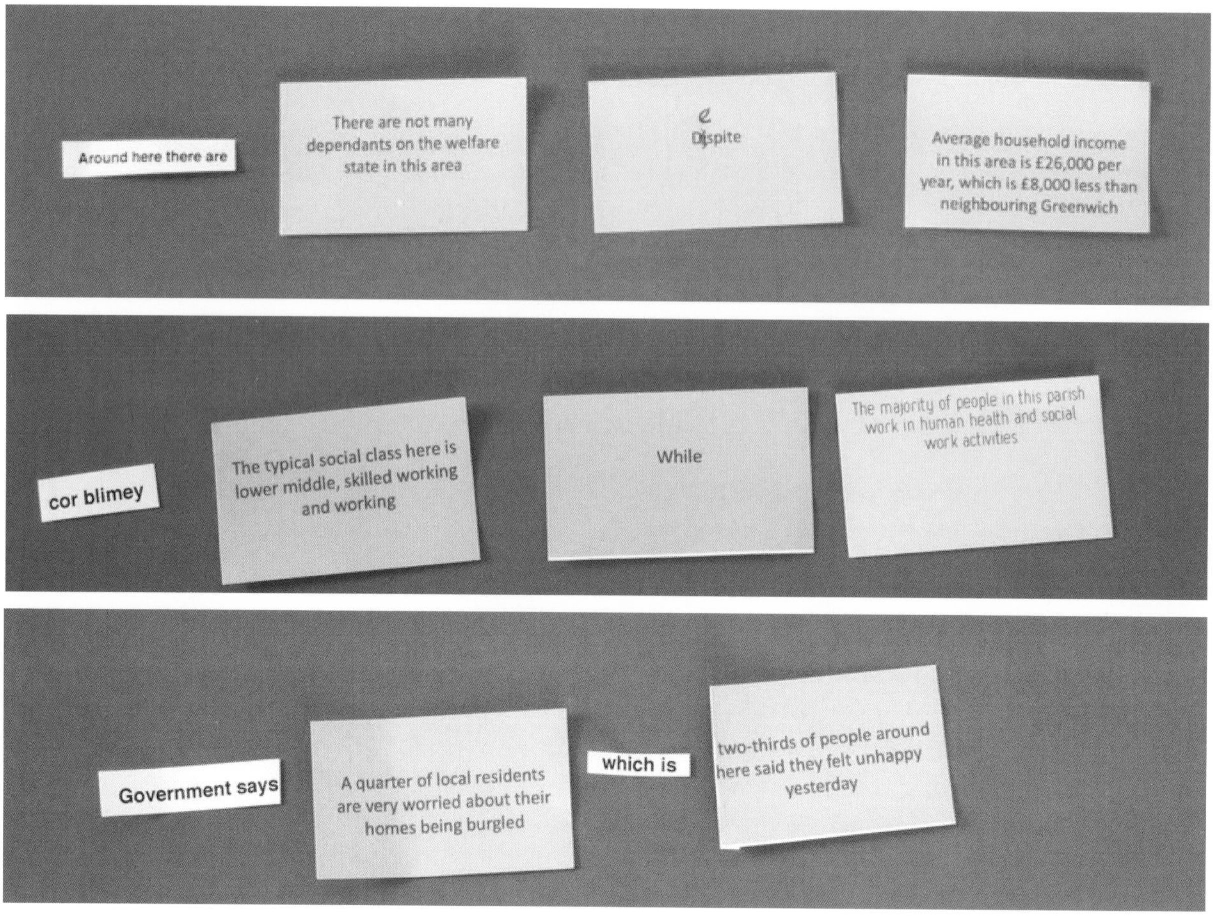

Around here there are
There are not many dependants on the welfare state in this area
Despite
Average household income in this area is £26,000 per year, which is £8,000 less than neighbouring Greenwich

cor blimey
The typical social class here is lower middle, skilled working and working
While
The majority of people in this parish work in human health and social work activities

Government says
A quarter of local residents are very worried about their homes being burgled
which is
two-thirds of people around here said they felt unhappy yesterday

We used cut-up techniques to explore how narratives could be formed by linking sentences about data with a few connecting phrases.

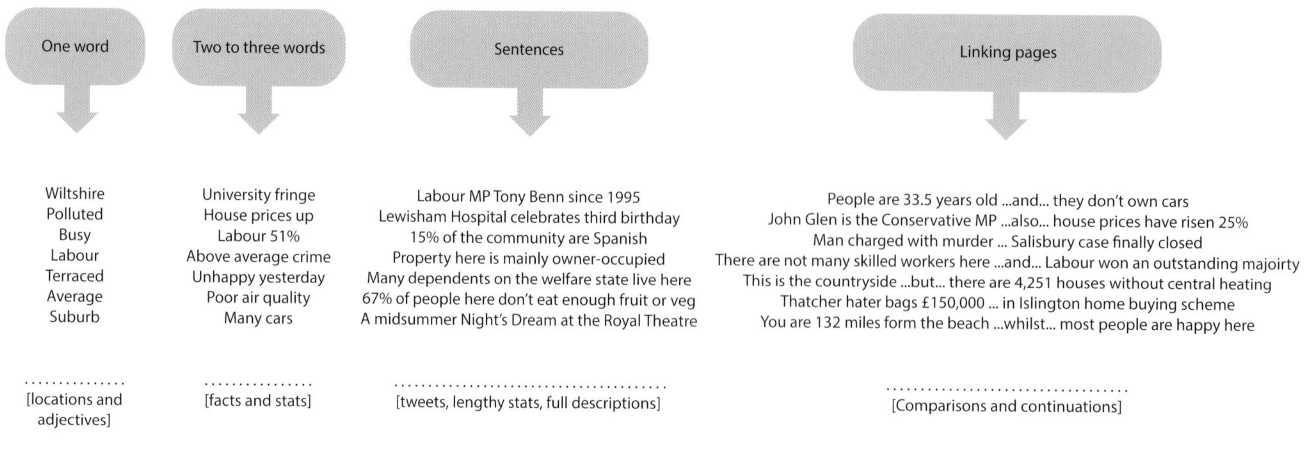

One word
Wiltshire
Polluted
Busy
Labour
Terraced
Average
Suburb
[locations and adjectives]
Two to three words
University fringe
House prices up
Labour 51%
Above average crime
Unhappy yesterday
Poor air quality
Many cars
[facts and stats]
Sentences
Labour MP Tony Benn since 1995
Lewisham Hospital celebrates third birthday
15% of the community are Spanish
Property here is mainly owner-occupied
Many dependents on the welfare state live here
67% of people here don't eat enough fruit or veg
A midsummer Night's Dream at the Royal Theatre
[tweets, lengthy stats, full descriptions]
Linking pages
People are 33.5 years old ...and... they don't own cars
John Glen is the Conservative MP ...also... house prices have risen 25%
Man charged with murder ... Salisbury case finally closed
There are not many skilled workers here ...and... Labour won an outstanding majoirty
This is the countryside ...but... there are 4,251 houses without central heating
Thatcher hater bags £150,000 ... in Islington home buying scheme
You are 132 miles form the beach ...whilst... most people are happy here
[Comparisons and continuations]

Single word messages were used in the final system to provide 'area glimpses' when entering new locations, thinking about the pace of message delivery.

RISK CURATOR

(for example data that might be used
to calculate insurance)

Around here you are at more risk of having a trip or a fall
Lower life expectancy here
You are at a place with medium flood risk
Higher rate of cancer
You are more likely to have your car stolen
More chance of caesarean section
You are more likely to get mugged here
Higher teenage pregnancies
Clay soil, moderate subsidence risk
Pollution is higher here
Household burglary is low
You are more likely to smoke here

INEQUALITY CURATOR

Houses here are worth less than they are one mile away
Neighbouring Herne Hill has much higher salaries than here
Council Tax is lower here
Street parking is free and they pay lower council tax
You have to pay extra to find out the sex of your child here
Higher house values but lower council tax
Higher salaries one mile away
People here are better off
Air quality is worse here than where you were yesterday
Affordable housing is not found here
People here have more green space than where
you've come from
Higher density yet higher council tax
More people on benefits here than where you've come from
Much higher unemployment here
Residents here have a much lower quality of life

Worried that our data might become too static, we considered ways to 'curate' it in various ways. For example, an 'inequality curator' might alter the tone of messages, or different datasets might be weighted by fluctuations of the stock market, or to reflect current news headlines.

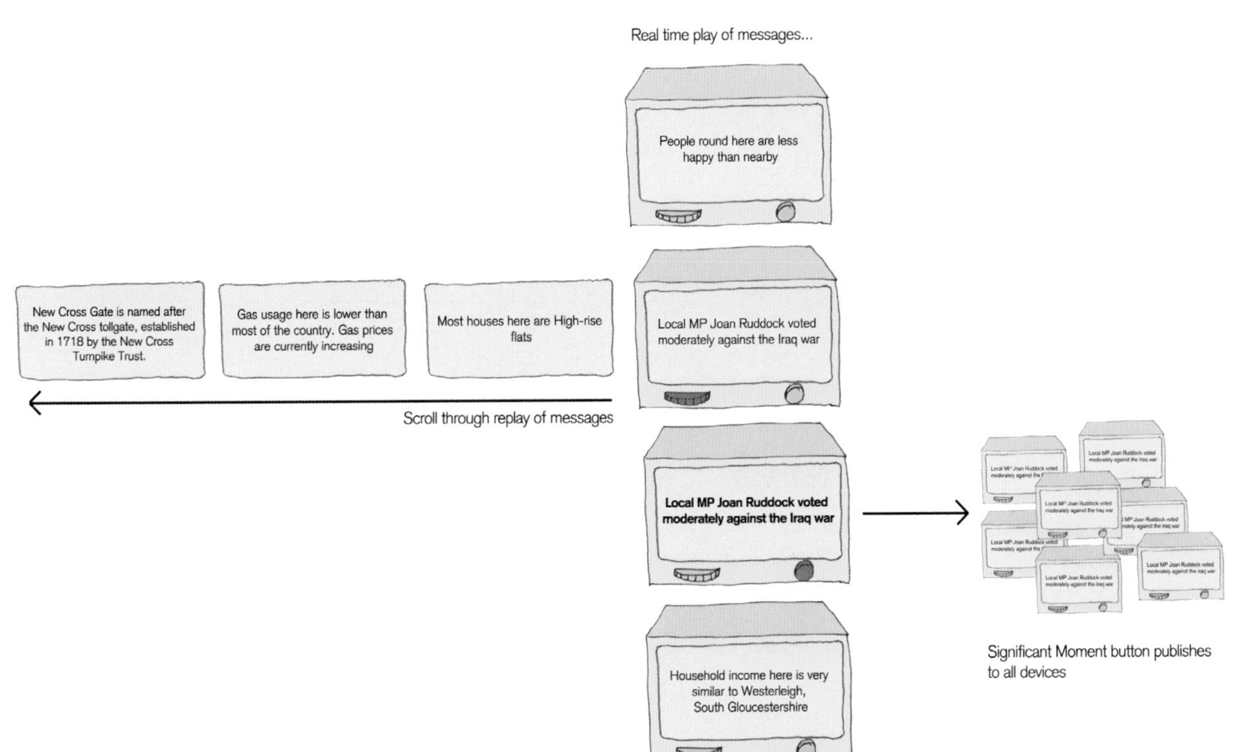

We originally envisioned a 'significant moment' button that would allow the user to send the message displayed on one device to all other devices.

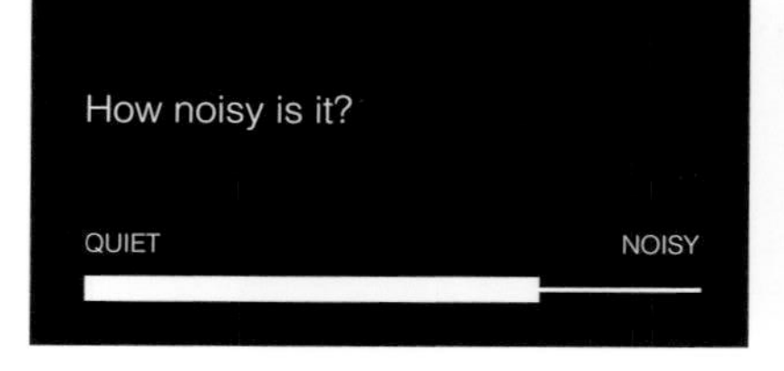

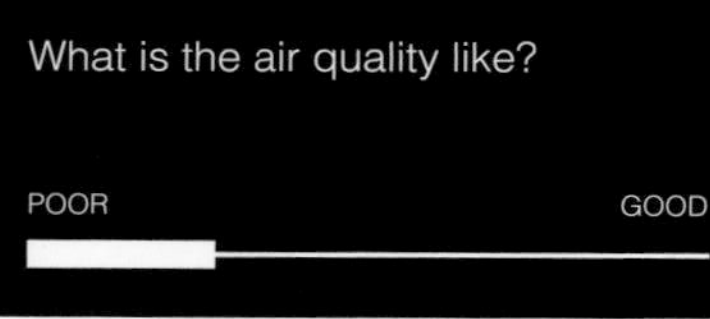

Yesterday in Brixton the air quality was poor.

Brixton, yesterday 13.05

Yesterday, 47% of Data Catchers were in areas of poor air quality.

BROADCAST

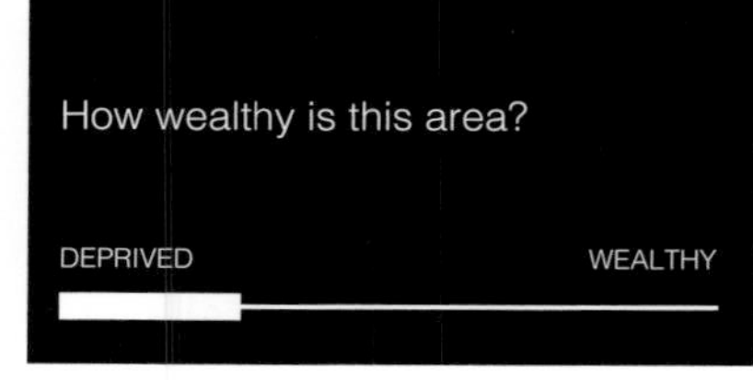

Two days ago Loughborough Junction looked deprived.

Brixton, January 10th, 14.08

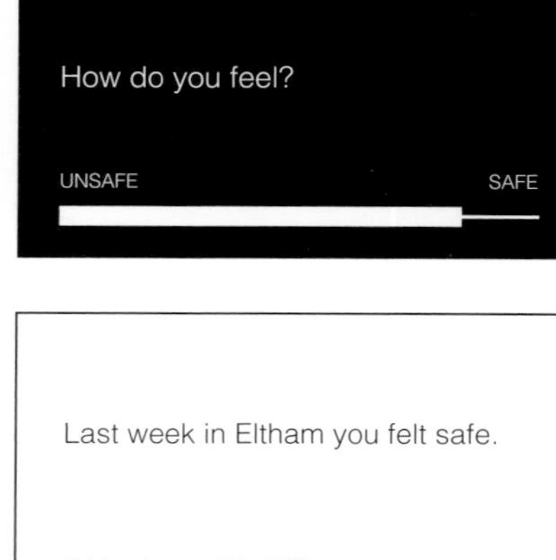

The final major feature to be added to the Datacatcher was the Participant Poll. This builds on the impulses behind the ‘significant moment’ button and data curator explorations. In the final version, people can express their own opinions of an area using a set of 20 questions and multiple-choice answers, many of which were deliberately humorous. Their answers are geo-located and distributed to Datacatchers along with the regular datafeeds, sometimes aggregated with other people’s answers.

Title

The polls: From data subject to citizen

Author

Nadine Jarvis

At a time when data about us is growing exponentially, when large credit agencies know what newspapers we read, what cars we drive, how we vote and socialise, and even what pages we are likely to visit on the web; when insurance companies know the likelihood of everything from needing a hip replacement to having a car stolen; when internet giants know what we are talking about on email, where we are and where we go; when government security is monitoring just about everything we do; when we are shedding more and more of ourselves online, it can be difficult to feel you have any control of your own data and how it is used. Both public and private sector use this data to put us into 'populations'. We are being systematically generalised in order for us to be useful 'data subjects' for the development of products and services. A large portion of this data, however, is available to the public.

The Datacatcher makes much of this data accessible, by bringing together a large corpus of datasets from a variety of public and private sources, turning them into human-readable sentences and displaying them on a handheld device. But what are we to do with this data? Without the motivations that drive large corporations and state systems, how is the person on the street able to find meaning in all this data? One of the key motivations behind the development of the Datacatcher was how we could make Big Data relevant to us as 'little people'. Through our prototyping, we realised that the experience of receiving sentences of data was limiting and less empowering than we'd imagined. So the final feature to be added to the Datacatcher was the Participant Poll.

People are the best sensors — no electronic sensor will be able to give you as clear a sense of a location as you'd get by standing on a street corner yourself. We started to imagine 'activating' our participants as sensors; a system whereby they could respond/disrupt/contribute to the datasets used by the device. So as well as allowing people to view data they could not otherwise access easily on the move — we also wanted them to be able to contribute to political or social data about a location, shifting the role from passive to active participant.

In the final version, people can express their own opinions of an area using a set of 20 questions and multiple-choice answers. The wording of the questions deliberately parodies questionnaires and the census. We ask questions that require an individual sensing of a place such as: 'How does it smell here?', 'How far can you see?', 'Are you safely above sea-level?' and 'Who looks after this place?' Some of the questions point at familiar datasets such as those associated with insurance companies — for example, a concern with flood risk. Others might sound absurd but hint at more sombre issues by asking, for example, 'Is this a dog/cat/fox/rat/horse place?' or 'What are the dogs like here?' (The options for the latter question are: handbag/working/family/weapon/fighting/blow-dried.) The multiple choice answers are not on a linear scale. We don't seek accuracy — there's no agenda behind the questions, we're just trying to open a space for contemplation.

The answers are geo-located and are treated in different ways before being broadcast as sentences across the devices. These first person sentences, which we have come to refer to as 'I say…' and 'We say…' sentences, act to bring forth the individual, something which is lost after data is crunched into categories. It also seeks to counter the voice of 'Them' in our system, the authority of government and other data collectors.

Manufacture

The Datacatcher was the most challenging device that the studio had ever planned to make and we were proposing to batch produce hundreds of them. In parallel to this physical making effort was the task of scaling content delivery for each device. For a number of years the studio had been building devices that relied on remote computation of content. The Prayer Companion, for example, is a fairly simple web device that streams messages sent from a computer based in our studio which scrapes and sorts data from various news and social media feeds. This procedure greatly improves the reliability of the devices we have in the field and allows us to remedy any problems fairly quickly. The Datacatcher uses the same methodology but at a huge scale. Rather than maintaining one feed for a device, we would now be generating hundreds of individual feeds that were reacting in real time to location changes.

These feeds were built from a huge corpus of data, at a scale bigger than anything we had previously worked with. Data from public bodies like the Office for National Statistics, the Department of Energy and Climate Change, and crime statistics from the police were supplemented with data from sources such as Twitter, Experian and Zoopla. The first step in managing this mixture was to translate data points into meaningful and legible sentences. For instance, health-ranking indices for different postcodes were turned into messages such as 'The census shows that 25% of people around these parts are smokers'. Each of these translations is built around a crafted sentence structure that accepts an automatically inserted variable. In total, there are there are around 600 individual translations in the system for each UK postcode.

In this section we describe our processes for managing this data and building a system to deliver individual message streams to each Datacatcher. There are contributions from each of the experts we hired into the project to help build the technical infrastructure that underpins the devices, and we provide reflections on the numerous technical problems we encountered along the way. We also detail the evolution of the Datacatcher form and the subsequent development to rationalise the design for batch production, a process that also necessitated the development of a new method for dyeing the 3D printed housings.

We document a walking tour that we organised prior to the completion of the technical infrastructure. We used this to gather first-hand experience of using the Datacatcher with a simulated data feed and to get feedback from other participants who joined the exercise. Finally, we conclude with a section about the production and assembly of the working Datacatchers.

Census — Office for National Statistics
data.police.uk
Department of Energy and Climate Change
FixmyStreet
Mosaic — Experian
Open Data Communities
The Environment Agency
Weather Underground
They Work For You
Twitter
UK Postcode Data
Wikipedia
Yahoo Finance
Zoopla

Final list of data sources.

Opposite: The earlier experiments with look-up tables eventually became the 'Source Definitions' document; a kind of master reference file that pointed the server to the different datasets and the various categories and ranges that the system would extract.

Name	Source Screen Name	group	priority	likelihood	duration	type	ranges	enabled	description	change Props	query	tone	notes
MosaicDebt Comparison	Experian	mosaic	2	1	10	comparison	[{max: 0, text: "A major credit agency says residents in <%=A.location. gazename%> are in less debt than <%=B. description%>."}, {max: 1, text: "A major credit agency says residents in <%=A. location.gazename%> have about the same amount of debt as <%=B. description%>."}, {max: 2, text: "A major credit agency says residents in <%=A. location.gazename%> are generally in more debt than <%=B.description%>."}]	y	Compare levels of debt with other areas	["auto"]	MOSAICDEBT		is this right? Debt has four categories to data – so do I need to include four?
AirPollutionMessage Comparison	DEFRA	pollution	2	1	10	comparison	[{max: 0, text: "Air pollution levels in <%=A.location.gazename%> are lower than <%=B.description%>."}, {max: 1, text: "Air pollution levels in <%=A.location.gazename%> are the same as <%=B.description%>."}, {max: 2, text: "Air pollution levels in <%=A.location.gazename%> are higher than <%=B.description%>."}]	y	Compares air pollution levels with another lower layer	["auto"]	AIRPOLLUTION		not sure this is right!
CrimeType Comparison MessageSource Vehicle	Police	crime	2	1	10	comparison	[{max: 0 , text: "More vehicle crime here in <%=A.location.gazename%> than <%=B.description%>."}, {max: 1 , text: "There is roughly the same amount of vehicle crime here <%=A. location.gazename%> as there were <%=B. description%>."}, {max: 2 , text: "Less vehicle crime here <%=A.location.gazename%> than <%=B. description%>."}]	y	Compare level of vehicle crime with another area.	["auto"]	CRIMEPOLICE		risk
HipReplace MessageSourceArea Comparison	Census	hospital admissions	2	1	10	comparison	[{max: 0 , text: "Less hips have been replaced in <%=A.location. gazename%> than in neighbouring <%=B. description%>."}, {max: 1 , text: "About the same number of hips have been replaced in <%=A. location.gazename%> as in neighbouring <%=B.description%>."}, {max: 2 , text: "More hips have been replaced in <%=A.location. gazename%> than in neighbouring <%=B. description%>."}]	y	Compare number of hips replaced with other areas	["auto"]	HOSPITAL ADMISSIONS	provocative	
NearbyPlaceOf WorshipComparison MessageSource	Google	nearby	2	1	10	comparison	[{max: 0 , text: "More places of worship here in <%=A.location.gazename%> than <%=B.description%>."}, {max: 1 , text: "There are roughly the same amount of places of worship here <%=A.location.gazename%> as there are <%=B.description%>."}, {max: 2 , text: "Less places of worship here <%=A.location.gazename%> than <%=B.description%>."}]	y	Compare number of places of worship	["auto"]	GOOGLEPLACES		

Title

Notes from a data wrangler

Author

Robin Beitra

At the core of each Datacatcher message is some data taken from one or more sources. This was an ambitious project which required the aggregation of many data sources into one system.

This process involved several steps, although not in strict order; we were developing ideas, discovering new sources and finding problems throughout the development process. The steps were:

1. Identifying desirable datasets or categories
2. Searching for usable sources
3. Acquiring the data
4. Converting it to work with the system
5. Integrating the data into the system
6. Building sentences to use the data

By the time I joined the project, a lot of work had already gone into identifying and searching for sources, as well as some acquisition. As the project went on, we continued to find more desirable datasets so these tasks were never really finished!

Each of these steps also presented some interesting technical challenges. Some data could not be used because of copyright or legal concerns, or required approval from the provider. Other data simply did not exist in a usable form. For example, flood risk data was only available in a complex vector data format; integrating it would have taken too long, to the detriment of other data sources. For a long time we did not have data on a location's distance from the sea — eventually I created some software to generate this from mapping data.

Data is available in many forms. Sometimes raw data files can be downloaded from a website, whereas others require custom software to communicate with the data provider. The data from the Office for National Statistics (ONS), for example, is accessible via a web API [Application Programming Interface]. There were almost 20 ONS datasets we were interested in, so I built some custom tools to search, download and convert the data specifically from the ONS.

Almost every data source we worked with used a different type of geographic coding, including postcodes, GPS coordinates and governmental coding schemes. These were further complicated by changing schemes. There are 2,750 new postcodes created every month, whilst 2,500 are discontinued. This presented problems for some older data.

All of these difficulties made the process take longer than we anticipated! Nevertheless, after a lot of time discussing, investigating and implementing we were able to build a system that uses a diverse collection of data in a unified manner.

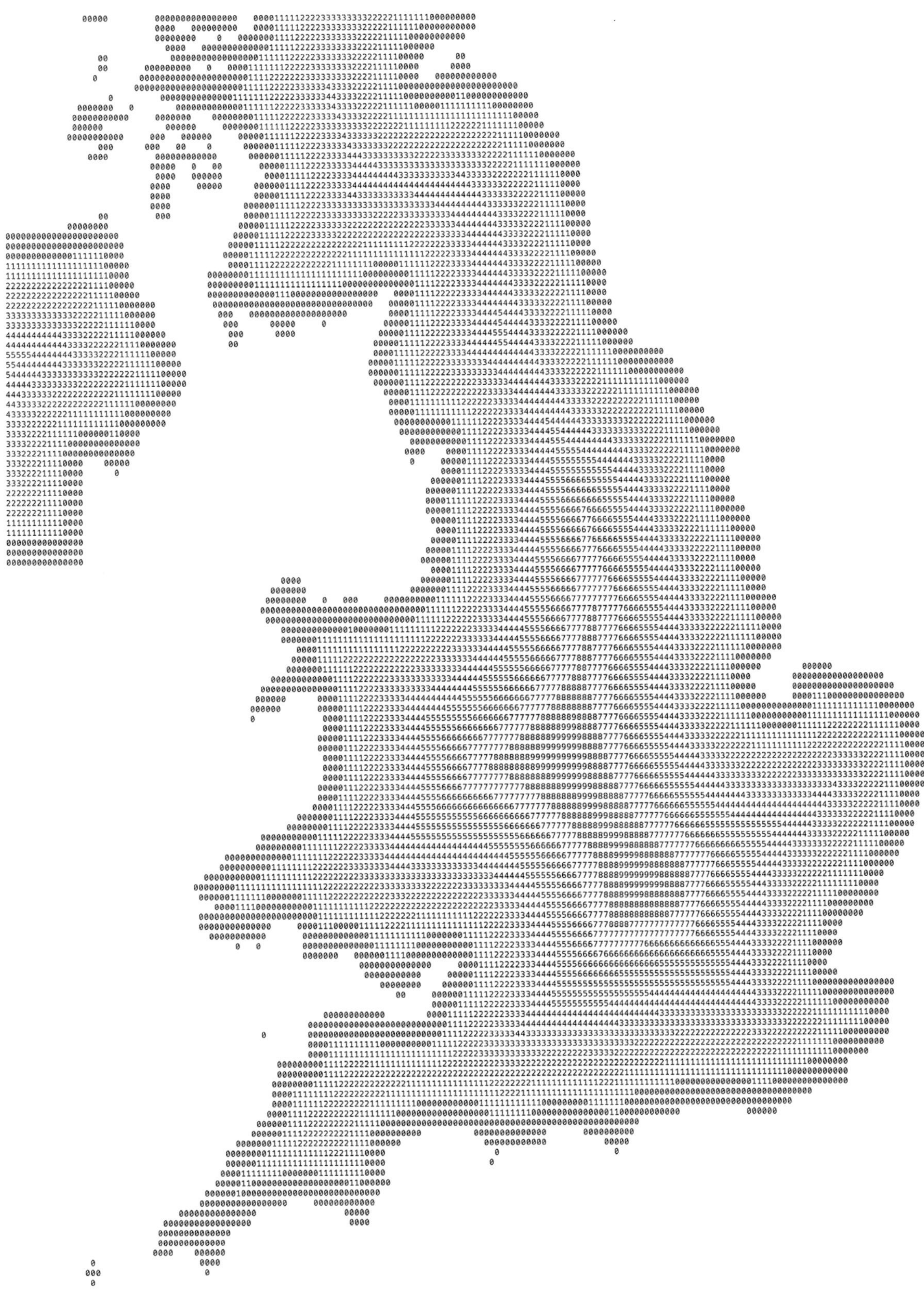

Robin’s look-up table to return information about ‘distance to the sea’.

Title

Developing the message

Author

Richard Cook

One of the central aspects of the Datacatcher project was the refining of raw data into formed sentences that would be read by users of the device. In trying to determine how sentences should be formed, their content, tone and structure, it was first necessary to establish what the sentences as a whole were trying to achieve. It became apparent upon discussion with the design team that the purpose was to engage readers with their area, to make them look up from the device and take in their surroundings. Each sentence had to balance the following elements:

— Authenticity: the data had to be feasible and reflect the surroundings to seem 'real'
— Contrast: comparisons of data within a single sentence provided room for thought and provoked greater interest
— Transparency: it should be clear where the data came from and sentence structure and language should not undermine this, e.g. through use of words such as 'possibly'

Building on these initial foundations, it then became easier to focus on areas such as tone and language. The team felt it was key to use language that did not lead or direct the user, and in addition that the tone should not be too highly politicised — although some room to provoke through the message was welcome. This enabled us to create a range of sentences that could be tailored to integrate a range of data, providing engaging messages about different locations for datacatcher users to interact with and respond to.

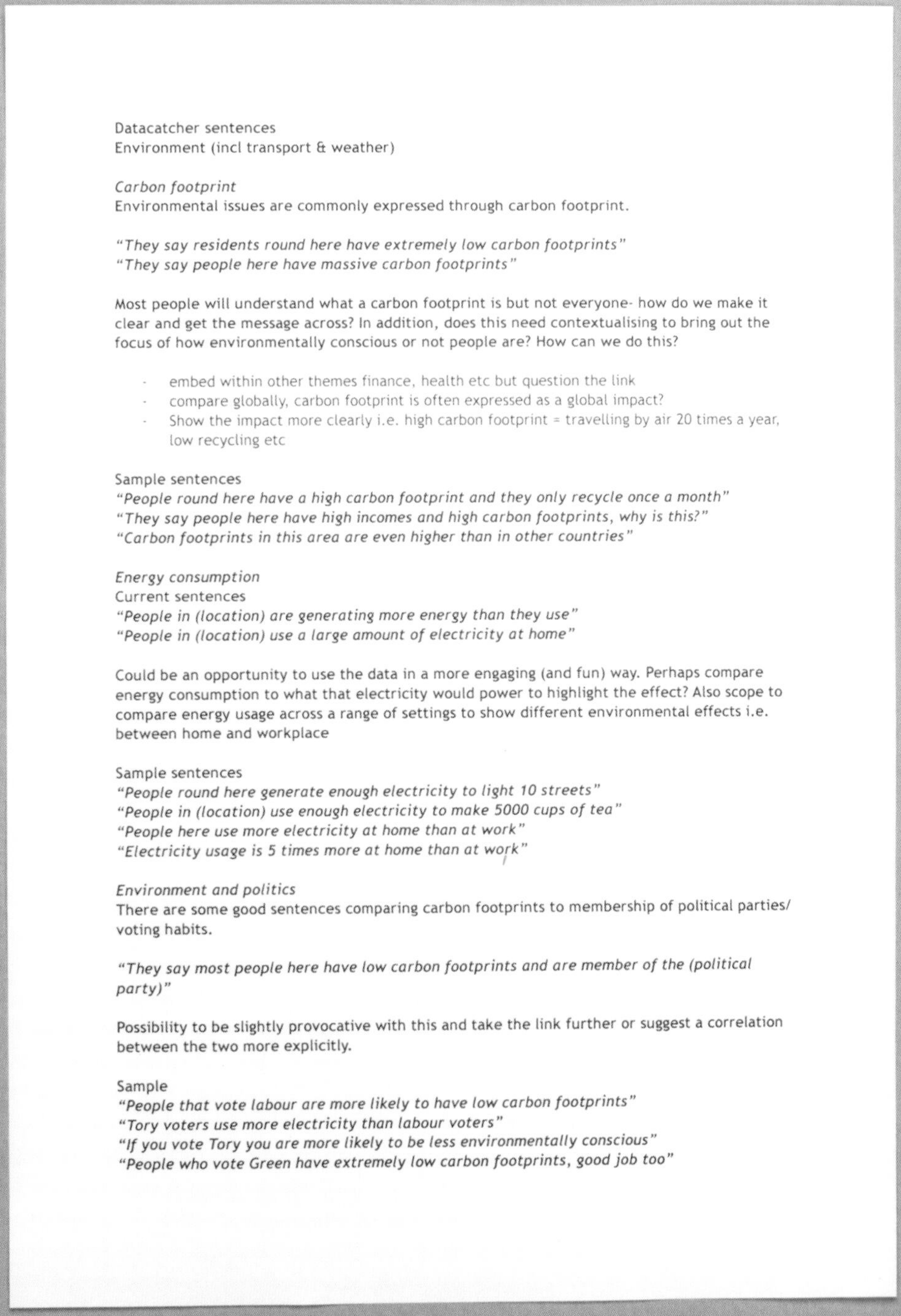

Datacatcher sentences
Environment (incl transport & weather)

Carbon footprint
Environmental issues are commonly expressed through carbon footprint.

"They say residents round here have extremely low carbon footprints"
"They say people here have massive carbon footprints"

Most people will understand what a carbon footprint is but not everyone- how do we make it clear and get the message across? In addition, does this need contextualising to bring out the focus of how environmentally conscious or not people are? How can we do this?

- embed within other themes finance, health etc but question the link
- compare globally, carbon footprint is often expressed as a global impact?
- Show the impact more clearly i.e. high carbon footprint = travelling by air 20 times a year, low recycling etc

Sample sentences
"People round here have a high carbon footprint and they only recycle once a month"
"They say people here have high incomes and high carbon footprints, why is this?"
"Carbon footprints in this area are even higher than in other countries"

Energy consumption
Current sentences
"People in (location) are generating more energy than they use"
"People in (location) use a large amount of electricity at home"

Could be an opportunity to use the data in a more engaging (and fun) way. Perhaps compare energy consumption to what that electricity would power to highlight the effect? Also scope to compare energy usage across a range of settings to show different environmental effects i.e. between home and workplace

Sample sentences
"People round here generate enough electricity to light 10 streets"
"People in (location) use enough electricity to make 5000 cups of tea"
"People here use more electricity at home than at work"
"Electricity usage is 5 times more at home than at work"

Environment and politics
There are some good sentences comparing carbon footprints to membership of political parties/ voting habits.

"They say most people here have low carbon footprints and are member of the (political party)"

Possibility to be slightly provocative with this and take the link further or suggest a correlation between the two more explicitly.

Sample
"People that vote labour are more likely to have low carbon footprints"
"Tory voters use more electricity than labour voters"
"If you vote Tory you are more likely to be less environmentally conscious"
"People who vote Green have extremely low carbon footprints, good job too"

Crafting sentence templates that could frame data in readable and varied ways.

tweets if more than 5 times.

e is zero, with exceptions (please add):
es
s

d be lowercase unless a noun e.g. the Guardian.

nce should be capitalised (script needed).

marks around values, unless it is a particularly obscure phrase e.g.
saic's population categorisation.

les around population size - to decide w/b 7/7

= 'the streets around here', 'thePostcode'
layer = 'around here' or 'within one mile of here'
ward of WardName'
= 'nameofLA' or 'in this borough'

nd 'TheSource say' to non descipt - to decide w/b 7/7

)7/14

aSW9 tweeted "http://t.co/RzlZDyyxFQ". It was retweeted 0 times.
yMessageSourceWithRetweet
more than 5 times.

hat contain links (I think this was in the original plan but wasn't

aSW9 tweeted "http://t.co/RzlZDyyxFQ"
yMessageSource2

ue is zero I don't think it should be used

en 'that' and 'income':
cy says thatincome is this area is just over the national average.
MessageSourceWordedRobin2

sentences:
ating is in the top 15% of the country most people here are
class.
class

vork better than others, not sure about this one:
ople locally are obese and average income is £38,591
neMessageSource

tuency of .

onstituency of E9 5EN is .

ent of E9 5EN is "".

act all the sea level sentences seem to be missing a value)

5EN is "".

es in E9 5EN are "".

e cost of property here is "" and most are "".

E9 5EN is generally though to be "".

ple round here read the The Guardian and live in .

ote marks: "Tower Hamlets" County council.

dwellings in Tower Hamlets are vacant. OR OR6710

0.00 inches of rain today.
source: WeatherRainTodayMessageSourceGlimpse

Exception to zero value rule for datasets (see exception list in rules)

Phrasing:
They say that the majority of people have an average carbon footprint here and the Labour party is in power.
source: MosaicCarbonFootprintLocalPartyWordedRobin
Suggested alternative:
Around here the Labour party is in power and the carbon footprint is average.
source: MosaicCarbonFootprintLocalPartyWordedRobin

Use of caps for values
E.g.
They say house prices in SW9 8SA are Below average.
source: UKPostcodePropertyPriceMessageSource3
Make all datasets lowercase (unless a noun e.g. the Guardian)
Write script to always make first letter of a sentence capitalised.

Use of quotation marks
Remove all quotation marks around values, unless it is a particularly obscure phrase e.g. some of experian mosaic's population categorisation.
The house price in SW9 8SA is generally thought to be "Below average".
source: UKPostcodePropertyPriceMessageSource2

More examples of double quotes:
They say the average cost of property here is "Below average" and most are "Terraced, flats".
source: UKPostcodeHousingTypesMessageSource3
Sometimes double quotes can give a syndical tone (like miming the action with your hands during speech)

Phrasing:
Most houseowners in SW9 8SA are "Owner-occupied, private rental, social housing".
source: UKPostcodeHousingOwnersMessageSource
Should be:
Most houses in SW9 8SA are "Owner-occupied, private rental, social housing".
source: UKPostcodeHousingOwnersMessageSource
*check if works with whole dataset.

Phrasing:
1,068 crimes in May.

In this area, more land is used for other use land than for non residential buildings.
(I think "other use land" needs to be in quotes / or if you alter the data set it could say 'In this area, more land is used for other purposes than for non residential buildings.)

According to a major credit agency a lot of people round here were born in Far East.
(please add 'the' in front of far East in the original data set)

The census suggests 1,562 households in the area are in temporary accomodation leased to the local authority. (SP accommodation)

They say 1,562 households in the area are in temporary accomodation leased to the council but are still classed as homeless. (SP accommodation)

Needs quote marks or rephrasing: The Government say that 2% of people in Stratford are of "Other" ethnicity.

Needs tweaking: This area is diverse, with 5% of people coming from the Mixed community and 26% of people from the Asian community.

Needs full stop: There are not many people out of work who are State pension claimants

SP jobshare: There are a lot of Females in professional/managerial jobshere.

Should this say house rather than property: A major credit agency says it will cost you £600,001-£900,000 to buy a property here.

SP employment: One in five people are in full time employement.

Could we round these numbers up? : A major credit agency says there are 51,667 who are employed full-time and 10,087 part time and 8,644 self employed.

Change to Buddhism in dataset: According to a major credit agency Buddhist is a popular religion round here.

SP elderly: They say that many people round here need to spend money on residential care for elederly relatives.

source: CrimeCountMessageSourceGlimpse
Change to:
1,068 crimes here in May.
source: CrimeCountMessageSourceGlimpse

Phrasing:
Police say there were over 1,060 crimes report
source: CrimeCountMessageRoundedSource
Change to:
Police say there were over 1,060 crimes report
source: CrimeCountMessageRoundedSource

Unsure about phrasing:
13% of locals drink too much and there are 20
source: NearbyPubBingeDrinkMessageSource

this is nicer phrasing (so maybe delete last):
They say over one in ten people in this area bi
mile of here.
source: NearbyPubBingeDrinkWordedSource

ratio of 'they say' and 'X say' to nondescript. Do w
we have a running curated feed.

Wikipedia errors - code showing in sentence:
Adjacent landowners began to d
of the creation of new roads and a boom in the
and the absorption of South Kensington into L
Underground at Gloucester Road and South K
directly to the main railway termini and to the
of the city in Westminster, the West End and t
source: WikipediaNearbyMessageSource
The nearest Tube stations are Sc
last char is = d.
source: WikipediaNearbyMessageSource

Doesn't work for Conservative value:
Kensington is governed by Conservative.
source: 3
Change to: n
If value = conservative use 'the Conservatives'
(check code works for other variables)

Rephrase: They say many people living round he

Space needed: Censuses show that most residen
to work.

Could these two sentences become combined wit
they are compatible or contradictory:
People in Stratford are less healthy than nearby i
People in Stratford are better off than nearby in B
To become :
People in Stratford are less healthy than nearby in

Round numbers
from 999 to 000 e.g. (50,000 - 59,999 to 50,000 -
doable via a lookup table but there are around
take a long time so leaving this for now.

Need to commit google places changes to the

- MP Votes scraper has broken (web

Checks;

- RE-TEST WIKI CONDITIONS

- TIGHTEN UP COMMON FAMILY SE

- FINISH BENEFITS MESSAGES

- put the 'none' category in the political message?

CrimeLevelMessageSource <- do we have a national ave

The snagging list was central to my work developing the Datacatcher's messages. Everyone on the team had access to this document. It became the place to list potential data sources that could be added to the server; and it acted as a central platform to note and overcome issues, such as how to optimise the technical aspects of message curation, or ensure messages fit the linguistic standard.
Robin Hunter

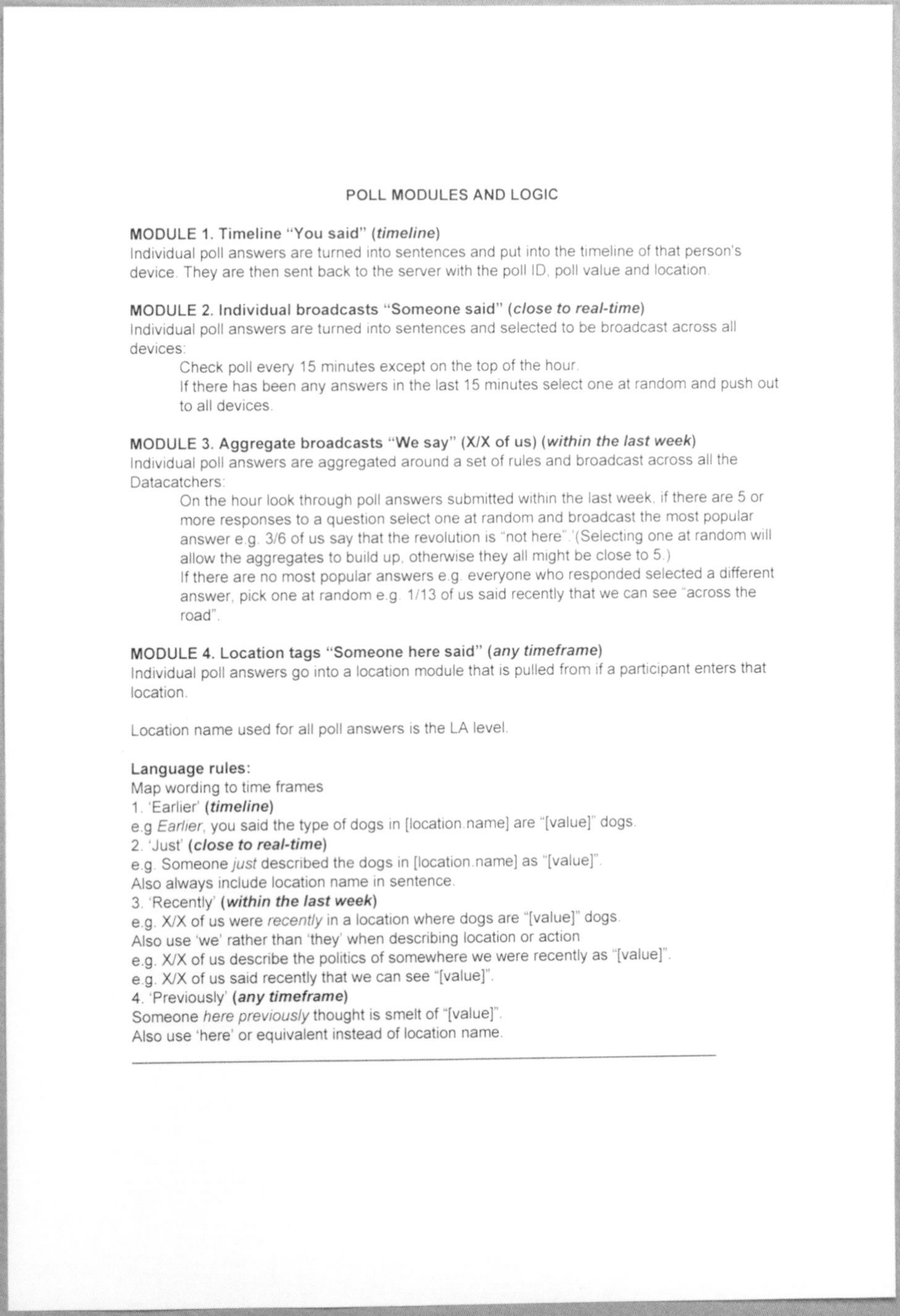

POLL MODULES AND LOGIC

MODULE 1. Timeline "You said" (*timeline*)
Individual poll answers are turned into sentences and put into the timeline of that person's device. They are then sent back to the server with the poll ID, poll value and location.

MODULE 2. Individual broadcasts "Someone said" (*close to real-time*)
Individual poll answers are turned into sentences and selected to be broadcast across all devices:

Check poll every 15 minutes except on the top of the hour.
If there has been any answers in the last 15 minutes select one at random and push out to all devices.

MODULE 3. Aggregate broadcasts "We say" (X/X of us) (*within the last week*)
Individual poll answers are aggregated around a set of rules and broadcast across all the Datacatchers:

On the hour look through poll answers submitted within the last week, if there are 5 or more responses to a question select one at random and broadcast the most popular answer e.g. 3/6 of us say that the revolution is "not here".(Selecting one at random will allow the aggregates to build up, otherwise they all might be close to 5.)
If there are no most popular answers e.g. everyone who responded selected a different answer, pick one at random e.g. 1/13 of us said recently that we can see "across the road".

MODULE 4. Location tags "Someone here said" (*any timeframe*)
Individual poll answers go into a location module that is pulled from if a participant enters that location.

Location name used for all poll answers is the LA level.

Language rules:
Map wording to time frames
1. 'Earlier' (***timeline***)
e.g *Earlier*, you said the type of dogs in [location.name] are "[value]" dogs.
2. 'Just' (***close to real-time***)
e.g. Someone *just* described the dogs in [location.name] as "[value]".
Also always include location name in sentence.
3. 'Recently' (***within the last week***)
e.g. X/X of us were *recently* in a location where dogs are "[value]" dogs.
Also use 'we' rather than 'they' when describing location or action
e.g. X/X of us describe the politics of somewhere we were recently as "[value]".
e.g. X/X of us said recently that we can see "[value]".
4. 'Previously' (***any timeframe***)
Someone *here previously* thought is smelt of "[value]".
Also use 'here' or equivalent instead of location name.

This specification outlined four 'modules' that would form messages out of the poll answers people submitted.

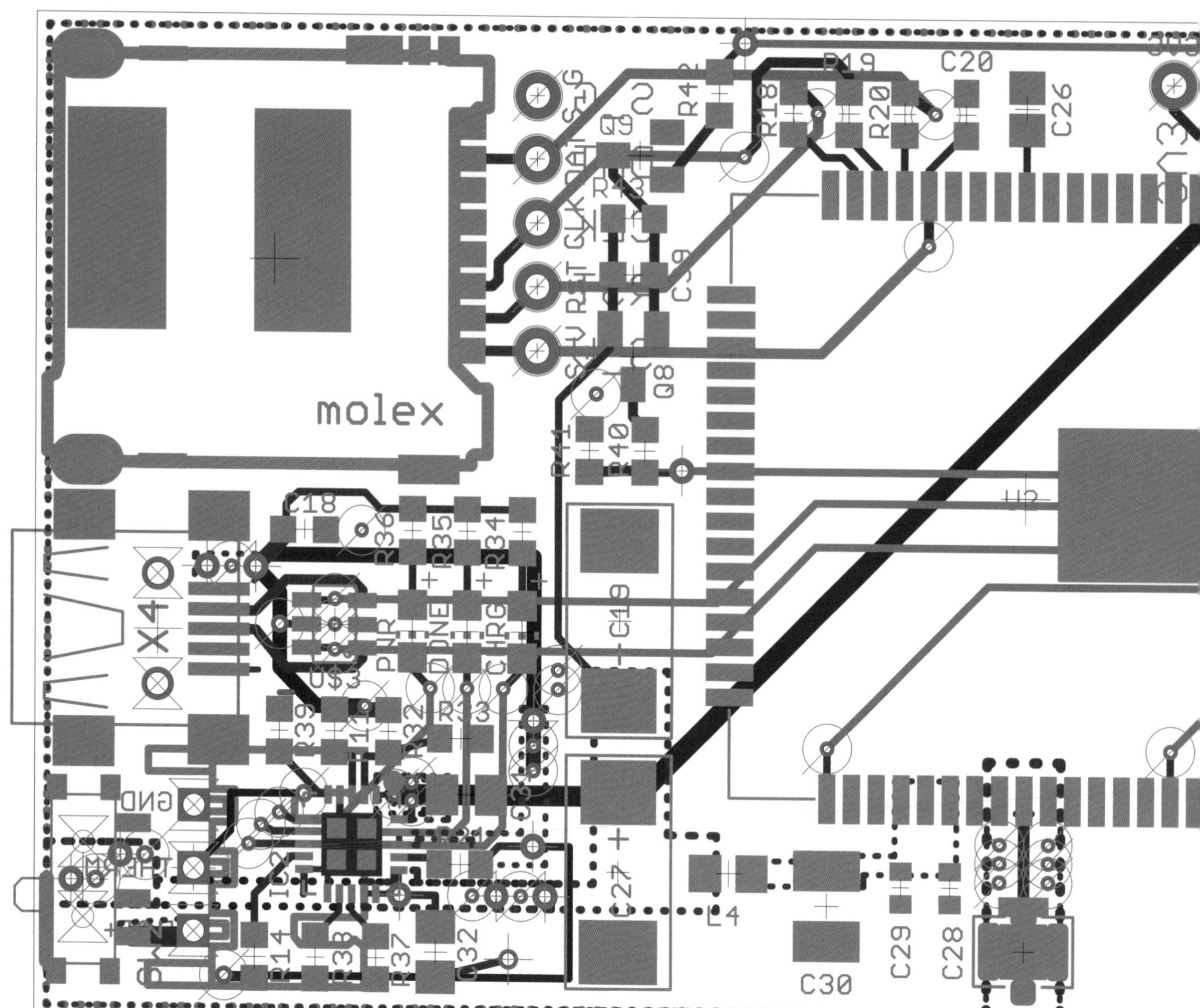

Design for version 2.1 of the Datacatcher's main PCB.

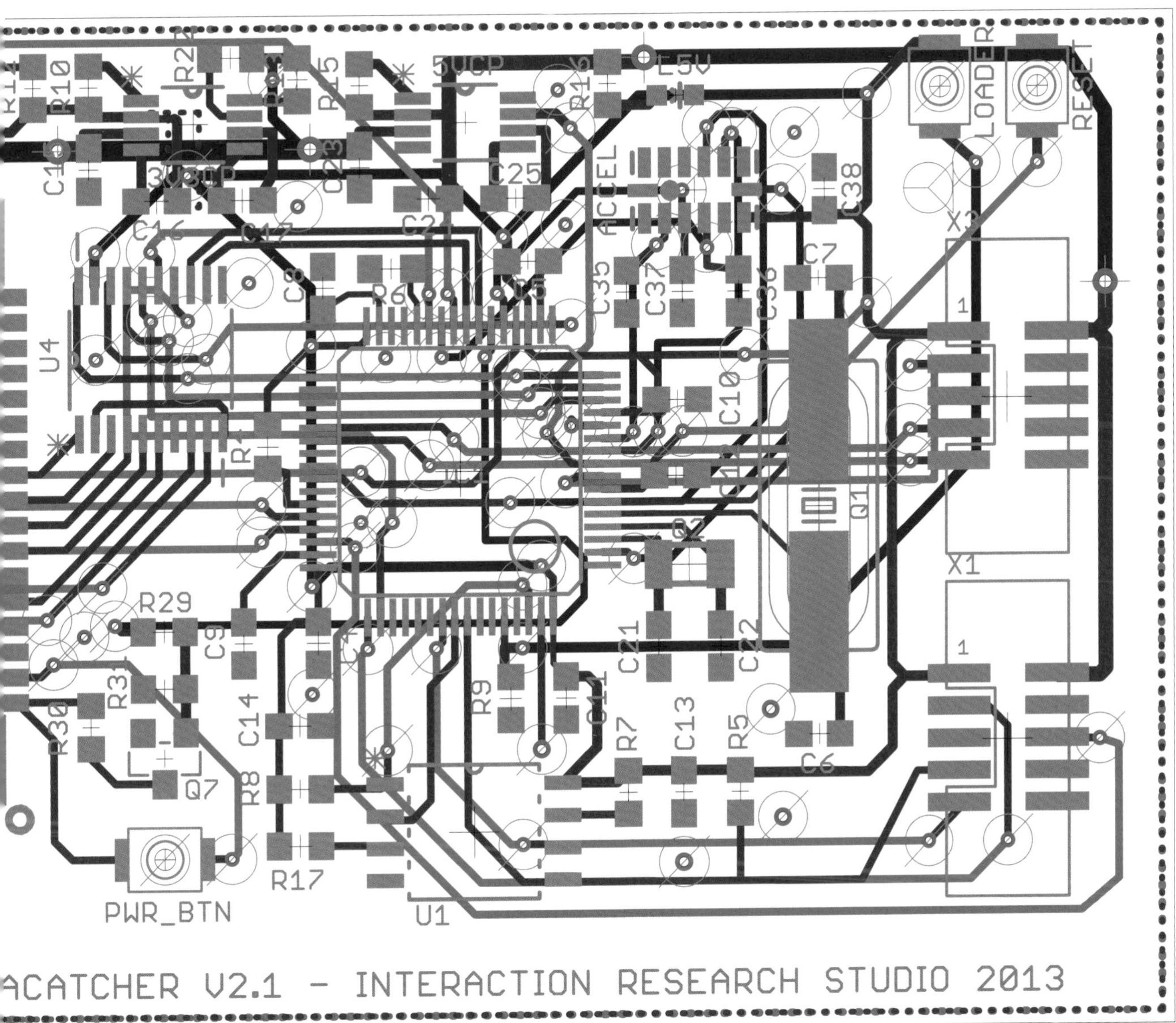
R10
5VCP
L5V
LOADER
RESET
C25
ACCEL
C38
X3
C16
C17
C35
C37
C36
C7
U4
C10
Q1
X1
R29
C9
C21
C22
R9
C11
C14
R7
C13
R5
C6
Q7
R8
R17
PWR_BTN
U1
ACATCHER V2.1 - INTERACTION RESEARCH STUDIO 2013

This is possibly the most complex project (both technically and conceptually) I have ever been part of — how do you collate and manage thousands of data points, while presenting the information to the user in a rich, yet simple format?

The challenge of developing the initial Datacatcher firmware — message transmission, storage and display, along with managing sensor readings and GPRS data connections was the most rewarding task I have undertaken.

Using the finished device in the field for the first time was incredible — I am still astonished that such a complicated, large scale project as this was designed and manufactured by only a handful of people.

The resulting experience should provoke years' worth of political discussion among every community it touches.

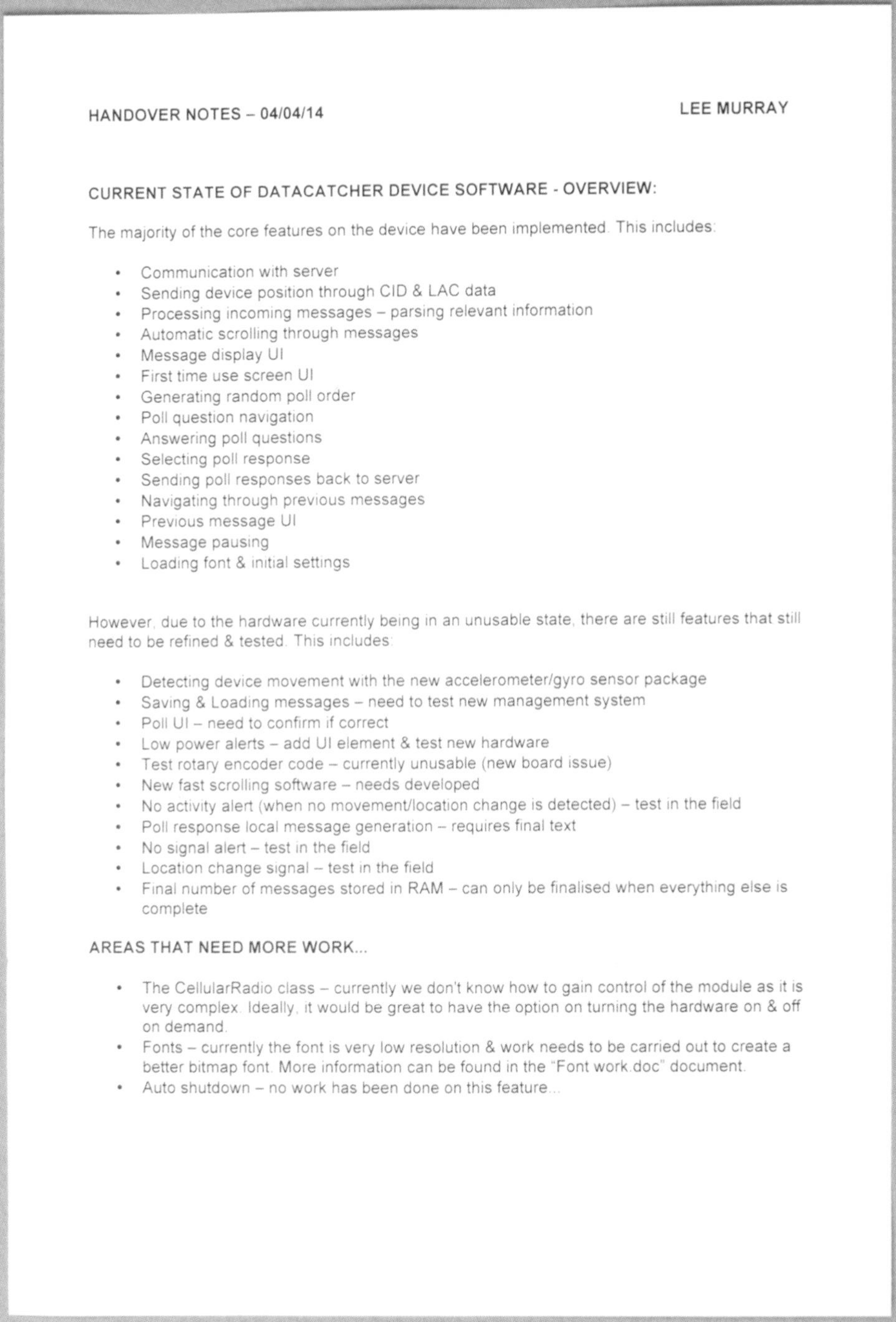

HANDOVER NOTES – 04/04/14 LEE MURRAY

CURRENT STATE OF DATACATCHER DEVICE SOFTWARE - OVERVIEW:

The majority of the core features on the device have been implemented. This includes:

- Communication with server
- Sending device position through CID & LAC data
- Processing incoming messages – parsing relevant information
- Automatic scrolling through messages
- Message display UI
- First time use screen UI
- Generating random poll order
- Poll question navigation
- Answering poll questions
- Selecting poll response
- Sending poll responses back to server
- Navigating through previous messages
- Previous message UI
- Message pausing
- Loading font & initial settings

However, due to the hardware currently being in an unusable state, there are still features that still need to be refined & tested. This includes:

- Detecting device movement with the new accelerometer/gyro sensor package
- Saving & Loading messages – need to test new management system
- Poll UI – need to confirm if correct
- Low power alerts – add UI element & test new hardware
- Test rotary encoder code – currently unusable (new board issue)
- New fast scrolling software – needs developed
- No activity alert (when no movement/location change is detected) – test in the field
- Poll response local message generation – requires final text
- No signal alert – test in the field
- Location change signal – test in the field
- Final number of messages stored in RAM – can only be finalised when everything else is complete

AREAS THAT NEED MORE WORK...

- The CellularRadio class – currently we don't know how to gain control of the module as it is very complex. Ideally, it would be great to have the option on turning the hardware on & off on demand.
- Fonts – currently the font is very low resolution & work needs to be carried out to create a better bitmap font. More information can be found in the "Font work.doc" document.
- Auto shutdown – no work has been done on this feature...

There were several changes of hard- and software technologists over the course of the project. These are Lee's handover notes for the coders who would take over the project.

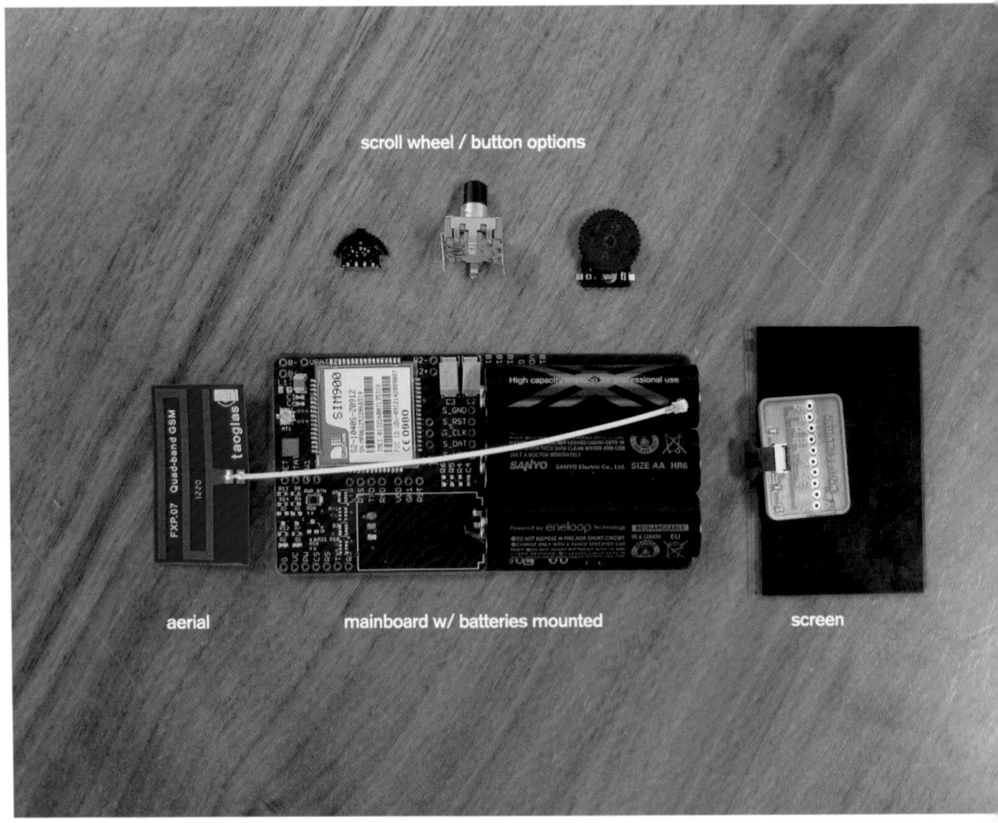

The first assembled PCBs arrive from the manufacturer.

The batch production of the Datacatcher brought up many unexpected issues, but perhaps the most surprising to us was the scarcity of electronic components and how quickly stockpiles of parts can evaporate globally. The largest problem we had was with our choice of display. We explored many different types of screen, but the best choice for the Datacatcher was a brand new component manufactured by Sharp with very similar properties to those found in eBook readers: it has a high pixel density that can render crisp legible text, requires very low-power, and works well in direct sunlight. These were qualities not normally found in small displays and would add distinctiveness to the design of the Datacatcher.

The Sharp screen became our preferred option mid-way through 2013, but it took months for us to develop the other Datacatcher hardware needed to confirm the viability of this part in the final specification. So it was not until October that year that we could be technically sure we could use this display. However, when we decided to order the screens for our planned production run of 250, we discovered the supplier had sold all of the 10,000 or so units that been in stock when we ordered the first sample unit.

We started to contact other suppliers only to find they had also sold thousands of units in the past few months. To make matters worse, we discovered that Sharp was not planning to produce any more until the second quarter of 2014, which was later than the deployment date we were planning. This presented a problem because we were committed to using the component and there were simply no alternative parts that we could use.

What followed was a global hunt for all the remaining stock in which we approached just about every electronics supplier in the world. Altogether we managed to scrape 139 screens from sources all over the world. In many cases, we made single digit orders from wholesalers selling us their last few units. We also contacted forum users who were discussing technical aspects of the component, and were fortunate enough to discover a developer who had 75 units remaining from a cancelled project. Had it not been for this haul, our production run would have been a great deal smaller; it seemed that we had managed to procure all of the world's remaining stock of this part.

The scarcity of the screen was a major issue for us, but it was not the only part that we found to be suddenly unavailable. We had similar issues with everyday components such as batteries, voltage regulators, memory chips and even the rotary encoder used in the dial. Thankfully, we found substitutes for those components, but these experiences led us to preemptively purchase a batch of a particular 9-axis gyroscope which was predicted to sell out quickly because of its use in hobby drones. Despite our forward planning with this part, the gyroscope unfortunately remains an unused component on the PCB in every Datacatcher, as we were unable to fully integrate the part into the software development.

Although in manufacturing terms our batch volume was comparatively low, we discovered that there is a fine line between under- and over-supplying parts, and this has to be balanced against the financial risk of procuring parts you may end up not using. We should have probably ordered the Sharp screens as soon as we were *reasonably* sure we were going to use them rather than waiting until we were *absolutely* sure. Likewise, we should have perhaps waited until we were *slightly* sure we could make use of a sophisticated gyroscope before contributing to the run on the global supply.

On reflection, we would in the future work much harder to ensure non-visible parts were as standard and interchangeable as possible, but for anything as device-defining as the screen was to the Datacatcher, we would seek to guarantee a supply long before we carried out development.

Evolution of the Datacatcher form

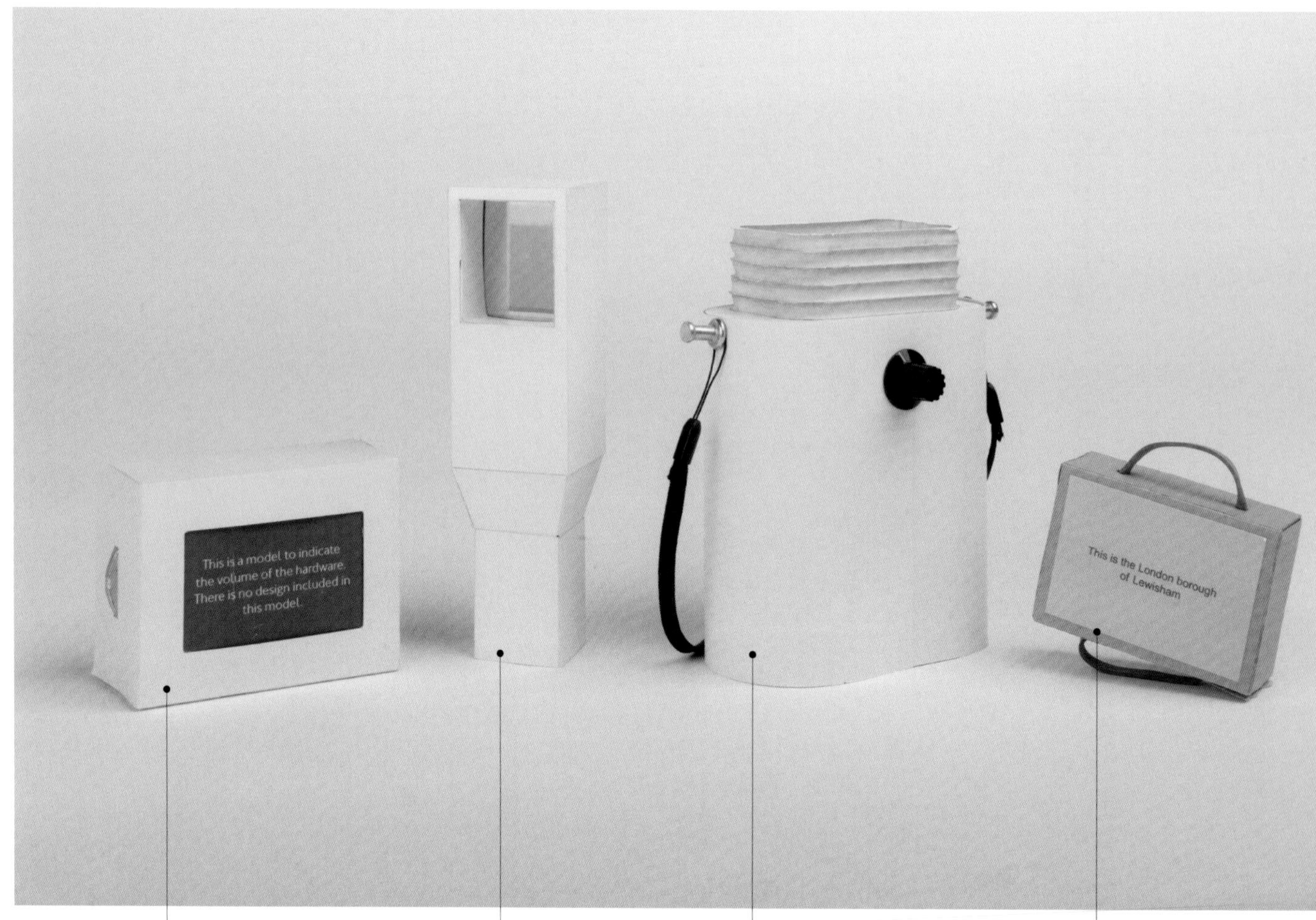

A bounding box around the proposed hardware, illustrating scale and the potential for a single dial interface.

Card model housing a transparent screen so the location is viewed as a background for the data.

A model of a device that would hang around the neck like a pair of binoculars, so the screen can viewed by glancing through the top aperture, much like a medium format camera.

Considerations of a device that loops or hangs onto other objects, to become a small personal or public display.

Evolution of the Datacatcher form

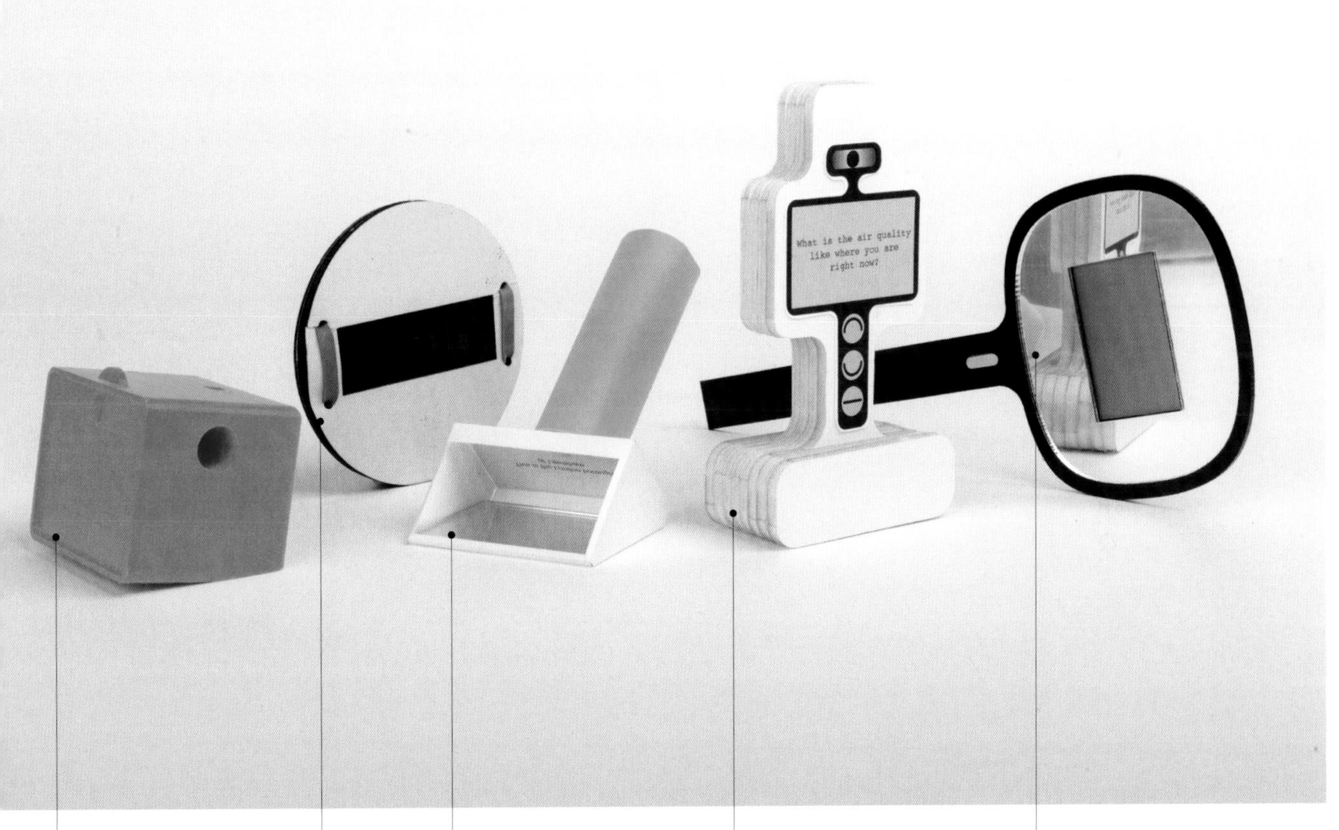
What is the air quality like where you are right now?

An iteration of the previous bounding box prototype, with subtle design detailing to tilt the object for desktop use and cut through holes to wear or lock the device.

Exploring flexible materials such as rubber and foam.

Periscope prototype with rotational handle as physical dial, presenting data on a mirror rather than electronic screen.

Two considerations emerge with this sketch. First is the inclusion of user-poll buttons which allow positive, neutral or negative responses to questions. Second, we added a large volume to house batteries, as early calculations showed the Datacatcher would need a substantial power source.

Ignoring battery or hardware considerations, this maquette incorporated the screen within a convex handheld mirror. This was a response to a proposal suggesting that the Datacatcher should focus users on their surroundings rather transporting them away, as is the case with most mobile technology.

Title

Evolution of the Datacatcher form

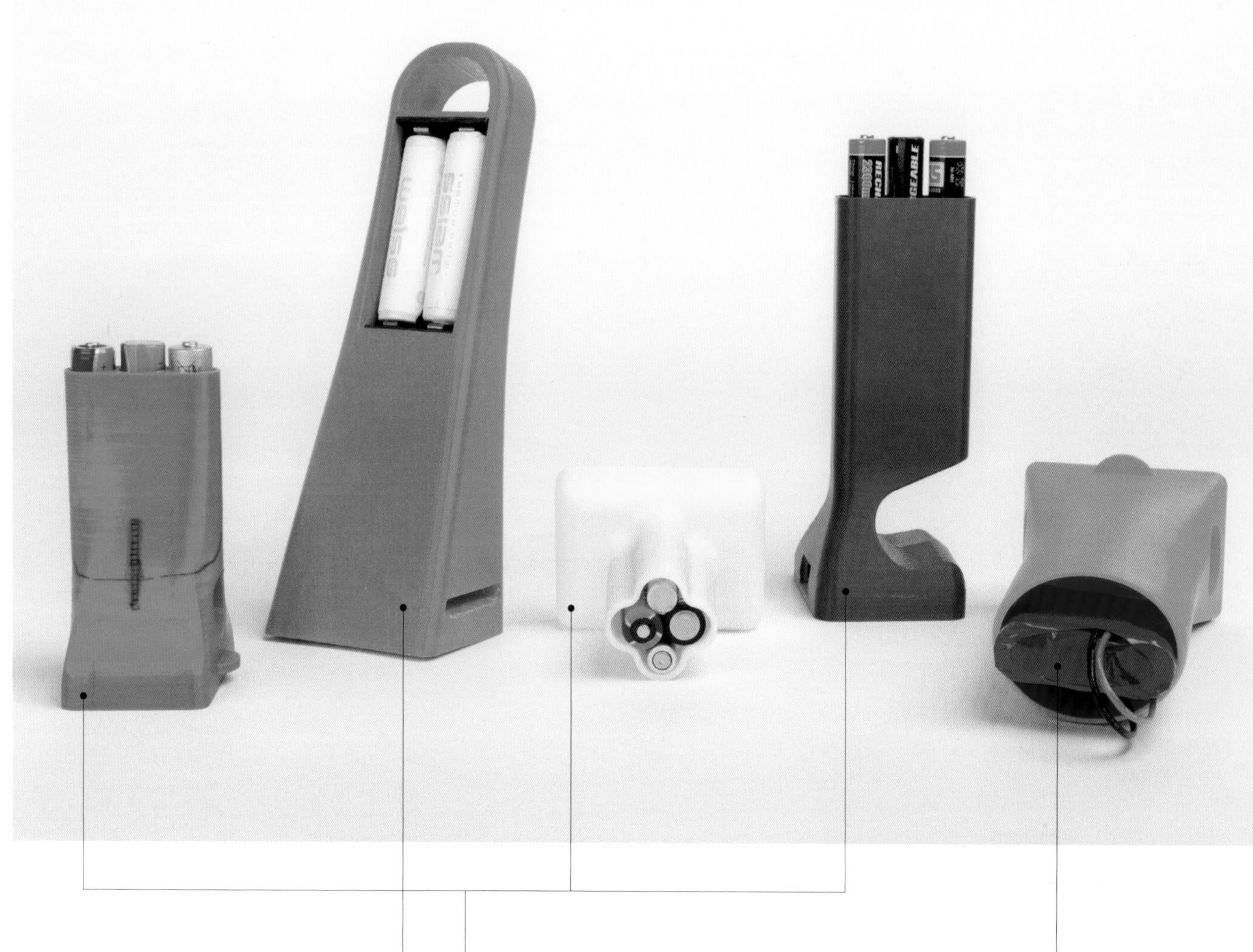

As we developed the electronic hardware, it became clear that we would need batteries that could deliver over 2500mAh. So we began exploring options using a rechargeable lithium-ion battery as seen in these two proposals.

We began incorporating batteries in proposals for the Datacatcher form. All the models on this page incorporate different specifications of high-performance batteries housed within the device's handle. These three use combinations of rechargeable AA and AAA batteries that suited our expectation of the power requirements.

Title

Evolution of the Datacatcher form

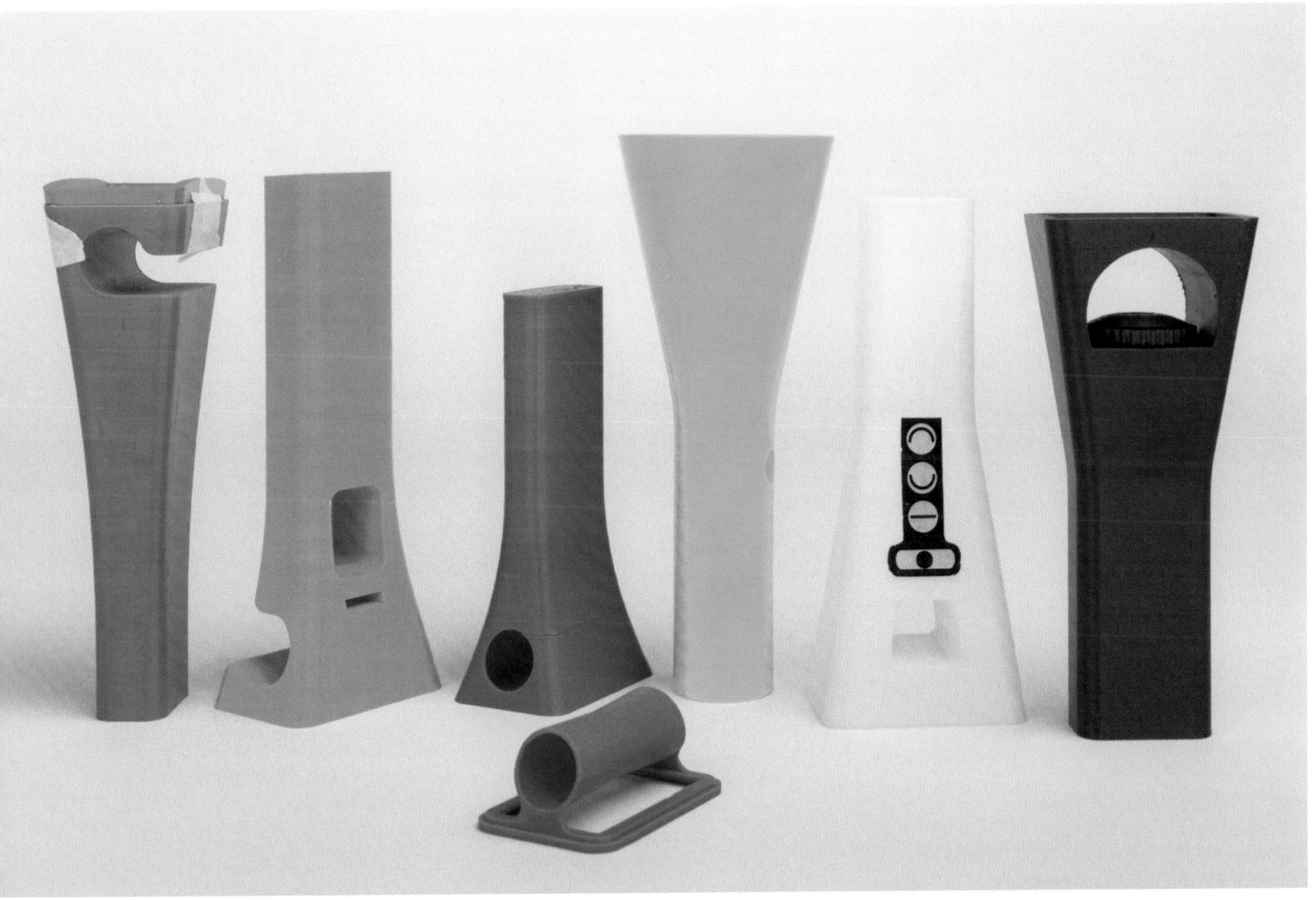

Around this time we started to explore different materials and production methods for the Datacatcher casing. We had been 3D printing these 'sketches' on our own machine which uses an additive process called fused deposition modelling (FDM), that builds objects by laying down molten plastic in layers. While this process is very useful for prototyping, it doesn't produce parts particularly quickly and the end results can be fragile.

In another project, we had bought batch produced housings from a company that specialises in producing low-volume injection parts, and finished them ourselves. The advantage of injection moulding is that the parts are very robust, they can be made in any colour and they are cheap and quick to produce. The disadvantage is that the tooling costs are quite high and that you cannot make any changes once you have committed to having the tool machined. Nevertheless we were keen on this process and were convinced that this would be the manufacturing route to take for the Datacatcher.

We were inspired by the engineering elegance of an Ikea torch (fourth object from the left), that was similar to the forms we had been sketching. It is cleverly and simply moulded using a tool with only two parts — this would lower costs. All the internal components such as the bulb, switch and batteries were clipped into a simple internal part that was secured to the outer case by one screw.

After spending some time considering how to we could replicate this simplicity, we discovered that one of the limitations of low-volume injection moulding is the length of 'core' that can be used in the mould. This meant the form of the outer case we were developing could not be made by this process in one piece (like the Ikea torch) and instead would have to be made in several parts. This would not only increase tooling costs but also introduce a pronounced seam where the parts joined, along the length of the Datacatcher.

We were very keen on making the Datacatcher out of as few parts as possible and we became quite determined to produce a seamless surface on the outer case, so we decided to abandon injection moulding and instead look at additive 3D printing.

Title

Evolution of the Datacatcher form

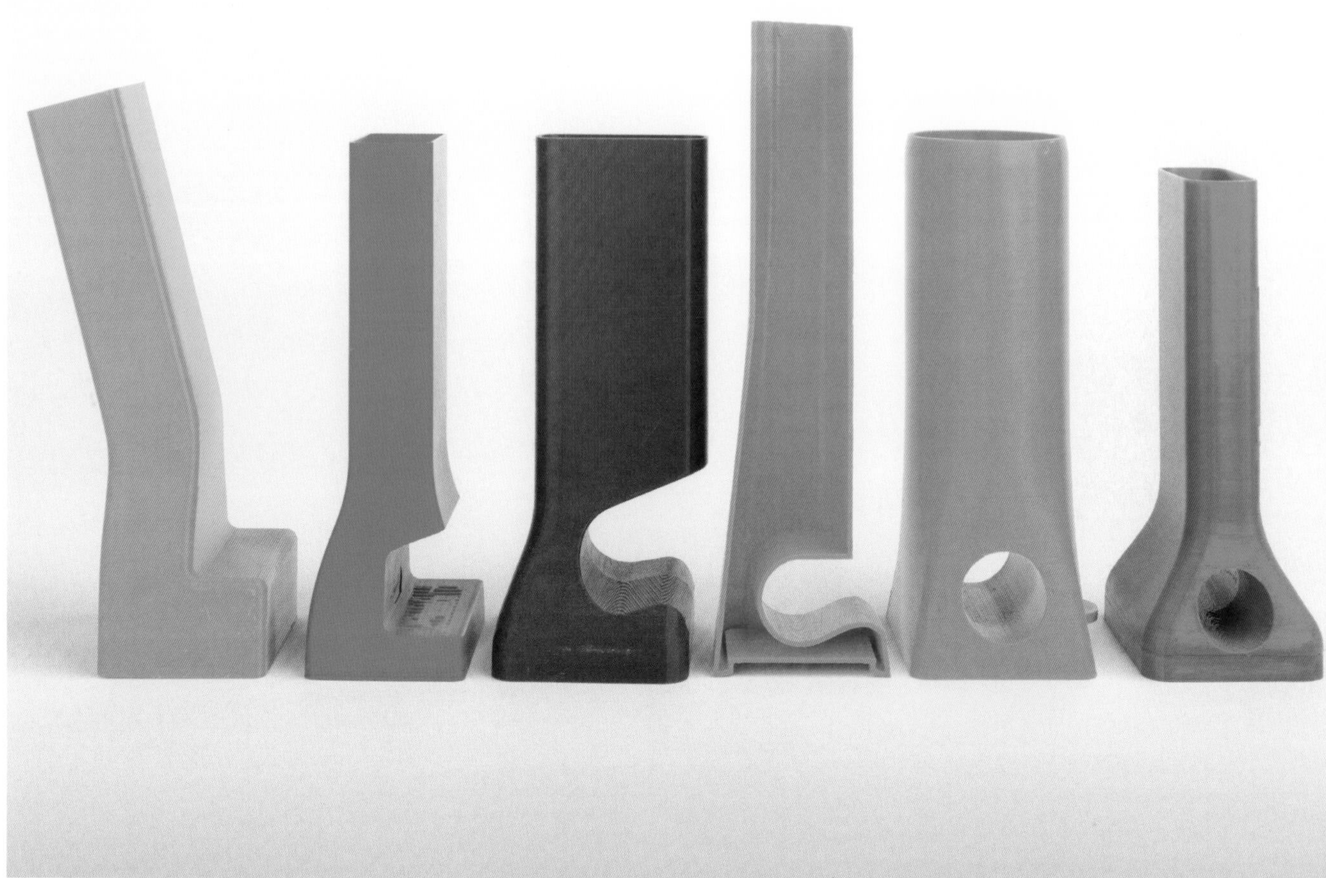

After approaching several bureaux that specialise in rapid prototyping, it became clear that a viable alternative would be to manufacture the housings using a process called selective laser sintering (SLS) with nylon powder. This method builds objects from layers like our FDM machine, but instead fuses nylon powder with a laser to produce incredibly robust parts. The supplier we contacted had very large machines that could print quickly, and the process would be slightly more cost-effective than injection moulding.

An additional advantage with this process was that we could develop the form using our in-house 3D printer, as the build technique is so similar, before handing the final design over to be manufactured. So we set about developing the Datacatcher with as few parts as possible, while taking full advantage of the fact that using the additive process we could make parts that are impossible to produce using traditional moulding techniques. The manufacturing process would enable us to maintain the cut-through hole that we were developing. The blue model, above on right [also seen third from left on the previous page in exploded form] was our first attempt at building the hole into the inner core or chassis of the Datacatcher.

The cut-through hole evolved from an early idea of incorporating a hook into the form. This would sit just over the thumb when holding the Datacatcher. We starting developing this hook to consider options where the Datacatcher could be hung from the other objects, but this evolved into a hole as we imagined scenarios where one might want to tie the device to bags, bicycles, railings and so on.

Eventually, the cut-through hole became the place to locate the thumb operated dial-interface of the Datacatcher, but it is also large enough to incorporate a bicycle D-lock.

Evolution of the Datacatcher form

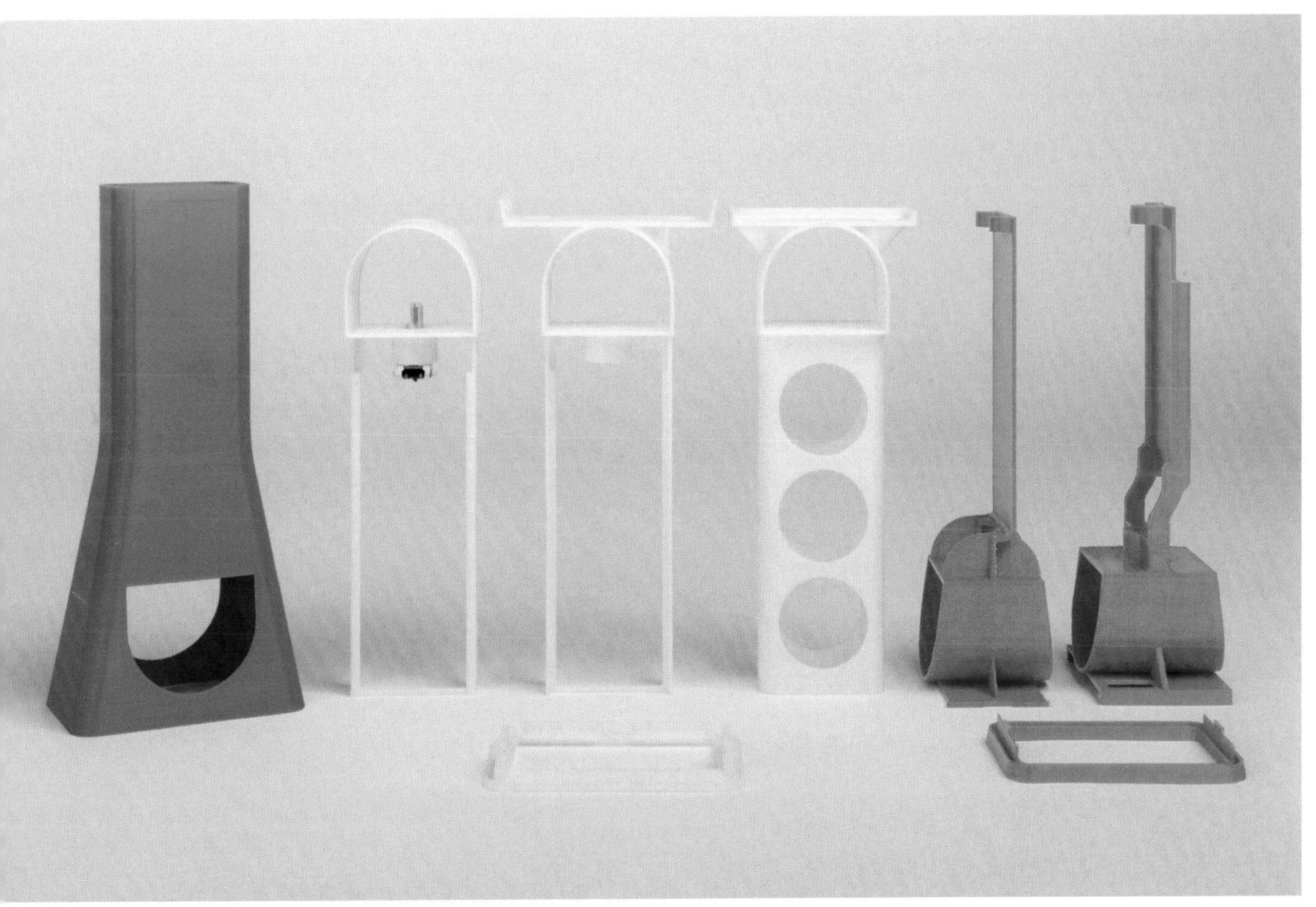

As we developed the form for production on a 3D printer, we narrowed the number of parts down to three. The cut-through hole proved challenging when rationalising these components, but was the perfect feature for showcasing the possibilities of additive manufacturing over conventional plastic moulding.

Shown above is the near-final form of the outer sleeve, and various iterations of LCD screen holder and inner core. The inner core was the part that had the greatest development as this had to incorporate the structure of the cut-through hole, the battery, electronics, encoder (dial), antenna and power switch.

Evolution of the Datacatcher form

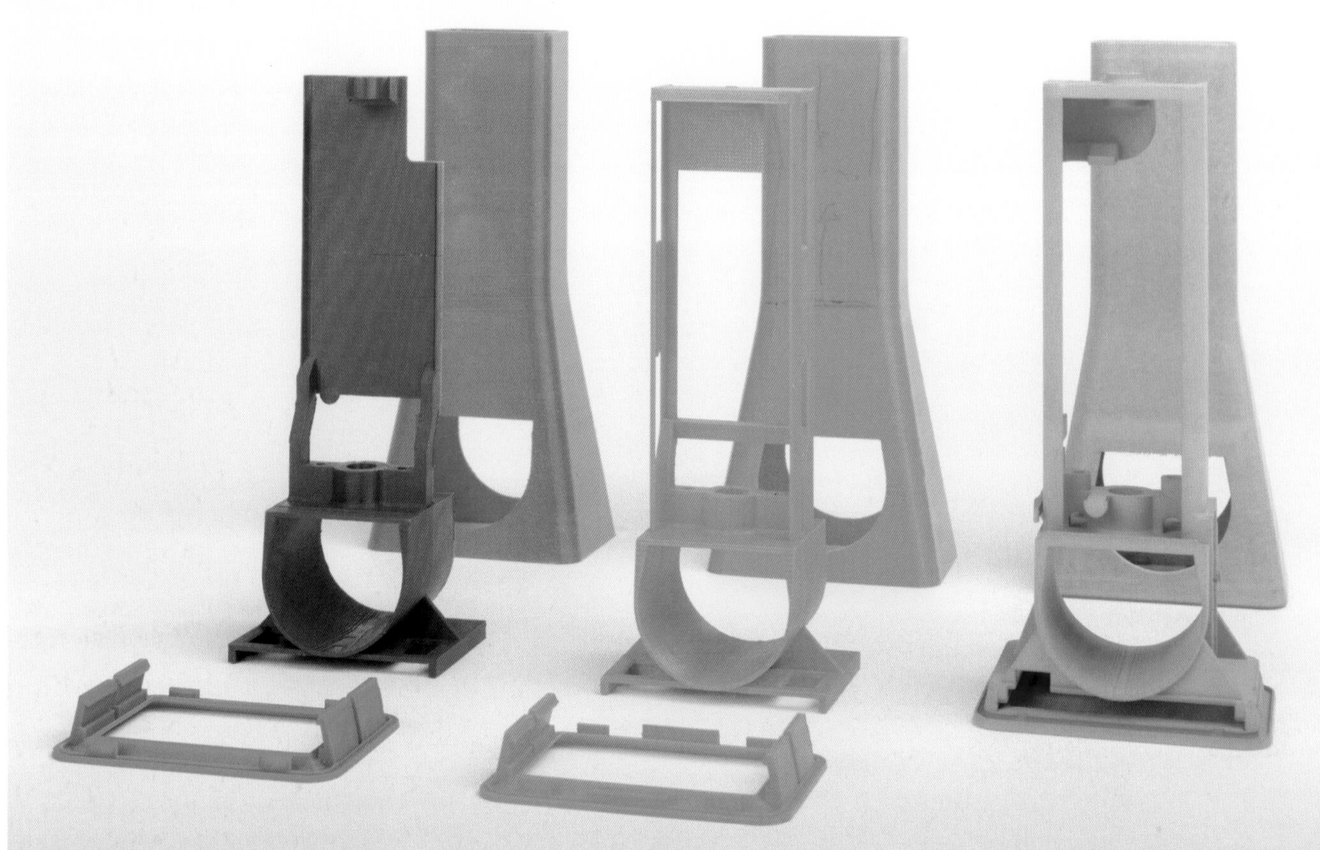

As we developed the inner core, we were able to reduce the number of parts from three to two as we worked out a way to incorporate the LCD screen holder by developing a slot for it to slide into. The inherent strength of SLS and the possibilities of additive manufacturing allowed us to develop components that would be impossible to produce by any other method. The simplicity of the outer core belies the complexity of the inner core. As with the torch that inspired us, the Datacatcher is held together with one screw.

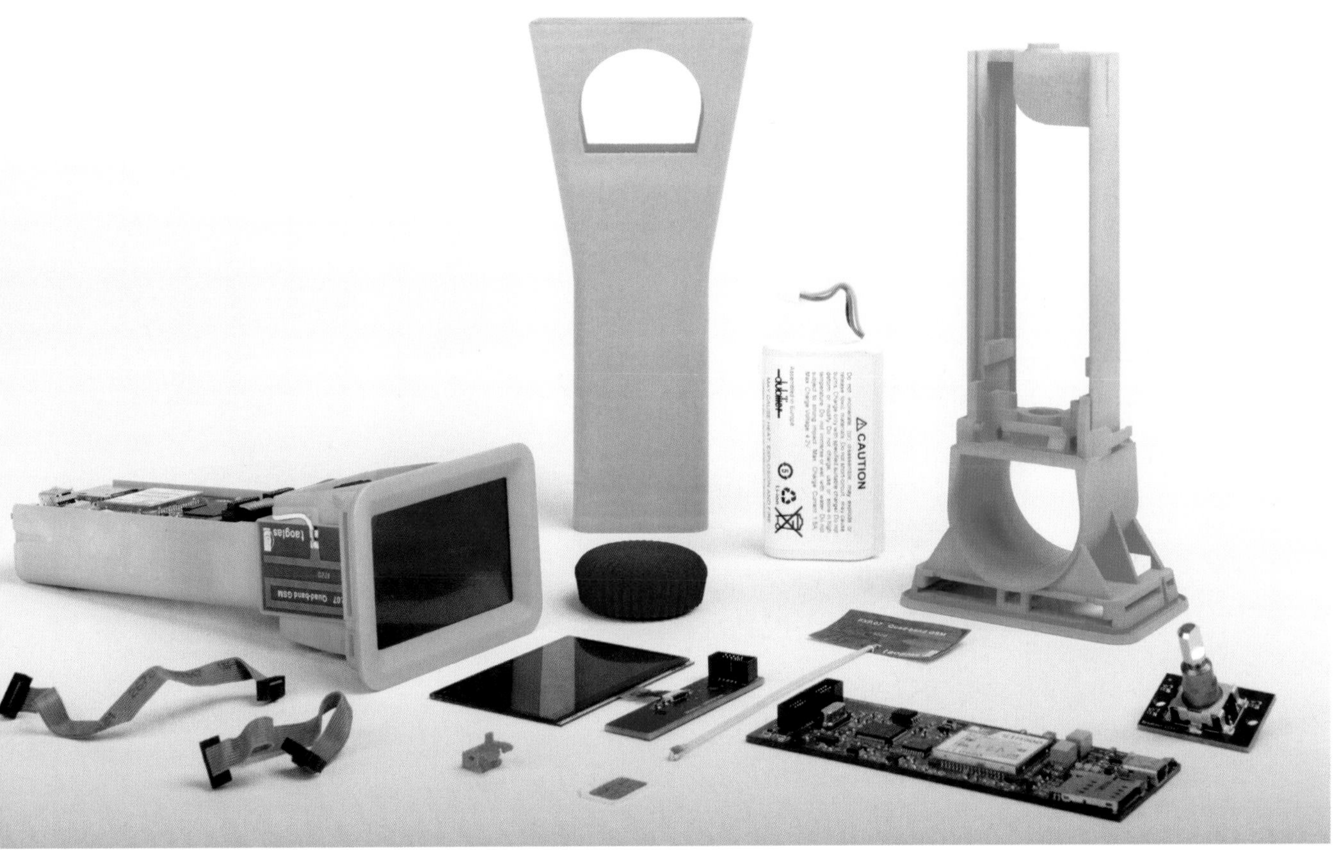

An assembled inner core of a Datacatcher next to a disassembled one. Parts that attach to the inner core are right to left: rotary encoder, mainboard PCB, cell phone antenna, battery, LCD screen and breakout board, dial, SIM card, switch cover, ribbon leads.

Evolution of the Datacatcher form

The first working prototype of the Datcatcher built with off-the-shelf Gadgeteer parts (left), and the finished Datacatcher built with our own PCB designs.

Evolution of the Datacatcher form

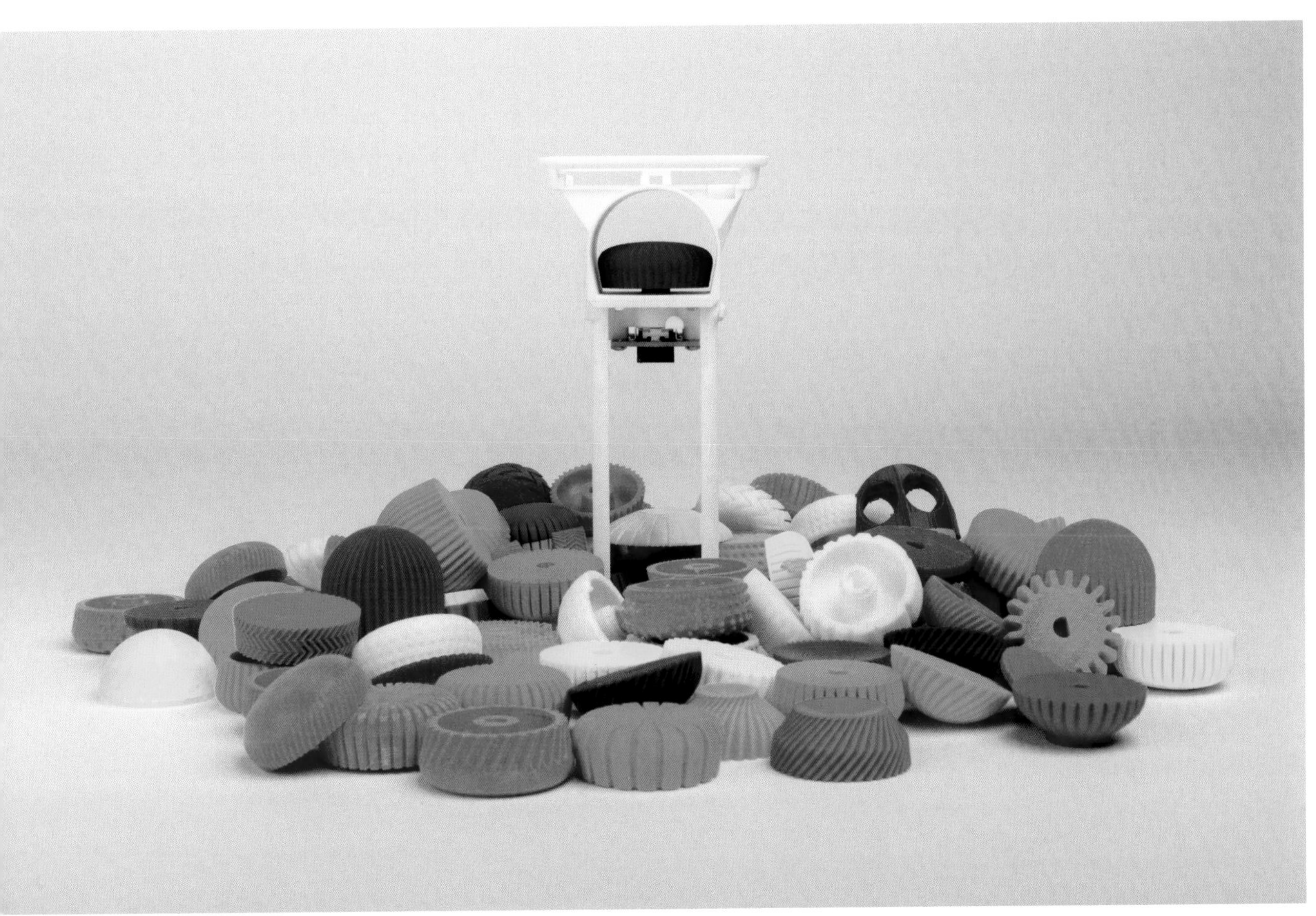

Although the final form of the dial may seem simple, it was the result of around a hundred different iterations of design.

Title

Designing specifications for batch production

Author

Dave Cameron

The design of the Datacatcher's casing was developed using our own 3D printer in the studio. This design was then batch produced at a manufacturing bureau using selective laser sintering [SLS]. However, due to a difference in tolerances between these two rapid prototyping processes, it was necessary to work with the bureau to further fine tune our designs. After running several samples and tests, we had developed a very specific process to craft a seamless two-part casing.

The final parts were built using one of the bureau's largest machines and then 'tumbled' to smooth the material's surface. Both stages of this process required detailed specification to ensure the highest quality of production. For example, the orientation of the parts in the machine's build chamber was crucial to create intricate details (such as the embossed text on the base of the device) as well as a consistent surface finish. Additionally, the tumbling of the casing required the parts to be half assembled to maintain a seamless join. With so many specific requirements for production, we found it essential to communicate these details directly to the technicians running the various machines. So we considered the design of this information to help it make its way beyond the service desk and into the machine room. Rather than convey this information in an email with the final job request, we collated a print-ready A4 booklet with images of every part, illustrations for assembly and diagrams of build orientation. As a result, this information travelled through the bureau's machine rooms and workshops with our parts to support the technicians who processed the job.

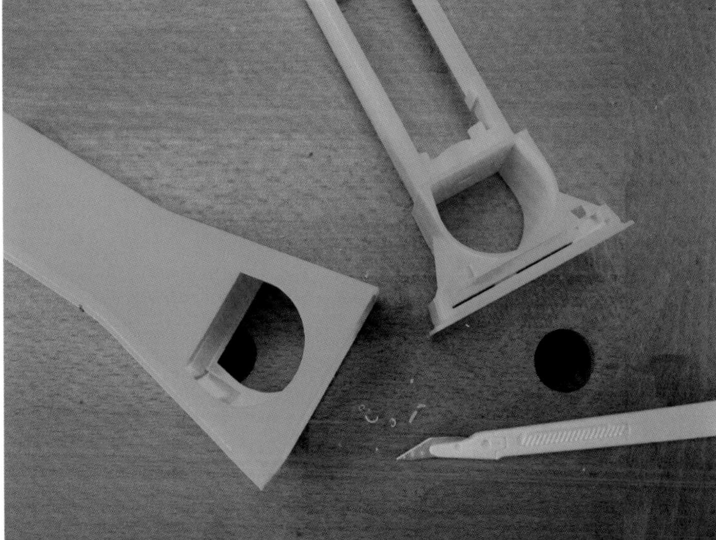

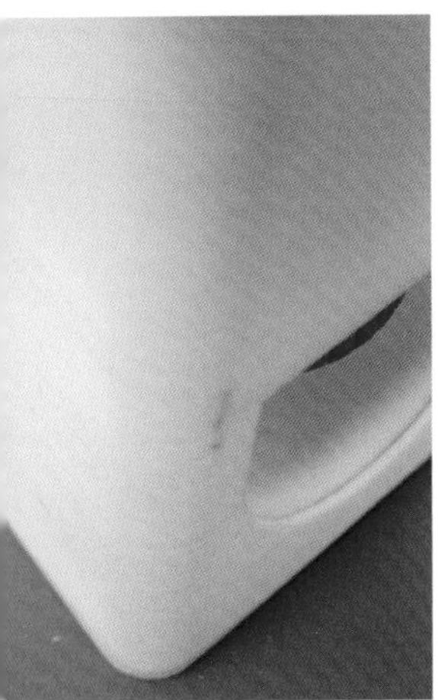

Making, testing and comparing. Bottom right, a page from the booklet created for the SLS machine operators.

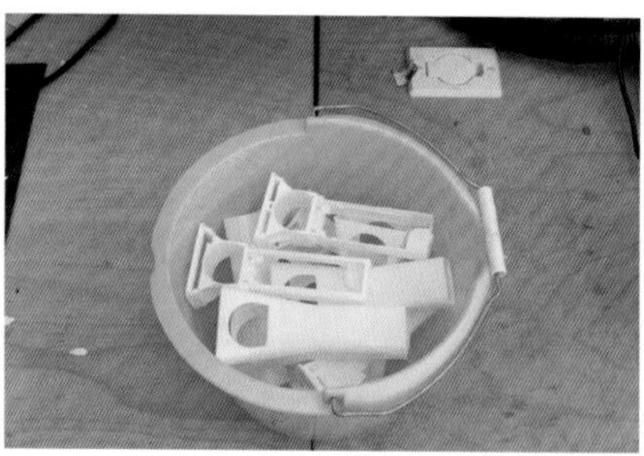

1. Clean SLS parts were gathered in batches of seven, which comfortably fitted in the tank. The parts were soaked for 10 minutes in clean water before the dyeing process began, which seemed to help with colour consistency. We filled the tank and heated the water to 95°C, which is the optimal temperature for the dye. It was important to thoroughly clean the tank before filling it with water — we found oven-cleaning cream and a green scourer worked well to clean the tank, which was then rinsed and dried using a micro-fibre cloth.

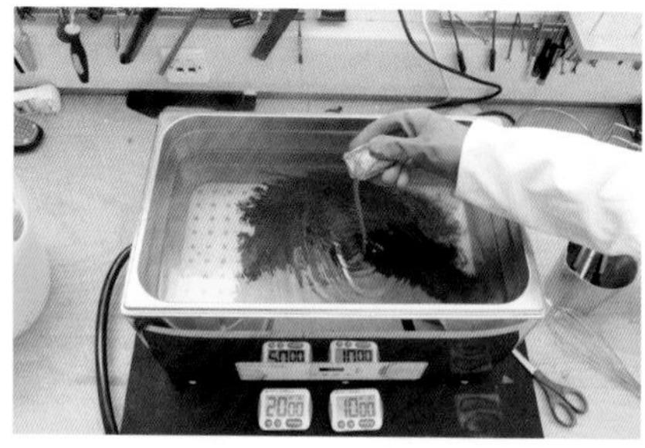

2. We used iDye Poly from Jacquard which comes in a soluble pack. However, to eliminate any contamination, we emptied the powder out of the pack into a clean bath of fresh water.

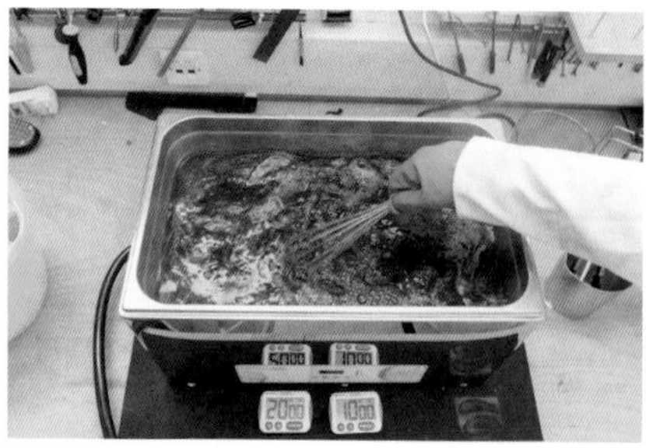

3. The dye was thoroughly mixed using a whisk. We then replaced the lid and allowed the water to return to 95°C before adding the parts.

7. After 10 minutes, all of the parts were flipped 180°. This was to allow the dye to evenly access the material, to ensure the bubble wrap did not interfere with the part.

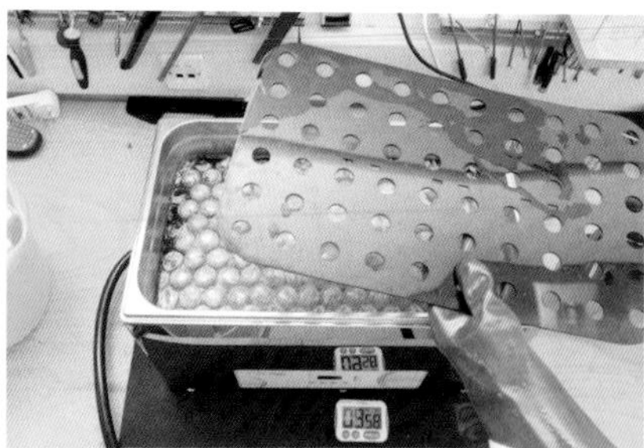

8. A fresh sheet of bubble wrap was laid on the surface of the water [as the first was distorted by the heat] and the same sheet of acrylic and the lid were replaced. The parts were submerged in the tank for another 10 minutes [a total of 20 minutes of dyeing].

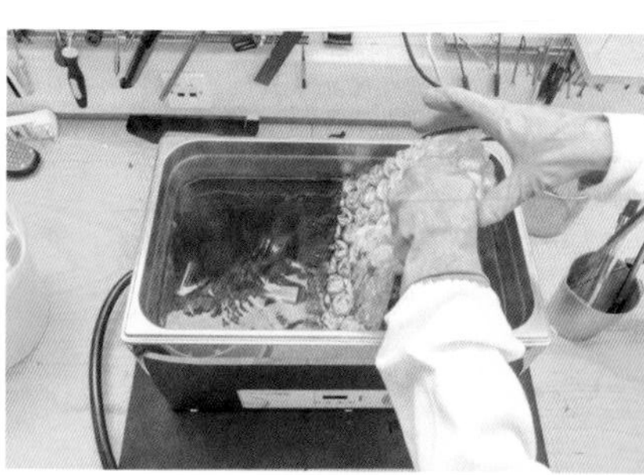

9. The parts were then removed from the tank into a clean bucket of water.

We developed a dyeing technique to colour parts that had been 3D printed using selective laser sintering [SLS]; and produced a booklet to share our process with other groups interested in dyeing this material. Reproduced here is the step-by-step guide to the dyeing technique we developed for the Datacatcher, using apparatus normally used for sous-vide cooking. A downloadable version of this publication is available at http://research.gold.ac.uk/id/eprint/11419.

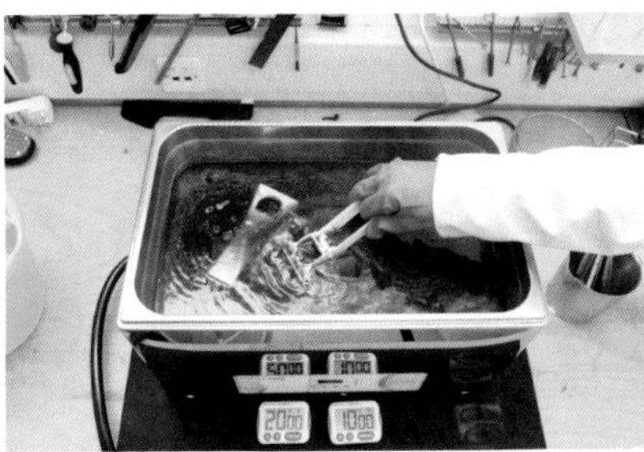

4. We prepared two timers, one for 10 minutes [to alert us midway through the process] and another for 20 minutes [to alert us at the end of the process]. The parts were fully submerged in the tank and allowed to settle back to the surface; we found all of the SLS parts we were dyeing floated.

5. We moved all of the parts away from the edges of the tank and carefully laid a sheet of bubble wrap on the surface of the water. A sheet of 3mm acrylic, laser cut to snugly fit the tank, was laid on top of the bubble wrap to weigh it down and ensure the parts were submerged just below the surface of the water. This stage of the process was crucial to ensuring an even, consistent finish.

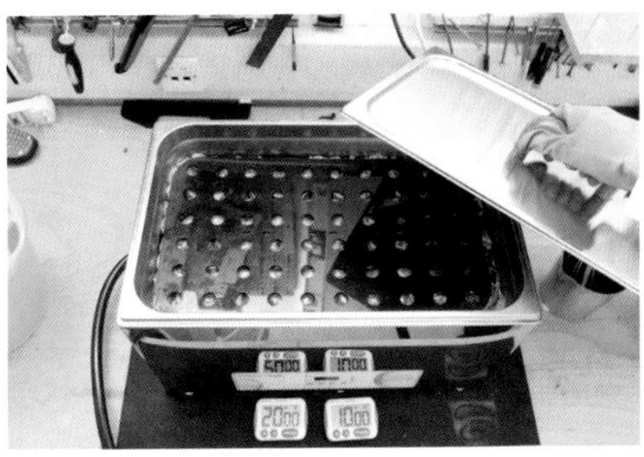

6. The lid was replaced and the two timers were started.

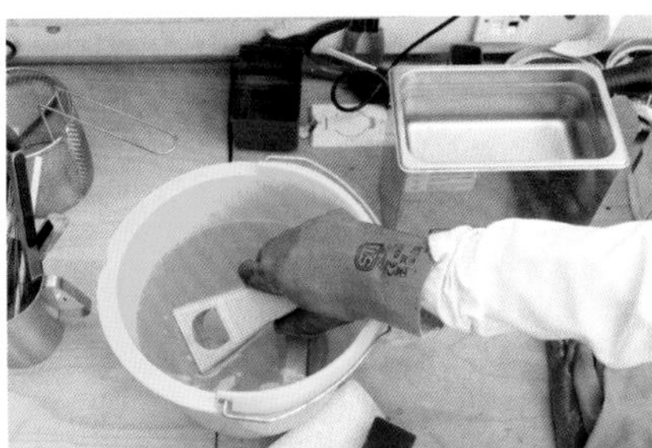

10. We rinsed the dyed parts in fresh water. Each part was inspected and lightly scrubbed to remove any obvious stains.

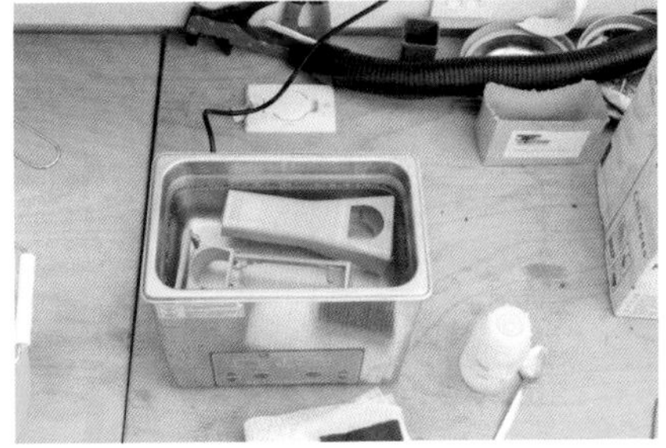

11. An ultrasonic tank was used during a final cleaning process. The tank was filled with water and a teaspoon of the levelling agent, Lavegal. This water was heated to 22°C and, wearing ear defenders, we switched on the ultrasonic tank for two minutes.

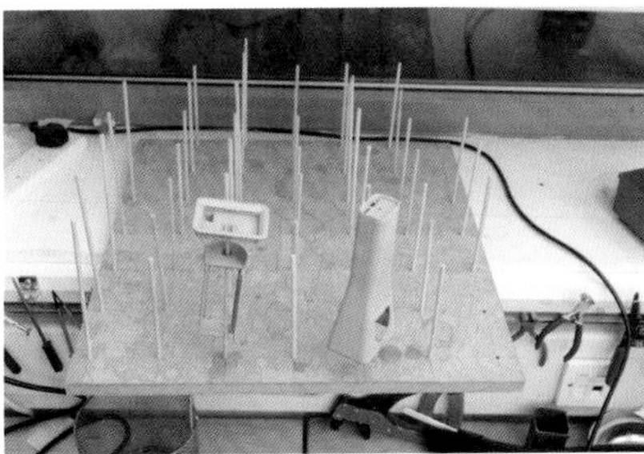

12. Finally, the parts were left to drip dry on a bespoke drying rack.

Extract from a conversation between Jonathan Rowley from Digits2Widgets, Dave Cameron and Sarah Pennington

Dave We encountered an issue with an inconsistent finish when dyeing SLS parts, which we are currently writing about in a publication about our dyeing process. This was due to a collection of dye that gathered on the surface of the water, similar to small oil slicks. A concentration of dye stained the parts as they floated in the tank, and many of our parts were left with intense spots of colour. To counteract this, we developed a way to submerge the parts and disrupt the surface of the water. We eventually found a solution by laying bubble wrap on the surface of the water, which was enough to disperse the dye and keep the parts from floating.

Jonathan You used a sheet of bubble wrap?

Dave Yes, so the bubble wrap floated on top of the water and the parts were submerged underneath.

Sarah I wonder how these conversations with us — about the dying of SLS parts in our studio at Goldsmiths for example — impact your practice, and whether you see this open dialogue as essential to your practice here?

Jonathan In all aspects of 3D printing, it's all pretty new. A lot of people are very traditional in their protectiveness of what they know. We're not really like that. If someone's open, then we're equally open. There's very little point in disparate groups of people reinventing the wheel. It's a wonderful technology, but it is very limited and we are trying to push it all the time. And if we're all pushing it together, we might be able to find good, proper, useful uses more quickly.

What I particularly enjoy is drawing in other people I know in related fields that can help with other aspects. And that's why whenever I get an email and the first question is, 'Can you sign a NDA [Non-Disclosure Agreement]?' I know it's going to be grim. I know that they are already locked into an idea. This prevents me from opening a dialogue with a network of experts who can contribute to improving an idea. They are not interested in a conversation about how you might modify it or adjust it or do it differently. They are set. And it tells me that they regard us as just the mode of production. They're not interested in understanding the craft of how to make something good. There is a particular problem when ordering multiples of things, in that people expect them to be identical. Dimensionally, surface finish, all of that stuff. The trouble is that the technology is not at mass-production engineering level. You have to accept wider tolerances and margins at the moment.

Dave We had a similar experience, I think, because we were being particularly fussy about the dials for the Datacatcher. Thankfully you were willing to entertain this! There were a few minor inconsistencies on the surface finish of our printed dials, which had been affected by the geometry of nearby parts in the build, and you were willing to explore a solution. We learnt from this — discovering that the geometry of parts in a build were cast across the chamber to affect other parts. You managed to find a solution, which obviously was a great help to us.

Jonathan I don't particularly like customers with calipers because all I can do is shrug my shoulders if they throw some of them back. And that's difficult. But that was an example of us learning how to address this situation. It doesn't make it very easy. Because if somebody wants 10 dials with nothing else surrounding them and everything else positioned above it and below it, that's difficult. That's a lot of wasted space.

Dave Yes, okay. I can understand that.

Jonathan So we have actually started dealing with situations like that off the back of that incident. [Now] we build not a cage around it, but little walls around it. So a sort of backdrop separates and picks up any shadowing between the two collections.

Digits2Widgets printed the Datacatcher's dials and switches.

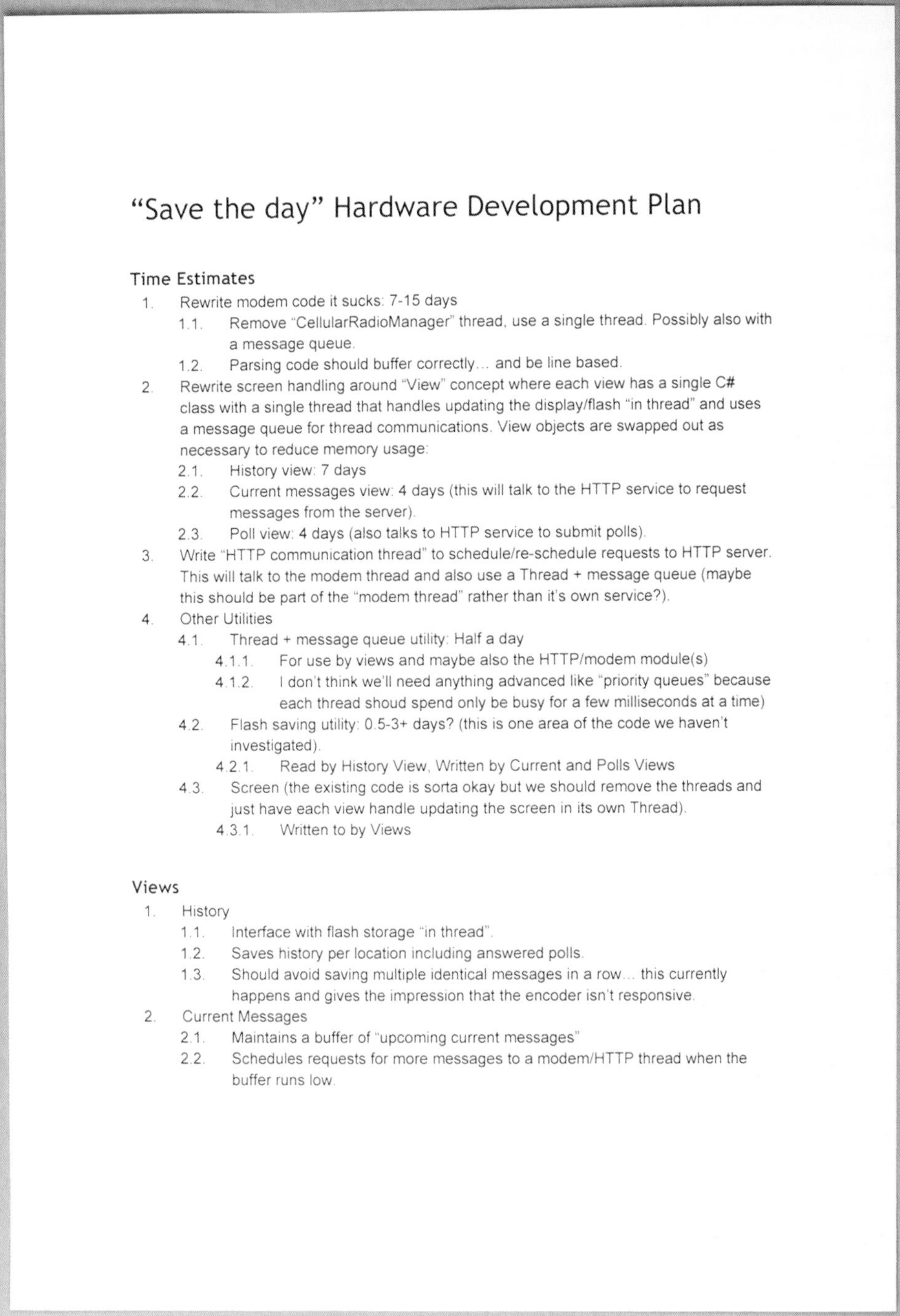

"Save the day" Hardware Development Plan

Time Estimates

1. Rewrite modem code it sucks: 7-15 days
   1.1. Remove "CellularRadioManager" thread, use a single thread. Possibly also with a message queue.
   1.2. Parsing code should buffer correctly… and be line based.
2. Rewrite screen handling around "View" concept where each view has a single C# class with a single thread that handles updating the display/flash "in thread" and uses a message queue for thread communications. View objects are swapped out as necessary to reduce memory usage:
   2.1. History view: 7 days
   2.2. Current messages view: 4 days (this will talk to the HTTP service to request messages from the server).
   2.3. Poll view: 4 days (also talks to HTTP service to submit polls).
3. Write "HTTP communication thread" to schedule/re-schedule requests to HTTP server. This will talk to the modem thread and also use a Thread + message queue (maybe this should be part of the "modem thread" rather than it's own service?).
4. Other Utilities
   4.1. Thread + message queue utility: Half a day
      4.1.1. For use by views and maybe also the HTTP/modem module(s)
      4.1.2. I don't think we'll need anything advanced like "priority queues" because each thread shoud spend only be busy for a few milliseconds at a time)
   4.2. Flash saving utility: 0.5-3+ days? (this is one area of the code we haven't investigated).
      4.2.1. Read by History View, Written by Current and Polls Views
   4.3. Screen (the existing code is sorta okay but we should remove the threads and just have each view handle updating the screen in its own Thread).
      4.3.1. Written to by Views

Views

1. History
   1.1. Interface with flash storage "in thread".
   1.2. Saves history per location including answered polls.
   1.3. Should avoid saving multiple identical messages in a row… this currently happens and gives the impression that the encoder isn't responsive.
2. Current Messages
   2.1. Maintains a buffer of "upcoming current messages"
   2.2. Schedules requests for more messages to a modem/HTTP thread when the buffer runs low.

We searched for some time for a .Net Gadgeteer expert to help in finishing the Datacatcher's hardware. We persuaded James Pike and Robin Beitra, who had been working on the server software, to take on the challenge. They proceeded with a plan entitled 'ProjectMaxtro5000'.

```
tag: v0.0.45, origin/stable, origin/
, master) restrict locations to uk lat/

0.0.44, stable) Remove device-by-imei
e alert. <James Pike>
0.0.43) Can give device to someone else.

wacky celllocation server results <Robin

nt-end: provide more sort options.

ei unique but optional in Mongo <Robin

 fix. <James Pike>
ypo corrections and comma removals.

g/typo fixes. <James Pike>
ditions. <James Pike>
cher essay - first draft. <James Pike>
0.0.42) Can change sort order on device

0.0.41) Send alerts in time order (they
mes Pike>
 where pollocation and pollaggregate
n Beitra>
lerts for later viewing when not on
ames Pike>
l reference error during paused mode.

 fix when thread exception handling is
ke>
able thread exception handling. <James

paused state after view thread crashes.

essage buffers to previous limits (due
cation errors, not certain this will fix

use of timeout helper when pausing LOCAL
James Pike>
 pixel alignment off by one. <James

evrons thicker. <James Pike>
pausing local data :( I liked this
Pike>
sing read param issue when ids list is
>
curated message buffers. <James Pike>
ow "press to continue" message for
>
e more message wording issues <Robin

lick to continue" message when paused.

onsistency. <James Pike>
 returns to current message when nothing
mes Pike>
update after pause in LOCAL DATA. <James

se in LOCAL DATA view. <James Pike>
AlertView. <James Pike>
 signal" -> "No signal" <James Pike>
 alert messages faster. <James Pike>
OCAL DATA during alerts. <James Pike>
 debug prints. <James Pike>
 Debug.Print with indexing logger. This
d 2 months ago. <James Pike>
-processor directives rather than consts
. <James Pike>
ble/disable battery stuff. Disable it.

0.0.40) avoid empty fixmystreet messages

off by 1 error in MosaicDataSource

e more message sources <Robin Beitra>
opulation age message source <Robin

e message wording issues <Robin Beitra>
0.0.39) make json sources the default

 battery logging, use entire flash for
ra>
rrent view show battery only when low

attery display filled rect to 0..1
```

```
* c00a411 - (tag: v0.0.37) Revert "ensure alerts always
have unique short id" <James Pike>
* f642fb4 - flip battery and make it easily flippable
<Robin Beitra>
* 9657d00 - Clean up, norfolk and western. <James Pike>
* 3cddcdc - Polls view ignores encoder acceleration
totally. <James Pike>
* 9b788fa - mergeohohoho <Robin Beitra>
* 60c5706 - Move pause icon to bottom and restyle, de-chev
when paused. <James Pike>
* 75fb388 - Build in Release mode by default and some
battery and config stuff. <James Pike>
* 2beb582 - (tag: v0.0.36) Server can send some static
config. <James Pike>
* 2b84157 - Change insecure session secret. <James Pike>
* a703e93 - Style consistency (the highlander, he cannot
act). <James Pike>
* 536f380 - Click in history pauses #189. <James Pike>
* b5cce23 - 0-3 chevs, not 1-4 chevs, otome no policy.
<James Pike>
* 62f3ab8 - Fix bug with acceleration algorithm and tune it
a bit. <James Pike>
* 4cebe42 - Fix floating point rounding error affecting
chevrons. <James Pike>
* 4d71e57 - Use 10^x for acceleration weights (from 5 to 4
steps). <James Pike>
* e66b967 - Log battery by default for now. <James Pike>
* 27bd791 - Disable battery logging by default, provide
constant to enable it. <James Pike>
* 9df8109 - add battery logging <Robin Beitra>
* c8c99eb - (Last?) cleaning up of yukan tree display code.
<James Pike>
* b5e5a49 - Half poll answer confirmation time again.
<James Pike>
* 951ab8e - Clean up display maths using integral
operations. <James Pike>
* 046d172 - "I'll give you the moon, Mary."  "How about you
just vertically center my text instead." <James Pike>
* df2ac94 - Re-fix text padding at cost of vertical
alignment. <James Pike>
* 9cb6ca3 - Cleanup more yukky yuk display code. <James
Pike>
* 858dd32 - Comment on ballsness of code. <James Pike>
* 5f1544d - More display alignment fixes. <James Pike>
* aa5cffa - display: remove height/width parameters, prefer
HEIGHT/WIDTH. <James Pike>
* 0efe222 - Fix vertical alignment issues with display.
<James Pike>
* c3c1354 - smooth the battery voltage input <Robin Beitra>
* 43d771e - Shift history location text down to correct
position. <James Pike>
* 4e69702 - Replace font size magic numbers. <James Pike>
* 2d2c959 - reduce frequency of fixmystreet <Robin Beitra>
* b0994ce - ensure alerts always have unique short id
<Robin Beitra>
* c268245 - Remove chevrons from poll view. <James Pike>
* c5ae241 - Move acceleration chevrons to bottom. <James
Pike>
* 4badc32 - Use hollow box for answer bar. <James Pike>
* f4df066 - Be extra paranoid about re-inverting display.
<James Pike>
* 1bc08ec - Fix display of answer selector. <James Pike>
* 730adac - Replace magic numbers about screen, clean-up,
no status on LOCAL DATA. <James Pike>
* 75281b7 - (tag: v0.0.35) fix comparison sources <Robin
Beitra>
* d5786d5 - some work towards fixing comparison sources
<Robin Beitra>
* 00e2ef6 - Fix anti-clockwise chevrons. <James Pike>
* a7cda8d - Show scroll chevrons (not quite working).
<James Pike>
* 3d3dee4 - Clean-up screen handling in preparation for
status bar. <James Pike>
* 5041358 - Remove unused parameter. <James Pike>
* 1985b64 - Display API consistency. <James Pike>
* 3274041 - TestApp display cleanup. <James Pike>
* beb9fa5 - Color vs Colour consistency. <James Pike>
* e90f9e5 - More clean-up of yukky display code. <James
Pike>
* b684f14 - Fix Vbat according to Justin. <James Pike>
* 452c74c - Remove DisplayHelper. <James Pike>
* fea8bec - Clean up text drawing routines + remove
commented out dead code. <James Pike>
* 18e2415 - Attempt to detect faulty encoder direction
changes. <James Pike>
* 9a63ca3 - Restart threads that escape their Run method
```

```
* 75eedf0 - Fix status message timing
"Connected/Disconnected" statuses. <J
* f452c0a - Show "no signal" messages
* 4feeb6f - GPRS attachment message +
<James Pike>
* 0a2d4d4 - tidy up message type logic
Beitra>
* 97e277f - fix click buffering issue
Beitra>
* ee4dcd1 - Reset encoder weight when
Pike>
* e7efffd - Fix broken build. <James
* 8b2b016 - make poll answers bar ren
efficient <Robin Beitra>
* 209b401 - Remove location history v
* bc0f620 - history view can now scro
view <Robin Beitra>
* 28124df - add the sleep back to enc
variable <Robin Beitra>
* 32c9e4e - merge encoder messages to
<Robin Beitra>
* 3de3ab7 - add filesystem seeking <R
* bd30b1a - ThreadSafeQueue bug when
Reject. <James Pike>
* 2aadba9 - Improve acceleration beha
* eeb74de - fix bug with filesystem o
<Robin Beitra>
* 83cec62 - Accelerating Encoder algo
quite working). <James Pike>
* 331d2e0 - Pattern for accelerating
* f3ebcf3 - Code convention violation
<James Pike>
* c46ec5f - Clean up Encoder class &
<James Pike>
* 0fbcdf7 - History view supports acc
events. <James Pike>
* ace3edd - Convert CRLF to LF again.
* 151d0f4 - Change Encoder interface
acceleration. <James Pike>
* a8b5ee3 - Style consistency. <James
* 2ddf06c - hardware: clean up History
FilesService. <James Pike>
* 24d1693 - Hook up VBAT, fix it a bit
* 9e049d8 - Fix compilation warnings.
* 55115fa - VBAT: log battery level,
* 6135ea1 - Avoid server messages gett
switching views. <James Pike>
* b3d4381 - Reduce overly-long poll c
<James Pike>
* 7438dd0 - Invert polls screens, this
Pike>
* f5f3d10 - fix server text wrap check
* a6e9115 - Remove HISTORY/POLLS splas
Pike>
* 30fd2c6 - add error loop detection
<Robin Beitra>
* 2ae4501 - Fix double counted modem
* 61b7fac - modem: driver more resili
Pike>
* bf43e51 - Location history prototyp
* 88e8a1b - requestCuration shouldn't
numbers, to preserve leading 0 <Robin
* 73fee0e - add command line tool to
Beitra>
* c4a25a3 - add imeis, and fix tool f
<Robin Beitra>
* 1791a37 - Code style consistency. <J
* ce2c795 - tidy up MessagesService:
code, add comments <Robin Beitra>
* 7152abf - fix pound character in de
Beitra>
* 0fccb32 - Device now checks lac/cid
hex <Robin Beitra>
* 47fc5a7 - Remove "x" bit from files.
* d03c299 - Move remaining DataCatche
DataCatcher.Hardware. <James Pike>
* 1e6d37e - Remove references to Tiny
libraries. <James Pike>
* d046a82 - Remove FlashHelper + refe
Pike>
* 703b8f8 - Move DisplayHelper into D
<James Pike>
* 76033e3 - Remove unused code + ques
structure. <James Pike>
* 2e822ab - Remove EncoderTest project
* c522f4e - device keeps track of fai
resends polls/readids <Robin Beitra>
* 53772f1 - Reprioritise location in
entry. <James Pike>
* 093d880 - Fix messages being tagged
#165. <James Pike>
* dbc10ea - device sends read message
* d9f5894 - update device to interpre
```

James and Robin's ProjectMaxtro5000 chat log, some 45 pages long.

```
* 4903009 - (tag: v0.0.33) respond to lac/cid updates
immediately, per-location data buffers. <James Pike>
* d7e6eb3 - add request checksum verification and response
error messages <Robin Beitra>
* 1b18adb - add response status code checking to hardware
<Robin Beitra>
* 86d4287 - Update modem state TODO to reflect current code
status. <James Pike>
* 5638c90 - modem/messages service: refactor + pass
messages on lac/cid update. <James Pike>
* d217daa - device sends query checksum <Robin Beitra>
* a461982 - fix some more line endings <Robin Beitra>
* f472e5f - modify message dates on device to reflect
display time <Robin Beitra>
* f4e9c09 - add modem fail loop detection <Robin Beitra>
* 9c3045b - (tag: v0.0.32) send server responses as
iso8859. set content-type header correctly <Robin Beitra>
* 7233897 - runner_tests.sh contains wget sample. <James
Pike>
* 2c9cbe8 - Revert "Revert "filter out super long messages
on the server"" <Robin Beitra>
* 5e5c57f - Revert "filter out super long messages on the
server" <James Pike>
* 42fe9ed - avoid problems reading messages after a flash
sector is reclaimed <Robin Beitra>
* 8fac4e4 - Remove old website code that is no longer used.
<James Pike>
* 9515cef - Revert "Server uses latin9 rather than utf-8
encoding, #148." <James Pike>
* 06ba01a - increase history flash partition size <Robin
Beitra>
* 86a691c - (tag: v0.0.31) Server uses latin9 rather than
utf-8 encoding, #148. <James Pike>
* 2105528 - Revert "add padding to server response
messages" <James Pike>
* 904cc9d - Comment about loading message. <James Pike>
* 715b717 - add a variable to imcrease timeout for send ok
wait in cellsergfvice thread <James Pike>
* 921c815 - Avoid MessagesService getting stuck. <James
Pike>
*   db5194b - (tag: v0.0.30) Merge branch 'master' of
bitbucket.org:datacatcher/datacatcher <Robin Beitra>
|\
| * 76f50ac - Silence compiler warnings about unused
variables. <James Pike>
* | 1161b4f - filter out super long messages on the server
<Robin Beitra>
|/
* 6f81347 - invert history screens <Robin Beitra>
* 96a7d25 - fix a small overrun error in Message.cs <Robin
Beitra>
* 681990b - modem: Disable CIPHEAD mode for now. <James
Pike>
* 783eb99 - Show "current message" when returning to "local
data" view. <James Pike>
* abc1e9c - use checksum on device to filter bad messages
<Robin Beitra>
* f69f9dc - (tag: v0.0.29) add message checksum <Robin
Beitra>
* 7e9869d - Squash "unreachable code" warning. <James Pike>
* a34254a - add padding to server response messages <Robin
Beitra>
* de69183 - Attempt to maintain 10-20 messages in server
message buffer. <James Pike>
* 228ea4e - keep track of lac/cid of poll responses <Robin
Beitra>
* 60e3a77 - WHYYYYYYYYYYYYY CRLF <Robin Beitra>
* 83617f7 - Send poll responses to server <Robin Beitra>
* 0095baa - fix adler32 <Robin Beitra>
* 22f163c - make history display properly <Robin Beitra>
* 4bff35d - move adler32 to separate file <Robin Beitra>
* b28f02b - add Lac/Cid handling to Message.cs <Robin
Beitra>
* 3c50a26 - WTF VISUAL STUDIO WHY MORE INCONSISTENT LINE
ENDINGS <Robin Beitra>
* 03c1696 - Improve ChunedFS performance a bit <Robin
Beitra>
* a70d5a2 - Reintroduce Encoder Thread.Sleep(10) to improve
performance <Robin Beitra>
* de3042d - Massively improve seek times for ChunkedFS
<Robin Beitra>
* 085e6e8 - Use fast read. Improve history speed a bit
<Robin Beitra>
* b053750 - Store message to history after being read
<Robin Beitra>
* 4479dfe - Make line endings unix again. thanks visual
studio. thanks. <Robin Beitra>
* 03becb0 - Get History to display parsed messages loaded
from flash <Robin Beitra>
* 1d4f390 - Interface between modem and messages service
threads is now asynchronous. <James Pike>
* ae1efd3 - More broken build fixes and CR removals. <James
Pike>
```

```
<James Pike>
* 7160b3f - "public static class" um how did this get
committed. <James Pike>
* 8c336ce - Load file system in background thread <Robin
Beitra>
* 916f964 - replace some line endings back to unix <Robi
Beitra>
* 8ad7401 - Integrate files with history view <Robin
Beitra>
* 35cc90e - .editorconfig: charset = utf8 <James Pike>
*   aabf660 - Merge branch 'master' of
bitbucket.org:datacatcher/datacatcher <Robin Beitra>
|\
| * 3f8d181 - Log modem line length due to unprintables.
<James Pike>
| * eec27c5 - Hack for bug Robin saw that is currently
unexplainable. <James Pike>
* | 77f1ee4 - Merge in filesystem changes <Robin Beitra>
|/
* 929b2cb - Cleanup, remove DataCatcherServices. <James
Pike>
* 716c940 - Remove unused code. <James Pike>
* 210992c - Actor model naming consistency and cleanup.
<James Pike>
* 90582c1 - Interface with modem serial line using Read
rather than ReadByte. <James Pike>
* 73f5aa7 - modem: Prepare for serial line interface
change. <James Pike>
* d10e86e - Fix LCD crash. <James Pike>
* 561095b - Modem reliability improvements, shouldn't ge
stuck anymore. <James Pike>
* bf84196 - Modem reliability + current messages kinda
working. <James Pike>
* d453417 - C C <James Pike>
* c88f3e4 - Replace bogus line in .editorconfig <James
Pike>
* 3aaf97d - Simplify HTTP request. <James Pike>
* 6cfc137 - Carriage return/trailing space consistency.
<James Pike>
* a9fd4c6 - Modem: Recover from ALREADY CONNECT status.
<James Pike>
* a25c7e6 - Work on messages service. <James Pike>
* 8e6c5fa - Fix file modes of c# files. <James Pike>
* ae276b6 - .editorconfig for consistent style across
editors. <James Pike>
* 9644eb4 - modem: close open TCP connection when

improvement. <James Pike>
* 15620c3 - (origin/modem-status) modem: Another status fi
attempt. <James Pike>
* a9bcff0 - Improve modem status handling, connects faster
in some cases. <James Pike>
* 4197cff - update test program <Robin Beitra>
* 114e154 - Work on escaping PDP DEACT mode (#134) <James
Pike>
* a2e9dbc - Modem uses Buffer object, Buffer.Reset and
Buffer.Substring(offset). <James Pike>
* b906924 - Bug where AT command could be withheld due to
incorrect sent. <James Pike>
* 65dc386 - Avoid re-powering modem when already in a gooc
state. <James Pike>
* cf49a78 - Code cleanup. <James Pike>
* 3e01923 - for (;;) <-> while (true) consistency <James
Pike>
* ffc4b54 - Fix potential null reference error and
accessibility. <James Pike>
* c718998 - Another debug verbosity decrease. <James Pike>
* c02705b - Make code less noisy. <James Pike>
* f94b9e2 - Remove a bunch of old and unreachable hardware
code. <James Pike>
* eb70062 - Remove unused (+ 1 invalid) member from
EncoderTest Program class. <James Pike>
* b362a45 - CurrentMessagesBuffer -> MessagesService.
<James Pike>
* 17cb38a - add a comment to CurrentMessagesBuffer <Robin
Beitra>
* 6618c56 - Relaxing modem timing after testing. <James
Pike>
* b4577e0 - replace Dequeue with DequeueAccurate <Robin
Beitra>
* cc76de5 - add test app <Robin Beitra>
* 30a9bcb - hardware: less noisy logging. <James Pike>
* 501cb1f - Remove source safe bindings. <James Pike>
* 1c980c2 - hardware: RLPnative.bin is needed? <James Pike
* 8551539 - update .sln to include missing file. oops
<Robin Beitra>
* 4742f8e - Add MessageQueue.DequeueAccurate for clock
based timing <Robin Beitra>
* e52b6f9 - fix timeouts in History and Polls view to use
TimeoutHelper <Robin Beitra>
* de91e67 - Very simple char buffer class. <James Pike>
* 219c4ad - add CurrentMessagesBuffer <Robin Beitra>
```

Working on the Datacatcher

James Pike

It was a pleasure to work on this project due to the trust Goldsmiths showed in allowing us to divide work between myself and Robin as we saw fit and to make fundamental architecture decisions without being bogged down in endless meetings or calls for justification.

Working both from home and in the office allowed us to collaborate when necessary and also enjoy the quiet working environments that enable rapid development to take place. In the four months we worked on this project as a two-man team we were able to commit over 30,000 lines of code which is well beyond the amount of code most small teams can provide in such a short time. It reaffirmed my belief that working in a small team using an informal, relaxed and trusting mode of working rather than creating an environment of pressure leads to greater productivity.

Server code

Four months before the Datacatcher server software was due to be deployed it was necessary to revisit many of the fundamental architecture choices that had been made when the project began.

Removing Backbone

Backbone is a popular framework used in the development of front-end web technology. It's a fairly modern event driven system, however its use on the server side was completely inappropriate. We discovered through profiling that 80% of the work the system was doing was firing Backbone events.

In a typical front-end environment these events are used to cause model updates to propagate to the user's browser display. On the Datacatcher server, these events weren't being used. In every case, a plain JavaScript array or object would have been a more appropriate choice. At the point when we began removing Backbone from the server, a single request would cause the system to use 100% CPU for several minutes. After 10 requests the server would exhaust memory and crash.

We also removed Backbone from the front-end component, replacing several thousand lines of code with some scaffolding produced by a yeoman generator and writing just a few hundred lines of code that used the Angular framework.

Lack of automated testing

The formalism imposed by a statically typed language can provide a number of safety guarantees. Without them, an alternative is necessary to ensure correct operation of any server-side technology. It is my belief that test-driven development (or a similar alternative) is an essential practice when using a dynamically typed language as a back-end technology.

During the stage where we lacked a test framework small changes were constantly being made that would fix one issue but cause several other issues. For this reason we retro-fitted tests of all services in the system using Mocha/Chai and with heavy use of Promises, a technique fairly recently popularised in the JavaScript community for dealing with asynchronous algorithms.

As a final stage we wrote several end-to-end/integration tests to test all services in the system together.

We ensured that the tests were run before any code could be checked in. In the few instances where code that broke tests was mistakenly checked-in, that code was reverted until a fixed version could be reapplied.

Rewriting the device hardware

After the server component was finished it became apparent that the hardware code, written in C# using Gadgeteer platform, was architecturally unsound and of an unacceptably buggy state.

General architecture

The system was using multiple threads with a total lack of regard to thread safety. Multiple threads could access the same data concurrently, with polling of Booleans being used to protect critical sections. We rewrote the architecture of the system entirely using the Actor design pattern with channels (thread-safe queues) acting as the only communication primitive between threads/actors.

The modem driver
The modem driver code was based on open source code provided for the SIM900 driver. This driver software was too broken and basic to be used. It had been heavily modified by a former developer. This made things worse by introducing typos and an unacceptably primitive method of dealing with multiple threads.

This code was completely re-written. The main improvement was that the code would ask the modem for its current state before deciding to do next, rather than assuming the modem would be in whichever state was previously requested.

The former driver had assumed that the modem was unconnected each time the code started up — this would frequently reset the power to the modem. After many resets the modem would end up in a state where it couldn't be used for 10–15 minutes.

In the new version, a state-querying code would find out what state the modem was currently in and continue whatever authentication or state-modification process was necessary from that point. This meant we could upload new code to the device without being locked out of testing for a great deal of time.

The modem driver ended up being the most challenging part of writing the hardware code due to one significant flaw: AT commands sent from and to the modem would intermittently cut out. We couldn't rely on anything we sent to the modem actually being seen by the modem and worse, TCP data sent from the server to the modem was often cut up, making it hard to interpret the commands sent from the server. We suspected the reason for this was interference between the modem and the encoder.

Usually the TCP/IP protocol guarantees that data has not been corrupted during transmission, but we had to implement checksums everywhere, both server-side and client-side.

This led to some interesting problems. For example, the LAC/CID identifiers which identify a particular cell tower were getting cut up, and in one instance this led a Datacatcher to falsely report to the server that it was in India, rather than London.

State of .NET MF
It is interesting to note the lack of online resources relating to issues with .NET MF/Gadgeteer compared to alternative systems such as the Raspberry Pi or Arduino. It's not clear whether this is because the open source community is not able to trust Microsoft or because Microsoft is not able to engage the open source community, but the online resources that allow developers to quickly diagnose issues with many other systems are not present in the .NET MF community. Most online searches for issues with the hardware project led us to questions posted by a former developer of this project. We had to get inventive with working around issues rather than being able to rely on a community and the experiences of others.

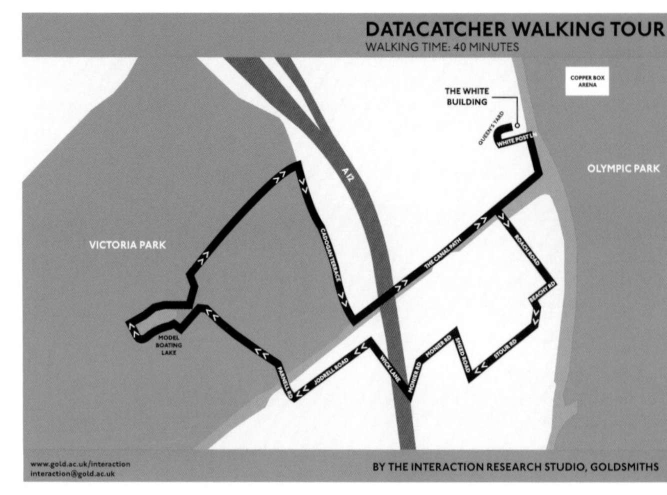

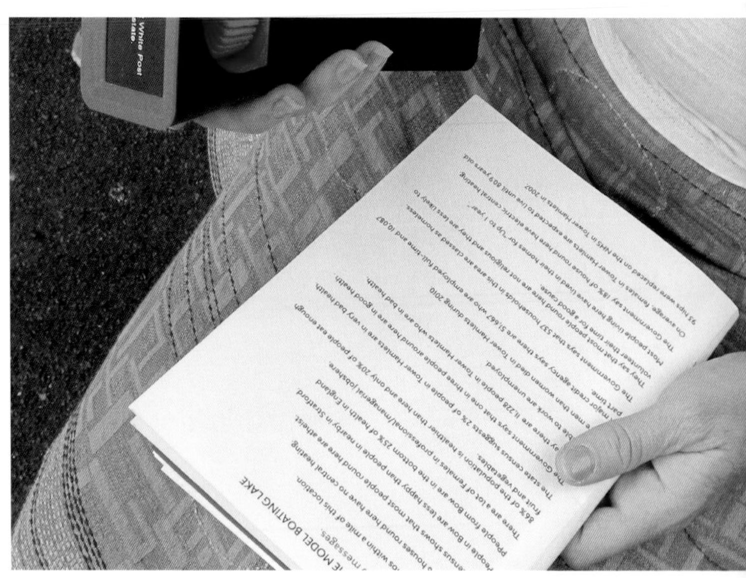

In June 2014 we ran a 'Datacatcher Walking Tour' in conjunction with an exhibition called 'A Sense of Energy' at The White Building in Hackney Wick. The final devices were not ready yet, so we brought Datacatcher cases with printed 'screens' as experience prototypes, and gave people booklets with maps showing the route and several hundred messages, produced by our server, to read along the way. Even this low-tech simulation of the Datacatcher in action stimulated a great deal of informative conversation about how people engaged with the messages.

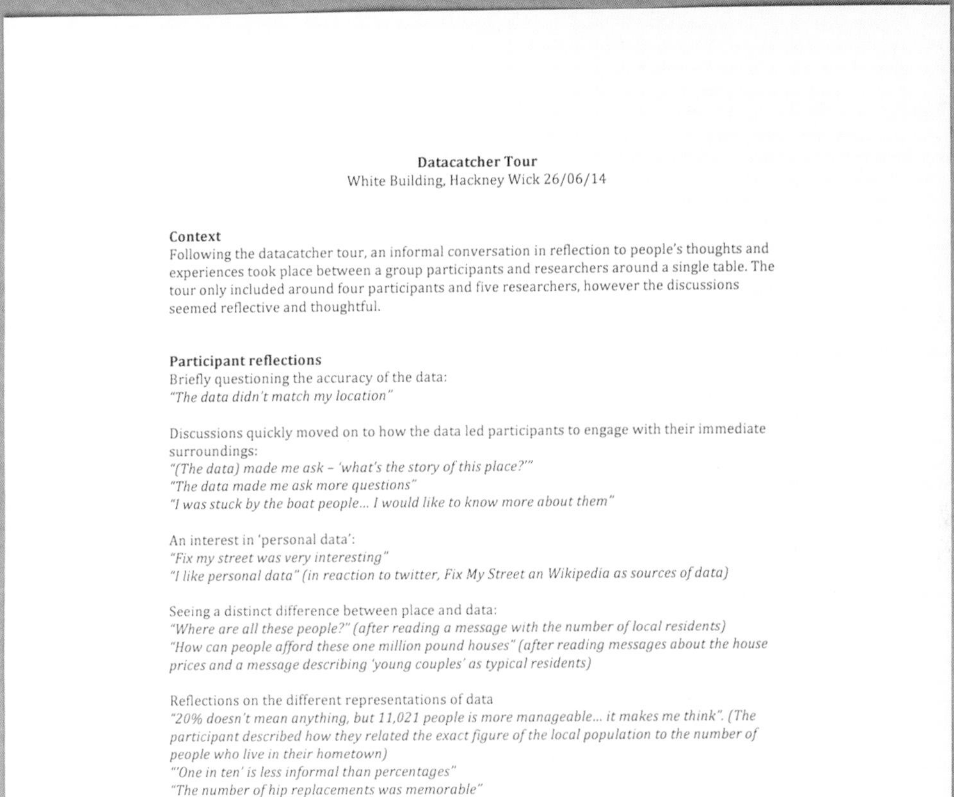

Datacatcher Tour
White Building, Hackney Wick 26/06/14

Context
Following the datacatcher tour, an informal conversation in reflection to people's thoughts and experiences took place between a group participants and researchers around a single table. The tour only included around four participants and five researchers, however the discussions seemed reflective and thoughtful.

Participant reflections
Briefly questioning the accuracy of the data:
"The data didn't match my location"

Discussions quickly moved on to how the data led participants to engage with their immediate surroundings:
"(The data) made me ask – 'what's the story of this place?'"
"The data made me ask more questions"
"I was stuck by the boat people... I would like to know more about them"

An interest in 'personal data':
"Fix my street was very interesting"
"I like personal data" (in reaction to twitter, Fix My Street an Wikipedia as sources of data)

Seeing a distinct difference between place and data:
"Where are all these people?" (after reading a message with the number of local residents)
"How can people afford these one million pound houses" (after reading messages about the house prices and a message describing 'young couples' as typical residents)

Reflections on the different representations of data
"20% doesn't mean anything, but 11,021 people is more manageable... it makes me think". (The participant described how they related the exact figure of the local population to the number of people who live in their hometown)
"'One in ten' is less informal than percentages"
"The number of hip replacements was memorable"

In response to being asked what they liked or didn't like:
"Negative data is difficult" (A participant imagining how a continuous number of messages revealing issues or problems with an area could become too much)

How the data revealed a 'split in the community':
A participant explained how contrasting data led to his imagining of a "split community". This was in reflection to reading a message describing the local community as 'guardian readers', which contrasted other descriptions of the local area.

Uncertainty of what to do with the data.
"Who reads which newspaper?" The participant explained he was not sure what he was supposed to do with this data, or how he should feel about this. The participant suggested that this reflective group chat was a way of understanding the data more, as well as to form more of a reaction to it. The group conversation continued to lead to a discussion of having a response in some way to the data, prompting the introduction of the poll questions...

There was an enthusiastic reaction to seeing the poll questions:
"Great. I love these. This is much better (in comparison to the data). This should be copyrighted".

There was a brief discussion about the likelihood of tripping over obstacles when reading the device. The participant questioned how the design of the device may overcome this *"design challenge"*.

Dave's notes reflecting on the Datacatcher Walking Tour.

What are the technologies for experiencing a place and what do they do with a person? Here are some: maps, guidebooks, flâneurism and détournement. The first two attempt to familiarise people with their environment by adding invisible data to the primary experience. Maps provide the layout of roads and houses beyond the visible space of a person in one moment. A map literally allows one to look around a corner. A map is also a defamiliarising tool, as it renders a place quite unlike what is visible. Surfaces are reduced to colours, details disappear for the sake of overview. A map gives control, in the sense of being able to plan the next steps even if unfamiliar with a terrain. While a map allows you to look around corners, a guidebook allows you to look back in time. It adds stories to places. We suddenly stand not in front of this house, but another house that stood here a long time ago. Again, a guidebook is also a defamiliarizing tool: it helps to replace existing colours, textures, smells with others that are not present.

Against these devices, there exist counter-technologies that aim to fuse the walker with the location, to eradicate all additional, distracting elements from a place. Flânerie is a technology for encountering cities not as shown on maps or guidebooks, but by flowing through the city without a goal. But the flâneur still goes with the flow, falling for centres of attention. In contrast to this technique, the dérive, the purposeful experience of a place through aleatoric means, produces surprises away from masses, by ignoring the pre-existing structures of centre and periphery, 'interesting' and 'less interesting' features of a place. A dérive is a wilful attempt to flatten features and draw attention to the boring and mundane.

The Datacatcher can then be seen as a curious device that intervenes in this already crowded space of creating connections between walkers and place. The intervention of the Datacatcher is quite particular as we could say it fuses the features of the flâneur with those of the guidebook, but it adds a very different notion of the 'stories' it tells about a place. It is based on the idea of the flâneur, as it does not attempt to make the user take a particular path. It follows a walk, wherever it leads to. It is not a technology to help with spatial orientation or to structure a place. Rather it is a technology to enhance a place with things that are absent. As such, it is similar to a guidebook: it adds stories to a place that are not visible in the place itself. To the locally existing smells, surfaces and noises, it adds what the device calls 'data'. But here is a difference from the guidebook: the Datacatcher does not add stories to singular objects that are thus turned into 'sights'. The guidebook highlights singular objects noted for their art historical, architectural, historical or political features at the expense of all other objects that thereby become a background to the singular objects. The Datacatcher adds compound data, statistical measures and, very often, averages to an area. It turns the background into the foreground, so to speak. Compared to a guidebook, the Datacatcher refers not to a visible object, but most often to a political entity, such as a local council, an area defined by invisible bureaucratic lines. The Datacatcher does not add stories or sequences of historical events as much as numbers aggregated over this bureaucratic space. But doing so, it connects in potentially new and strange ways to the visible: people we encounter on the street appear as specimens of average income or voting behaviour. Buildings appear as typical or atypical for what we imagine can be bought for the average house price. A walker with a Datacatcher is no longer a flâneur, who decodes status and habitus from appearance, but rather someone who adds status and habitus to the things she sees, using the numbers she now knows. The Datacatcher thus adds a new level of 'experiencing' the city. Far more radical than the guidebook, the Datacatcher abstracts from the visible city of primary senses. It fuses the flâneur, who gains experiences through the body, by being part of the masses, with experiences that are usually had only by statisticians, planners, and bureaucrats.

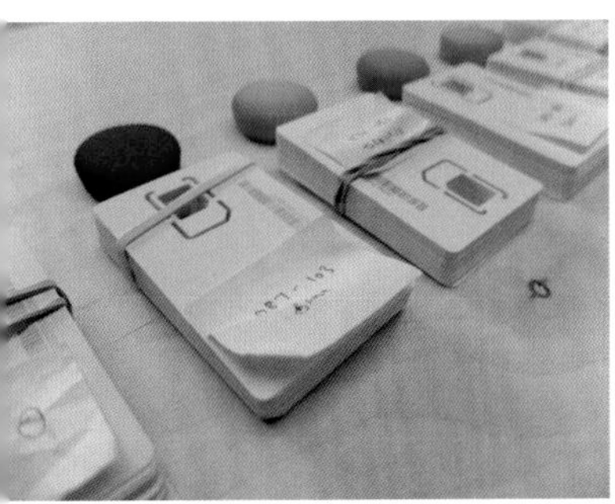

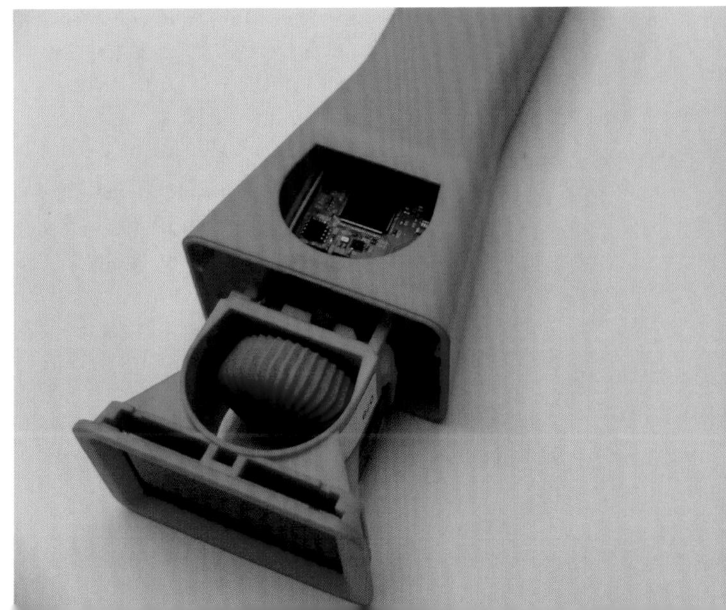

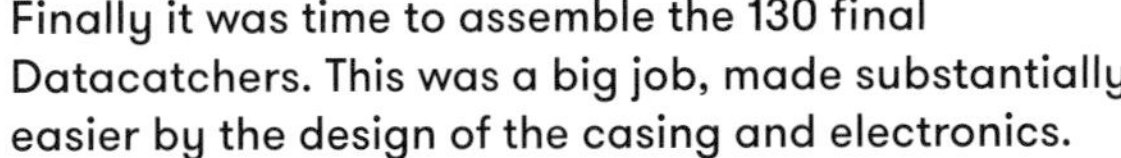

Finally it was time to assemble the 130 final Datacatchers. This was a big job, made substantially easier by the design of the casing and electronics.

Messages appearing on a working Datacatcher: the start-up screens, live messages, participant polls and past messages.

Do people like children here?
in theory
Attitudes here are?
misogynistic
Public space here is?
for sale
Religion here is?
mandatory
What are the dogs like here?
handbag
Poverty here is?
growing
A night out here is?
gnarly
This place is diverse...
ethnically
The shops here are?
fried chicken
Difficult on income.
A lot of people around here think that reports on violence and crime affect their lives.
People in Greenwich have a higher quality of life than nearby in New Cross.
New Cross is home to Goldsmiths, University of London, Haberdashers' Aske's Hatcham College and Addey and Stanhope School.
Someone has just described the politics in Greenwich as "neo-liberal".
The census suggests there are 3,240 people in this borough who are in very bad health.

Participants

Having produced 130 Datacatchers, we were in a position to carry out a field study far bigger than any we had ever tried. Most of our studies up to this point had involved between 5–20 participants — this study would be more than five times larger than the largest of these.

Just as manufacturing the devices forced us to let go of some of the craft sensibilities that have imbued previous designs and find ways to design for multiples, so this phase demanded that we rethink our tactics for deployment. We realised we would not have time or resources to maintain close personal involvement with the field trial as we had in past ones. Instead, we agreed to outsource a good deal of the deployment activities, hiring a 'strategic consultancy' firm to recruit volunteers and hand over the Datacatchers, and two teams of documentary filmmakers to collect information about engagement with the devices by filming people talking about their experiences.

Working with so little direct contact meant that we had to find new means to frame the project. We produced concise manuals to be distributed with the devices, and also independent sign up sheets and ethical clearance forms. For each, we sought to balance approachability with thoroughness, avoiding officialese while conveying the relevant information. We had to do an equal amount of work communicating our intentions and expectations to the subcontractors. This involved preparing detailed briefs, and buttressing these with meetings to describe the context of the project and how we saw their involvement. Nonetheless, as the field trial began it became evident that we could not simply prepare the teams and leave them to carry on the work independently. The further the Datacatchers moved from our core team, the less the devices and the project were framed as we would have done. This was brought home to us vividly when we visited a market where the first deployments were being staged and came across a member of the deployment team calling out: 'Want to try something for free?'

Incidents like these led us to recognize a balance to be achieved between working with subcontractors as colleagues or as employees. Originally we approached the teams as partners who would naturally understand and be sympathetic to our approach. It became clear, however, that they came, equally naturally, with their own expectations, objectives and commitments. We might, perhaps, have brought them into line via tightly written contracts and pre-written scripts. Instead, as Dave details in his essay later in this section, we worked with them continually to communicate our ideas and share our experience from past research projects.

The challenges we all faced were amplified by the practical difficulties of working with more than a hundred volunteers, representing a wide demographic range and spread over a large area of London. This was a significant endeavour from any point of view. In the end, we worked together successfully, if not without occasional tension, to find 130 diverse people across London willing to try the Datacatchers, and to film more than 50 of them.

GOLDSMITHS DESIGN RESEARCHERS

looking for people

to try out an experimental hand-held device that displays information about where you are and the kinds of people who live there.

Interested? Contact:

interaction@gold.ac.uk

We placed advertisements in various London publications such as *Metro* and *Camden New Journal*, to discover the level of potential interest in taking part. We had a few responses, but not nearly enough to make us confident this would work at scale.

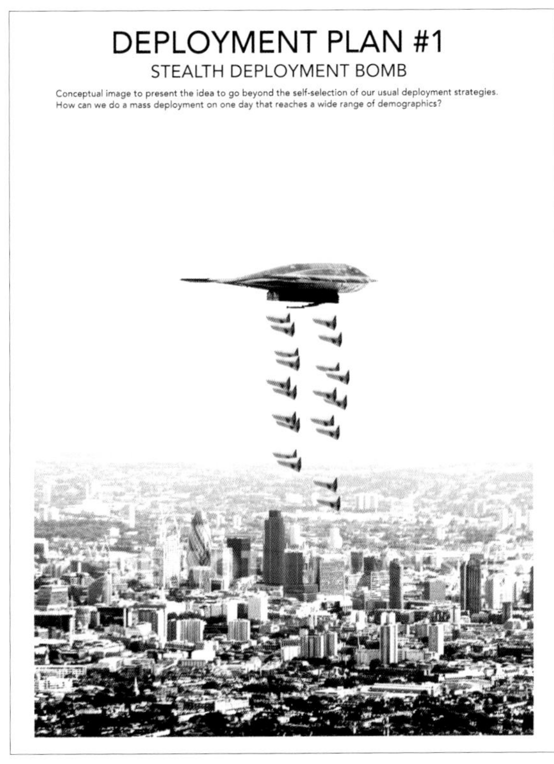

DEPLOYMENT PLAN #1
STEALTH DEPLOYMENT BOMB
Conceptual image to present the idea to go beyond the self-selection of our usual deployment strategies.
How can we do a mass deployment on one day that reaches a wide range of demographics?

DEPLOYMENT PLAN #2
'LOCAL EXPERTS'
EXPERT LOCAL DEMOGRAPHERS:
Cabbies
Refuse collectors
Our bins are our single biggest data collector.
Royal Mail
Local Action Group
Social workers
LOCAL SPIN DOCTORS:
Highly versed at producing local spin.
Estate Agents
Surveyors
Local Councillors
MPs
This was original meant to address the different levels of cosmopolitics (see Table 1) which I interpreted as the different political touchpoints within society. Should we target a society cross-section? Mosaic levels?

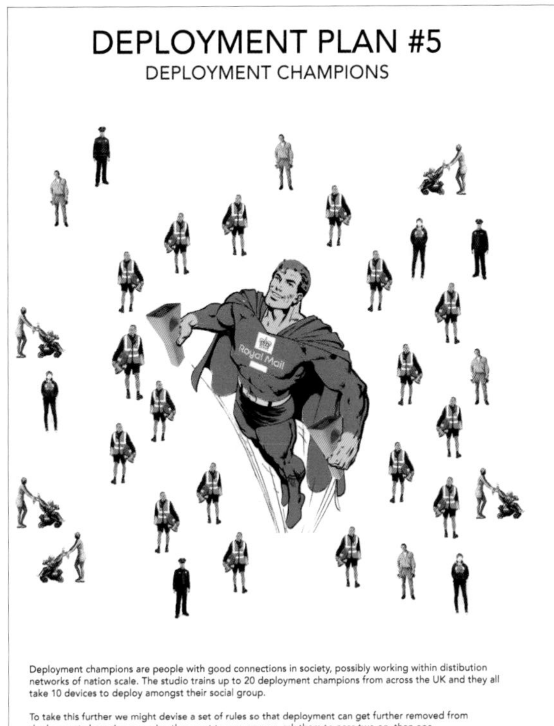

DEPLOYMENT PLAN #5
DEPLOYMENT CHAMPIONS
Royal Mail
Deployment champions are people with good connections in society, possibly working within distibution networks of nation scale. The studio trains up to 20 deployment champions from across the UK and they all take 10 devices to deploy amongst their social group.
To take this further we might devise a set of rules so that deployment can get further removed from deployment champion e.g. give three out to one person, ask them to pass two on, then one.

DEPLOYMENT PLAN #6
MARKET STALL DEPLOYMENT BOMB
This is the actual stealth bomber - set up several market stalls across the UK on one day to deploy to a random population / reach a wider socio-economic demographic. Consider local bootsales and farmers markets to get a range of participants. The benefit of this method is that we are bringing the deployment to the people, rather than expecting them to come to us. Would need a method of assessing the committment of individual participants.

We started exploring other options for recruiting volunteers, ranging from distribution via an e-commerce site to signing up existing communities. We started to fantasise about being able to sign up volunteers and deploy the devices in a single day.

YOUR DATACATCHER

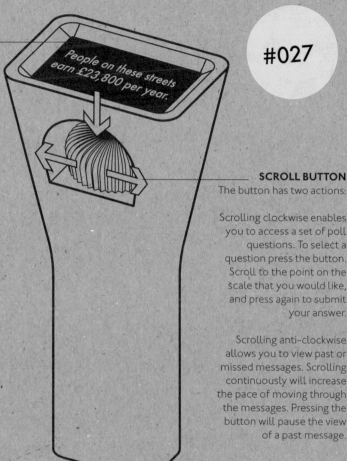

#027

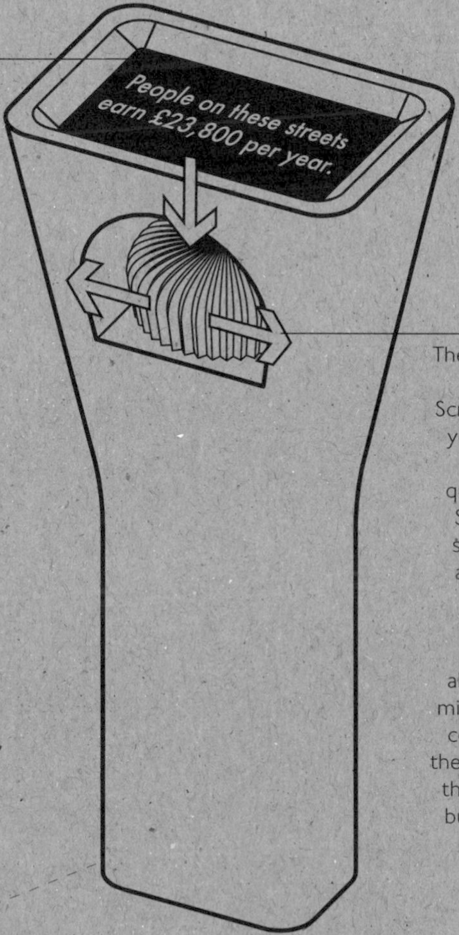

People on these streets earn £23,800 per year.

SPLAY SCREEN
e screen will display essages (data) about the ea you are in. You can so access a series of poll estions as well as a list past messages. From ne to time you may also e maintenance messages this screen containing portant information instructions.

ote: Like all electronic evices we recommend at you don't use the tacatcher in the rain.

ARD SLOT
o not remove. ard is not compatible th other devices.

CHARGING SOCKET

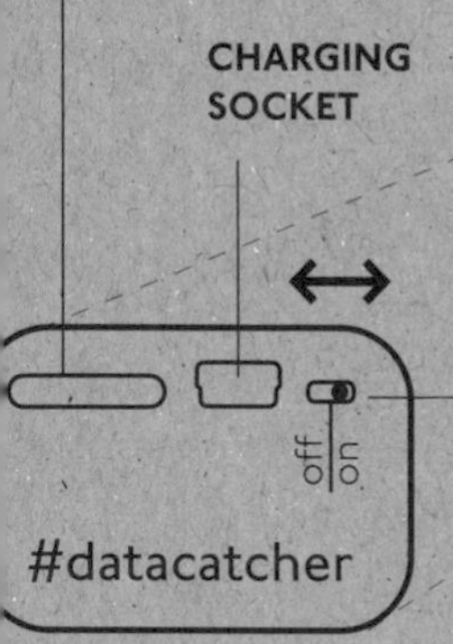

ease use #datacatcher in cial media.

SCROLL BUTTON
The button has two actions:

Scrolling clockwise enables you to access a set of poll questions. To select a question press the button. Scroll to the point on the scale that you would like, and press again to submit your answer.

Scrolling anti-clockwise allows you to view past or missed messages. Scrolling continuously will increase the pace of moving through the messages. Pressing the button will pause the view of a past message.

POWER BUTTON
When you first get the Datacatcher you will need to turn it on using the slider switch located on the base of the unit. You can turn the device off here whenever you like, although it will not collect messages unless you leave it switched on.

Problems? Contact us at: interaction@gold.ac.uk / t. 020 7078 5182

HOW TO USE YOUR DATACATCHER

Please use the Datacatcher in whatever way appeals to you. The devices were developed for research, and our primary interest is to see how you engage with the device, the data it displays, and the ways it ma affect your views of the world, so however you want to use it is interesting to us.

While you have your Datacatcher, treat it as your own. Don't be precious: we don't mind if you decorate write on it, attach accessories, or get it dirty. Feel free to leave it on all the time or to switch it on and off (though doing this repeatedly will cause the network to lock it out for a while). Leave it at home, or take on journeys with you (it should work anywhere in the UK). Tweet about it, put it on Facebook, or keep it t yourself. All we ask is that you try it out and be willing to talk with the filmmakers about your experienc

Thanks!

HOW TO CHARGE

Your Datacatcher battery should last several days but we recommend charging it daily so the battery doesn't run empty.

If your device is struggling to connect to a cell tower, the battery may be low and require recharging. Alternatively, try restarting the device.

Please do not leave unattended while charging.

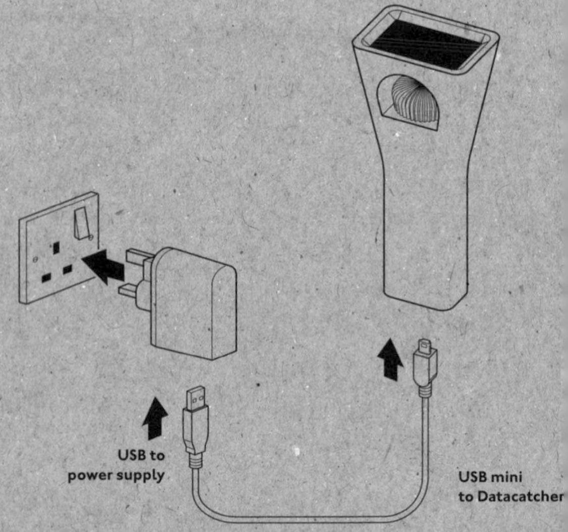

Problems? Contact us at: interaction@gold.ac.uk / t. 020 7078 5

To allow a hands-off deployment, the Datacatchers had to be packaged and accompanied by many forms, documents and accessories. These included a user guide, sign-up sheet and ethical consent form as well as a self-addressed label and postage for returning the devices. Detail was important here: for instance, each box had a sticker on its side indicating the colour of the enclosed Datacatcher.

The studio took on the appearance of a warehouse as we packed up the Datacatchers for distribution.

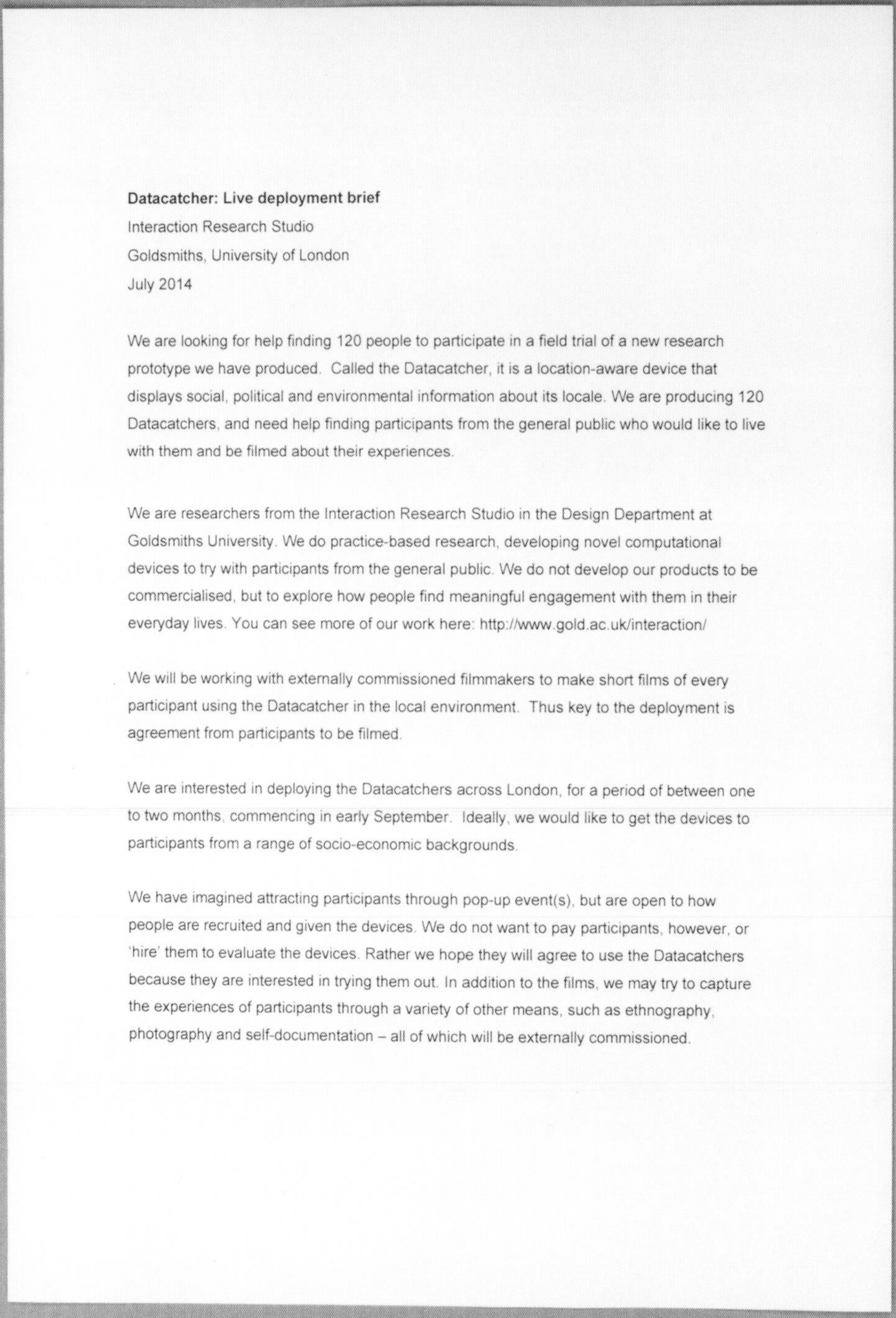

Datacatcher: Live deployment brief
Interaction Research Studio
Goldsmiths, University of London
July 2014

We are looking for help finding 120 people to participate in a field trial of a new research prototype we have produced. Called the Datacatcher, it is a location-aware device that displays social, political and environmental information about its locale. We are producing 120 Datacatchers, and need help finding participants from the general public who would like to live with them and be filmed about their experiences.

We are researchers from the Interaction Research Studio in the Design Department at Goldsmiths University. We do practice-based research, developing novel computational devices to try with participants from the general public. We do not develop our products to be commercialised, but to explore how people find meaningful engagement with them in their everyday lives. You can see more of our work here: http://www.gold.ac.uk/interaction/

We will be working with externally commissioned filmmakers to make short films of every participant using the Datacatcher in the local environment. Thus key to the deployment is agreement from participants to be filmed.

We are interested in deploying the Datacatchers across London, for a period of between one to two months, commencing in early September. Ideally, we would like to get the devices to participants from a range of socio-economic backgrounds.

We have imagined attracting participants through pop-up event(s), but are open to how people are recruited and given the devices. We do not want to pay participants, however, or 'hire' them to evaluate the devices. Rather we hope they will agree to use the Datacatchers because they are interested in trying them out. In addition to the films, we may try to capture the experiences of participants through a variety of other means, such as ethnography, photography and self-documentation – all of which will be externally commissioned.

We decided to investigate hiring an outside agency to recruit volunteers, complete sign-up paperwork and distribute the Datacatchers. We circulated a brief and talked to several agencies before choosing one to work with.

DATACATCHER FILM SPECIFICATION

IMPORTANT DATES

- Deployment week: 26th Sept - 3rd Oct
  (As agreed, you could attend one of the days to film 3-5 participants)

- 8x weeks of deployment: 4th Oct - 28th Nov
  (This gives 8 weeks to film approx 60 participants each)

- Final closing event: 29th and 30th Nov

RECRUITMENT OF PARTICIPANTS

- The design agency UsCreates will be co-ordinating and delivering a number of 'deployment events' over the week commencing 26th September.

- 120 participants will be recruited during this week, mainly located in Greater London, with a few potentially located outside of London.

- We have an additional ten devices. Both groups of filmmakers will each have one of these Datacatchers during deployment; this can be collected during the deployment events.

- UsCreates will co-ordinate details of deployment events directly with filmmakers

THE BOOKING SYSTEM

- The datacatcher will be packaged with instructions directing participants to an online scheduling system. This will have bookable slots clustered around five areas of London - Central, SE, SW, NW and NE.

- Participants will sign up for a 2-hour time slot, using one of the five calendars corresponding to an area of London. This will help to geographically cluster participants, reducing your travel time when filming.

- There will be a *maximum* of 4 bookable time slots on the days you are available to film. Sebastian - we can block out two time slots per day so participants can only sign up to two on the days you and your team are available. Time slots are scheduled for 9:00-11:00am, 12:00-2:00pm, 3:00-5:00pm, 6:00-8:00pm.

- Once the participants have committed to a time slot, you can contact them nearer the time to confirm a more precise location and time to meet.

- These time slots allow for at least one hour travel time between participants, which should be enough time for you to travel within the restricted areas of London (Central, SE, SW, NE, NW). Jared - as you are aiming to visit four participants per day, hopefully these times will also provide enough downtime for lunch etc.

- During the deployment events, participants will be asked if they want to sign up to a time for filming during week one of deployment. We hope to fill your schedule for this first week, so you are not waiting for participants to sign up to the online system when you ideally need to be out filming.

- After we have handed out 120 datacatchers at the deployment events, the online scheduling system will go live and participants will be able to sign up for a time during weeks 2 to 8. We will chase participants asking them to use the system if necessary.

We decided that the core of our 'data collection' strategy would involve commissioning very short documentary videos of each person who signed up to use a Datacatcher. This is the brief we sent to the two teams of documentary video-makers we hired.

'Playing with everyday life is just paying attention to what is conventionally hidden.'
Allan Kaprow

In the pursuit of elevated moments for everyday life, artist Allan Kaprow realised the biggest force holding back his genre-bending vision was the audience–performer divide. Ultimately, he reasoned, the divide could only be bridged when audience and performer were one. From this insight, Kaprow created a participatory art where conditions are established for people to engage in a heightened act of noticing the self, environment and experiences.

The Interaction Research Studio enacts a similar move with regards to participation. Participants engage in a kind of personal enquiry alongside others. This enquiry is situated in the everyday — in the detritus of classified ads, in household chores or routines, in daily commutes, in the work of intercessory prayer, in grassroots activism — but the scope of enquiry can reach beyond singular instances to reflections on concepts such as inequality, loneliness, spirituality, sustainability, community and intimacy.

Engaging in the 'act of noticing' is a slightly different framing of participatory design from how it is usually understood (i.e. engaging in the collaborative design of a process or artefact), although it is complementary to the original agenda of a design process to engage all stakeholders. What often drives participatory design is a collective process toward consensual or democratic decisions regarding a product or service. In the Interaction Research Studio's work, however, participants act as designers not of the artefacts but of their own enquiry process into questions of home life, relationships, community demographics, etc. This enquiry is provoked throughout a project's lifecycle through the artifacts of design and conditions of engagement that are informed by participants but created by the studio.

At the beginning of a project, for example, 'probes' provide a glimpse of rich personal and cultural experiences not just for the design researchers as points of inspiration but crucially for participants to engage in their own self-enquiry. Failing to support participant enquiry and the probes become a myopic questionnaire relevant only to the limited question and answer space provided. Likewise, the studio's artefacts such as the Drift Table, Prayer Companion, Plane Tracker or Datacatcher, all serve to create conditions for participants to engage in an altered, and ideally heightened, experience of their day-to-day lives. To the extent that engagement with these artefacts only provides the design researchers with new insights or stories to tell suggests a failure of the artefacts. This emphasis on aiding personal reflection and expression throughout the project lifecycle is what led to using Cultural Commentators as one tool for evaluation. In order to keep the artefacts of evaluation open for reinterpretation, the studio created the Cultural Commentators form to enable a multiplicity of interpretations.

The probes, devices, and evaluation tools work in concert along the arc of a project lifecycle. Probes do not solely provide input for a design, nor are evaluation tools simply for assessment — that is, they both do more than point forward or backward toward the designed artefact. Instead, all three elements form part of the larger game of enquiry into the conditions and nature of a particular space. For all of these points of intervention, we can ask: how do they stimulate enquiry and engagement? Do they open up exploration of various types of enquiry or do they tend toward one dominant narrative?

The studio has always described the type of enquiry participants engage in as a kind of playful pursuit — an experiment with current conditions and reflection on meanings and possibilities. The studio's term 'ludic design' was coined to emphasise the perspective that at heart we are all playful creatures and curiosity is a natural predilection. Many of our current designed tools and artefacts, in particular computational devices, ignore this playful nature. The studio's work serves as an alternative approach to design. The body of work the studio has established provides methods and strategies to design for the curious, and to design for participant enquiry. A broader implication, however, lies in the lessons we can learn from this body of work about the nature of play and curiosity as a cultural phenomenon. What have we learned from our participants about the nature of curiosity? In what ways is curiosity, like creativity, a cultural construct that evolves over time? Is the Curious Home of today different from yesterday's? If curiosity is a natural condition, how do we become un-curious? What do we lose when we lose curiosity? What conditions support or suppress curious engagement? How can we use design not only to design for curiosity, but also to understand the nature of curiosity itself?

'You invite people to play a game, in which the rules are explained and the expressive nature is clear. If they want to play, they will respond. Once they've made the commitment, you can play your game to your heart's content.' Allan Kaprow

Datacatchers being deployed by UsCreates at Ridley Road and Deptford markets, 13 and 14 November 2014.

DATACATCHER

People in this
part of town
can be called
"Urban Cool"

YOUR DATACATCHER

Deptford Market debrief – Alan
UsCreates
Friday 14th November

Today was a really good day, and we got lots of interested and engaged sounding participants signed up.

Reflections and thoughts:

- We were having much longer conversations with people, unpacking the ideas behind the project more, and people were asking more questions compared to yesterday
- Telling people about the polls seemed to get a good response with people liking the ability to contribute (whereas yesterday when the polls were mentioned there seemed to be trepidation about having to answer the questions)
- Turning their device on to demo live was really helpful, and got people answering the polls straight away. Also meant they took an active device away with them
- Focussed on emphasising the chance to be part of this exciting research project, and that they would get more out of the experience by using and interacting with the device
- 3 people once signed up brought/sent they friends to sign up
- A slower but much more consistent pace to the sign ups

We managed to get 26 people signed up: we had planned to cap at 15 or so, but the chance to get these engaged and enthusiastic users signed up was too good to miss!

This means that we have 23 devices left to give out, and I feel that going to both events over the weekend may be overkill.

What do you guys think about doing one or the other? I think of the two the Battersea carboot will be the more interesting opportunity. Obviously happy to attend both if you would like us to stick to the original plan.

End-of-day debrief from the agency.

Datacatchers being deployed by UsCreates at Battersea car boot sale, 16 November 2014.

Scaling up: collaborating with sub-contractors

Author Dave Cameron

The teams we hired to undertake deployment and filmmaking made the challenge of scaling-up our research manageable. These relationships presented new challenges to efficiently communicate the job at hand, however, and we found ourselves drawing up numerous briefs, specifications and proposals. Nonetheless, it soon became apparent these relationships needed to be more collaborative.

The strategic design consultancy, UsCreates was tasked with recruiting 130 participants to deploy an equal number of Datacatchers across London. The specifics were outlined in a brief, written by the studio, along with a set of our own proposals that explored potential methods for recruitment and deployment. In response, UsCreates designed pop-up style events to be delivered over three consecutive days at various London street markets, where prospective participants could sign up to the project and take a Datacatcher home.

On the first day of deployment, the studio joined the UsCreates deployment team at Ridley Road market. We soon realised that our brief alone was not enough to support the recruitment and deployment of the devices. Instead, it was important we worked together with the consultancy to shape the events in response to our learning from each day. This included modifying how the project was framed to prospective participants, as well as changing one of the event locations. Midway through the deployment events, we revised our original brief, changing our method of recruitment. In addition to the pop-up events, we deployed a batch of devices through social media and via existing contacts. We were able to redesign our deployment methods by working with UsCreates, drawing upon our own experience from past deployments, listening to their feedback from each day and joining them on location to experience the events ourselves.

Two teams of filmmakers were contracted to document the participants' experiences with the Datacatcher — Chaka Films and Jared Schiller Films. The studio produced a brief and specification to guide the filmmakers in holding a one- to two-minute conversation with each participant. This specification also outlined a system for participants to book an appointment with a filmmaker. This was a significant logistical challenge, in attempting to meet each participant's availability and location, whilst ensuring the appointments were geographically close to enable the filmmakers to travel from one participant to the next.

We anticipated the need to work collaboratively with the filmmakers to help shape the conversations with participants during filming, and set up a mechanism for edited footage to be uploaded as soon as it was complete, along with any notes from each appointment. This enabled us to respond to the footage and provide feed-back, with suggestions to develop the forms of conversations with participants, as well as to share any ideas to improve the style and content of the footage.

This ongoing collaboration enabled us to modify and improve our method of booking appointments for filming. Filmmakers fed back any issues and suggested improvements in coordinating these appointments. As a result, this system improved as the deployment progressed.

The relationship with both UsCreates and the filmmakers was ongoing throughout deployment. A single brief or specification was never enough — this work could not be 'handed over' to subcontractors. It was important we did not assume a shared tacit knowledge, and instead worked together to transfer the studio's learning and experience from past deployments. The ongoing collaboration with our project partners also allowed us to react to our learning from each challenge, so we could redesign our methods and be more experimental with our deployment.

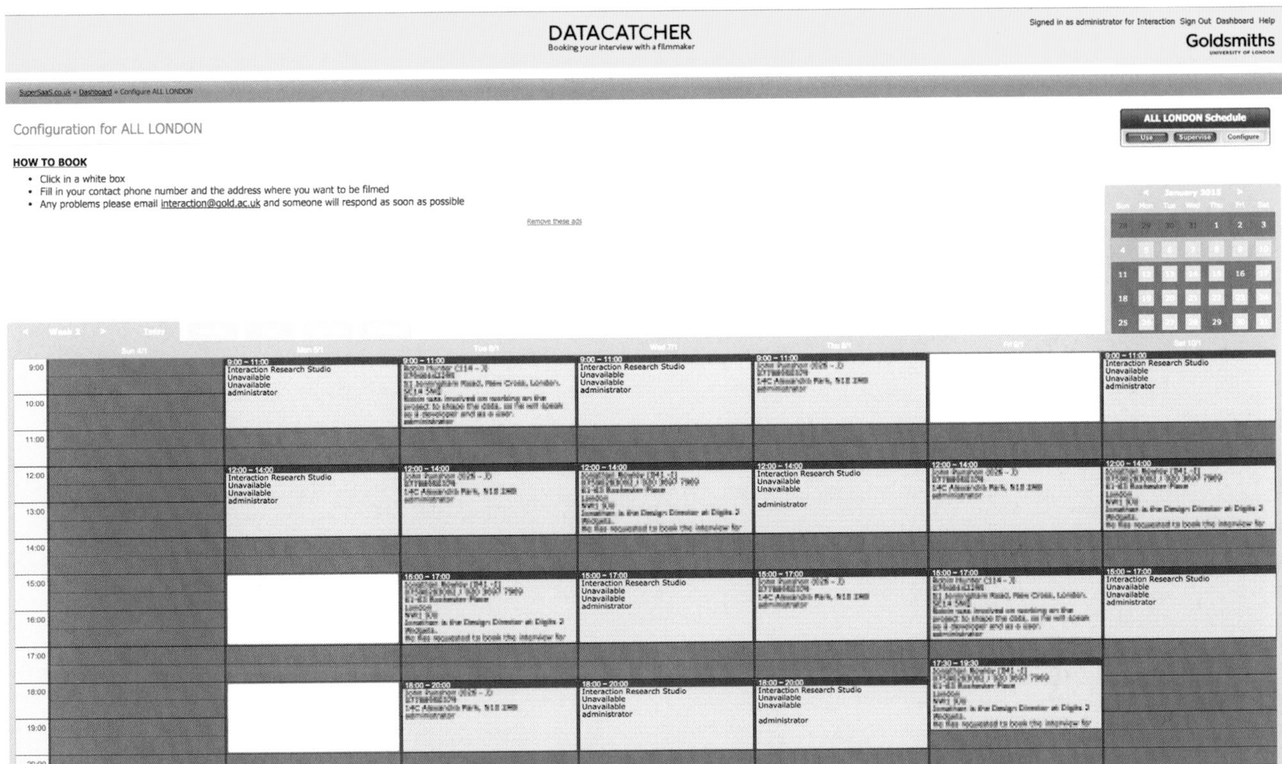

Online system for booking appointments with the filmmakers. This was an attempt to ease the logistics of booking participants by showing slots when the filmmakers would be available in different parts of London.

Title

Divide and conquer: adapting to personal details

Author

Belén Palacios

Diversity is enriching as much as it is challenging. The Datacatchers distributed around London moved into completely different homes only leaving behind their owners' contact details.

It was fast to send group emails but they proved inefficient. Over time, we had to build a relationship with those who were willing to share moments with our screen. It was laborious to handle the variety of personal cases a month after the deployment when the replies to our calls varied between 'Oh, yes, that torch!' and 'I'm not interested in buying anything'.

We had to become effective in our communications: categorising participants by use, but taking the time to talk to them personally and establishing an honest relationship in which they could say 'I don't understand it', 'I can't answer "yes" or "no": give me more options!' or 'I really enjoy looking at it'.

Our database started growing with notes from conversations. We discovered that some users were unable to see the text in the screen, that others decided not to open it because they were afraid of 'spoiling it' and even active users were concerned about incurring charges for using it over a certain time. Eventually, case by case, we started booking interviews to discover more about their experience.

The balance between statistical data and personal care was crucial in terms of our communication with the participants. They preferred to be greeted personally, rather than feeling like an extra contact on the BCC list of an email. In an age where everything needs to be quantified and processed through a database, the most effective approach became to pick up the phone and have a one-to-one conversation.

The documentary filmmaking teams started working as the devices were being distributed, interviewing several people as they received the Datacatchers to hear about their initial impressions.

The teams continued working throughout the two-month field trial. Getting volunteers signed up turned out to be very difficult, and there were many cancelled appointments or no-shows. One participant even demanded 'a present' for being filmed (we turned him down). Nonetheless, we succeeded in producing over 50 films in the end.

Stills from films of the participants.

datacatcher #066
week_09
ydenham
SPRESSO
ERROL STREET
E.C.1

We are God's unwanted children, people are fatter in Jesmond, a walk

Author John Bowers

At the turn of the 1960s into the 1970s, the Bank of England opened some new provincial branches around the UK. One of these was in Newcastle upon Tyne at the foot of Pilgrim Street. The building, designed by Sir Basil Spence — probably most well-known for the new Coventry Cathedral — was opened in 1971. A bold concrete and glass design, it was always controversial architecture, in particular because it comes starkly into view as the Tyne Bridge is crossed. When, in 1997, Tony Blair's government as one of its first acts changed the role of the Bank of England, the Newcastle branch closed and was sold. Being a highly specialised and somewhat inflexible office space, with massive underground vaults for the secure bomb-proof storage of gold and banknotes, the building had no new occupants and was demolished in 2012. Its site is now (early 2015) enclosed behind a tall wooden fence whose palings are tightly packed allowing only slits to view the absence. The loss of the Bank of England has raised questions not just about its site but about the future for the surrounding area known to planners and campaigners as East Pilgrim Street.

The Bank of England has fascinated me as a tightly knotted history of late capitalism and the state, and of the relationship between central government (and London and the South) and the provinces (and Newcastle and the North). But more than that. Pilgrim Street is so named because it was the route and resting place of pilgrims on their way to St Mary's Well in Jesmond to the north of the city — an important site for early English Christians up to the 15th century. It is now felt to be one of the most run down main streets in the centre of the city. From the Tyne Bridge, many would like to see a gateway to the city, not a stockade around a flooded area on top of infilled empty vaults with further dereliction and an abandoned police station, fire station and cinema nearby.

With colleagues Clara Crivellero and Tim Shaw, I plan a series of curated activities in relationship to this site. A gateway walk from the south across the Tyne Bridge. A pilgrims' walk to St Mary's Well. A massed witnessing through the slits of the security fence. And an encircling around the lost bank, tracing the perimeter of the East Pilgrim Street regeneration area. Today, I set off anticlockwise, as that is how pilgrims encircle the Ka'Aba in Mecca and how, for many Muslims, the world, the solar system and the universe are spun. I was accompanied by the Datacatcher. Here are our notes.

Just before noon, I touch the granite facing that remains from the base of the Bank of England. It glistens in the winter sun. I am eight miles from the sea. I think about the connections between (lost) commerce, (lost) shipbuilding and the (lost) port. People here are well-educated, wealthy and living in detached houses. But I see little to match that. There are few people on the streets and no residences. I begin to think that the Datacatcher is catching ghosts, from the prosperous port and the proliferation of printing and associated scholarship that took place right here in the 17th century.

I join my perimeter line (or my best approximation of it) after passing under the Pilgrim Street roundabout. You are in Gateshead where 14% are unemployed and 6,000 people are mental health service users. Ah no! That is the other side of the River Tyne. Very much the other side of the Tyne. The Datacatcher flickers between connecting to a cell tower in Gateshead, to one in South Jesmond, to one just above my head on top of 55 Degrees North, the building that dramatically straddles the roundabout and, before fashionable rebranding, was known as Swan House. Joseph Swan, inventor of a form of incandescent light bulb and creator of the first electrically lit city street in the world (which also joins the roundabout), still gives his name to the cell tower.

I follow the railway viaduct. In this borough 3,400 people are long-term unemployed. I stop at GG's for a bacon sandwich with brown sauce and see a characteristically layered Newcastle vista. Through the window of the modern office building containing the café, I see the railway arches, through them some low-rise, high-density recent housing. NE1 3JF has low house prices. Perhaps those ones. Outside again, a busy road takes the traffic from the A167 (M) that does not want to go over the Tyne Bridge. It separates me from the Holy Jesus Hospital which has been treating the sick for over seven centuries. Two lanes of fierce traffic. Bright blue painted railings. The hospital seems to sink at one end but my eye is tricked by the slip road rising. Town Moor has a lower standard of living than High Heaton. I am in neither place but perhaps the Datacatcher is doing for space what it did earlier with its out of time ghosts.

Jack Carter followed his dead brother's lover, Margaret, down the steps of Manors railway station. He confronted her, abducted her at gunpoint, and after forcing her to strip naked in his car's headlights, administered a fatal injection. The station is closed, its entrance blocked up. The building was once used by Tile World. There are old signs and ghost lettering. Another layered vista: the location from Get Carter in 1970, Tile World and, tucked by the dark, leaking, crumbling Trafalgar Road railway bridge, Generator, a 'music development agency'. Here 28% of households have central heating.

Under the suspended walkway over the urban motorway that took employees from Manors station to the Bank of England, I find a nook filled with beer cans, waste paper and a kind of botanical slime. Stenciled graffiti reads: WE ARE GOD'S UNWANTED CHILDREN. 5/6 recently described this location as stagnant. On Twitter, Shaun tells Anthony that he's hoping for moose blood.

I use the Datacatcher to advise me, as an oracle, how to proceed as the motorway cuts across my perimeter line. Happiness levels are very low. So I do not take the walkway over the motorway just yet, I keep low and pass through the car park of a development called Technopole and stop to appreciate a wilderness under a motorway access road. The people in this area are military dependents. I see no soldiers but some office workers, some students. Mostly I am walking alone.

Eventually, I have to cross the motorway. A long high walkway is the only way to do it. The motorway is set in a natural valley known as Pandon Dene although it looks like its route was specifically cut. Pandon Dene seems idyllic in 18th century engravings. A romantic fold in the earth just adjacent to the city. Shepherdesses and sophisticated gentlemen-of-commerce-and-learning pictured together. The traffic roars in six lanes above the Dene buried deep in a concrete culvert. 42% drink too much. I have a severe vertigo attack on the walkway and nearly faint. The traffic roars. I hold the handrail hard and cut myself on a curled-up metal edge. The idyll of Pandon Dene. Roar. Vertigo. Low air pollution. (Surely impossible.) Lost idyll. Roar. Vertigo. 7% pensioners. Dene. Shepherdess. Traffic. Roar. Labour Council. Damn you T. Dan Smith and your visions of the city in the sky and your disregard of my dizziness. Damn you Datacatcher for your heartless statistical and demographic tabloid headline news. In the culvert, the Dene roars.

An ambiguous zone the other side. Long, thin, partially covered. All entrances bricked up. Maybe there were once shops here and a nightclub and a restaurant. The smell of piss is intense. 32% of us are in good health. You are in Jesmond. You are in Low Team. I just want some timberlands. Why am I so poor (and basic)? I take a spiral stairway down to street level (from the level of an illusory street, vacant and piss-drenched). I am outside the club where Jack Carter chased the nervous Thorpe, eventually cornering him as Thorpe cowered in the toilets — toilets which were actually located at Newcastle Airport, some six miles away. Jesmond people are fatter than those of Town Moor. Another swift cut to some other parts of town. And their problems. There is blood on my hand.

I am moving between the backs of buildings. I have not seen, full on, a building's front façade since the (sinking) Holy Jesus Hospital. I faced and touched the entrance of the Bank of England. But it was not there. I am skirting around things. Looking out from the East Pilgrim Street regeneration area. But seeing the faces of no buildings. No urban grandeur. I cross a car park and pick up a dropped raw potato. 2/5 said they could hear birds. As I read this, I hear a birdcall and then the traffic noise returns. 4% of people here smoke. I inform the Datacatcher that I too have heard a bird. I also am reminded to smoke.

The line of the regeneration area is differently drawn in different planning documents. This, and the Datacatcher's flickering sense of where I am, make me reflect on just how problematic place can be. I am approaching Northumberland Street — the major shopping street of Newcastle, surely. The plans differ as to whether one side of it is in the regeneration area or not. And perhaps they should do. At the front, the bright windows of H&M. At the rear, something half-built, half-demolished. On the same block. I approach on a street called Saville Row. Vegan foods. Hairdressers. Loan shop. A Londoner would laugh (but, Jack Carter, we all drink from straight glasses now). Ahead Samsung promises me virtual reality experiences while I wait. Above the shop are four statues in the 19th century façade. Sir John Harley. Roger Thornton. Thomas Beswick. Harry Hotspur. To the right of the Samsung shop, a clothing chain called Bank is, of course, closing down. This is a Muslim area.

I walk downhill towards Pilgrim Street. 48% are in good health. Yes, these shoppers do look good, maybe 100% of them. I hug the west side of Pilgrim Street, walking my line. To my right, the windows of the Northern Goldsmiths Company. Watches and jewellery. On the other side of the road, the empty and crumbling Odeon. Commercial House straddles one lane of the road above the traffic — a building out of line, in the air, in the city of the sky. Occupied by artists on low, short-term rents. 5/14 feel comfortable here. I feel comfortable, oddly. I tell the Datacatcher. Happiness levels are low. One in eight are obese. A six bedroomed house costs £250,000. 7% ride a bike. It is 4.5 degrees. 7% pensioners.

By the abandoned police and adjacent, also empty, fire station, I can just see the Tyne Bridge as Pilgrim Street begins to fall away. A lone newsagent's in an otherwise derelict, scaffolded building. New York Haircutters was once next-door. (New York was once next-door.) The Army and Navy shop with its window display of camo and air guns. I return to the Bank of England and take photographs through the slits in the fence. They look like 19th century photographic experiments. A drunk congratulates me on the photos and tells me he sometimes climbs over the fence and splashes in the puddles. I make a bloody handprint on the granite facing to finish my circuit. People are fatter in Jesmond.

My walking partner and co-author, the Datacatcher, has an extended sense of time and place. It speaks of places I am not in but could be. And, perhaps, of times which once were here. It draws on a cloud of cells which somehow hover above us as we walk, creating ghosts and non-sequiturs. It is a harsh companion, monotonously giving me its mock shock horror headlines every few seconds, never mind my feelings or concerns, or the hubbub or stillness around us. It smears the city. It places us where it can find a cell tower, never mind where my foot falls. The cloud I imagine that feeds it has no sense of our trajectory or where we are looking. The layered vistas of the city are just signal strength proximities to it. On a flat plane. A flat plane of concern too. Obesity and moose blood. Muslims and birds. House prices and fashionable boots. The city is already loosely fixed in my imagination. Shoppers, drunks, inventors, pilgrims, bankers, soldiers, shipbuilders, Jack Carter, King Charles in exile. They are all here. The Datacatcher unfixes the city yet more. Porous boundaries. Hither and yon. Where the hell are we? Uncertain futures. Dropped potatoes. Data are everywhere, even though we do not know where we are. The Bank Of England and its gold and its promissory notes from the Queen cannot help. It's gone. We only catch glimpses from a distance of where it once was. The Datacatcher is a cold paranoid statistician. I will walk with it again. And perhaps, at the point of vertiginous despair, another city will come.

Datacatchers that have been returned through the post.

And then

It's a cliché because it's such a widespread experience: waiting for the party to start, and becoming convinced it's going to be a disaster. The invitations are stupid, too many got to the wrong people, and those who did get them probably don't understand what the party is supposed to be about in the first place. The whole theme didn't turn out the way you'd hoped anyway — the decorations seem awkward and boring, the music is embarrassing, you'd do better just turning on the radio. And the food is wrong too: there's probably not enough, some never got made, and the rest might be overcooked. And so you wait, convinced that nobody will turn up and that if they do they'll make their excuses and leave early…

Research through design can seem like the most difficult thing in the world: so much can go wrong.

It's not enough to find a fertile area for exploration, investigate it without letting facts overwhelm possibilities or alternatively spinning off into fantasy, develop a feel for the space of possibilities that might be pursued, decide on a strong idea, and then actually design, produce and field test a device that works technically, aesthetically, socially, etc. etc. etc.

No, beyond all that you have to avoid the countless small and stupid problems that can spoil the best of projects.

Proposals can be developed endlessly until they become impossible to navigate. Good ideas can be nixed by knee-jerk reactions. Designs can be iterated and reiterated until they lose all their life.

Parts can go out of stock. Mobile phone protocols can be obscure and finicky. Cell towers can be sparse and connections difficult to establish. Battery life can be precious, and a few lines of code can make the difference between a charge lasting days or just a few hours.

And once you finally produce a working research device, it can still all go wrong. Devices might be given to people who don't understand how to use them, or the sorts of engagement the project is looking to explore.

Participants might suddenly find themselves with obligations, or interests, or passing whims that mean they stop engaging with the device. They might get tired of recharging it after a couple of days, or take against it for some reason that seems trivial. They might simply stop answering the phone.

And when you finally get a number of people to participate, and moreover arrange to talk with them about what they think of the design that you and your colleagues have spent years, literally years, making, they might reject it, or even like it, in ways that seem utterly predictable and uninteresting.

As the guests arrive, you greet them, hang up their coats, and lead them to the refreshments. You scurry around, turning up the music, moving dishes, changing the lighting. Somebody seems to be standing awkwardly on their own, and you bring them into an interesting conversation. When a couple has to leave to pick up their kid, you're convinced they were just looking for an excuse to go. You get a little frantic, serving drinks, making connections, changing the music again. Finally, you begin to realise that everybody seems to be having a better time than you...

It's no wonder that we spent the first few weeks of the field trial worrying that everything would go wrong.

First of all, we had spent a lot of devoted work fine-tuning the Datacatchers, but that meant that we were more aware than anyone of their limits.

The final form may have been the result of countless iterations (seemingly hundreds of the dial alone) but perhaps it was a too torch-like, or toy-like, or simply the volume taken by an extra-large battery made the whole thing too big.

And why was it a device anyway? We knew already that one of the most frequent reactions we could expect would be that the whole thing should be an app. We were confident that a stand-alone device would be used very differently from an app, but less convinced others would get this.

Far more important than these concerns, however, we worried about the data and the messages we created from it. We were using a substantial range of sources, some accessible to us only because of our academic status. These gave extraordinary access to the locations the device visited: their finances, infrastructure, politics, environmental practices, even the number of pubs nearby.

The Datacatchers made routine use of a range of data that is historically unprecedented. But the data is limited as well. For instance, many of the sources are updated infrequently or not at all, which meant that messages might become out of date, or repetitive if the devices were not moved around much — and even if they did travel, the categories of messages remained the same.

In any case, it wasn't always clear what area a given message might be about. If it said that 203 households 'around here' were without central heating, for instance, well... what is 'around here'? Is that within eyesight? Or is it in that general part of London? It didn't help that the Datacatcher might be locked onto — and thus assume it was located near — a cell tower that was far from its actual location.

The Datacatchers also revealed a more insidious limitation of the datasets that increasingly characterise our world — and determine the ways corporations and governments act within it. They are all about people, not individuals. Datasets do what Holmberg and her colleagues call 'populationisation': they aggregate individual characteristics into distributions and then use these distributions to understand individuals. The group becomes the norm, against which any single instance is compared. And this happens at multiple levels, so that a household can be compared to its neighbourhood, the neighbourhood to its district, the district to the city, and so on.

Populationisation is a powerful logic, enabling an enormous range of individual things, from housing prices to taste in music, to be placed with respect to others like them. But it is a totalising logic as well, obscuring other ways of perceiving the world. On the one hand, it relies on isolating things of interest from their contexts and categorising them for comparison. On the other, in suggesting that the norm of an existing population is, well, normal, it can be deeply conservative. Perhaps all houses cost too much? Perhaps the range of incomes is simply too large?

Perhaps we had made a fundamental mistake in seeking to create a 'mobile political intelligence' based on the logic of populationisation?

We worried. And once the deployment started, we worried more.

It's late now, and most of the guests have gone. The only ones left are a few close friends, and a guy who seems to have forgotten to leave. You don't know him well, but you don't mind. Now that it's over, you've finally started to mellow and feel

magnanimous. In the end, the party was fine — no, it was good.

After the field trials ended, things looked a lot better.

It took a lot of anxious planning and replanning, innumerable cajoling phone calls, trips all over London, missed appointments, reformulated briefs and difficult conversations, but at last we got the data we could get. The devices were shut down, and most returned to us.

And in the end, we have more than 50 short videos of participants talking about the Datacatchers.

Fifty!

That is about two hours of tightly edited film. It represents about half the people who borrowed a device. As any social scientist will tell you, that is an extremely healthy rate of return.

Browsing through the films is like overhearing fragments of conversation. *A new layer of information to a city.... Like a dedicated tool to explore your areas... So different from anything else that is out there, it immediately gets people asking questions...*

Of course, not everything is positive. *It's bright and flashy... I found a lot of the data I picked up quite inane and boring... People were looking at me wondering why I was reading a torch... I went to Stratford for a swim, not to find out what the population was like...*

The tenor of most engagements, however, seemed to be good-natured, leaning towards appreciative. *It brings you to bigger issues in the area that normally in your day-to-day life you're not... It was mesmerising to keep staring at the screen... The Datacatcher gave me loads of information that I hadn't picked up on and wasn't on my radar... Capturing the data, like a net going through a glasshouse full of butterflies...*

Not surprisingly, many of the comments circle around the data itself, with stances ranging from interest to bemusement, belief to scepticism. *There was a big contrast between where I work and where I live. I knew that, but it was interesting to see that in the statistics... Like some of the things seemed quite shocking, actually, some of the facts, it was like 'really?' I almost question whether it was true. I mean obviously it is... It said the house prices around here are really low, I was like 'definitely not!'*

Overall, the videos show a large number of individuals, each working to make sense of an unusual device, presented to them in an unusual manner.

Of course, some people are ambivalent. They try out different orientations without seeming to settle on one that satisfies. Others don't try very hard at all, for whatever reason. They reject the Datacatcher without compunction and even with a hint of schadenfreude.

Many, however, find ways to value the Datacatcher. Some appreciate it as a tool for gathering information, and revealing dimensions to their surroundings that are otherwise inaccessible or unnoticed. Some appreciate it as a provocation, raising questions about the kind of society we live in, or about the ways that data characterise the world, or about how we think about our locations, or about our identities. Others appreciate it as a designed device, admiring the care we put into it, the simplicity of its interaction, its unusual appearance, and its distinctiveness in a world of smartphones and apps. Others still appreciate the questions it asks, for allowing them to share their impressions of their surroundings, for making them think in new ways, or simply for their humour. It becomes clear, over the course of the videos, that there are many ways to engage with the Datacatchers, and many ways to find interest in them.

What this emphasises is that any success of the Datacatchers is an *achievement.*

The success of the Datacatchers is an achievement of the device itself, of course. It is the payoff for all the fretting we did about how it looked, what interacting with it was like, and whether the data would be interesting.

It is also an achievement of the people that got the Datacatcher out of the studio and into the participants' hands. The deployment team didn't just give out the devices. They created a milieu that conveyed a sense of the kind of event this was, and what sort of device the Datacatchers might be. The filmmakers, too, framed the Datacatcher: as a thing to be discussed in front of a camera, about which certain questions might be asked, and about which certain remarks might be worth making. Both these groups shaped the field trial in profound — if sometimes uncomfortable — ways.

Moreover, the Datacatcher didn't make the journey from studio to participants on its own: it was accompanied by manuals and forms, packaging and websites that told its story in a multitude of ways. These things, too, were agents of its success.

The participants, however, are arguably the most responsible for any success enjoyed by the Datacatcher.

When it works, it is because the people who use it do the job of making it work. They link it to their concerns. They bring their aesthetic sensibilities to it. They reflect about data with it, or about their neighbourhoods. They carry the Datacatcher into their worlds, both literally and metaphorically. In a very real sense, the participants do a substantial part of the design and implementation of the system.

We are grateful to them.

Unloading another armload of dirty glasses into the sink, you look around the remains of the party in the early morning. Dirty dishes are stacked on the table, with leftover food and discarded packaging. There are crumbs on the floor, and a large smear of something that has been trod into the carpet in the living room. Several pieces of furniture have been moved and need to be replaced, and some old vinyl albums lie scattered on the floor near the stereo. You sigh. What's the point of throwing a party if all you're left with is a mess? Are they worth it?

With over a hundred Datacatchers deployed to volunteers, this project has been our largest study to date.

We took on development at this scale to see whether it would work as a methodology for 'Third Wave Human Computer Interaction'. This stresses the role of personal interpretation in interaction, and suggests that people's engagements with technology are situated and particular. Studying many people using a given design makes sense because it allows many different stories to appear, and reminds us that there is no single truth about a given design.

But such a large-scale deployment came at a cost.

Actually, it came at many costs, each step of the way.

We had to avoid the use of 'craft' techniques in designing the Datacatchers in order to make it possible to approach production at this scale. This was a sacrifice in itself, and, moreover, knowing this would be necessary constrained our designs from the very beginning.

We had to make the Datacatchers easy to assemble, write computer code that could handle hundreds of separate devices at the same time, deal with shortages of parts and many irksome hardware and software bugs.

We had to recruit, deploy and maintain contact with so many volunteer participants that we ended up outsourcing much of the work to third-party agencies. This limited our ability to frame the devices, the study and our relationship with participants. And instead of having regular, in-depth visits with participants to talk about the Datacatchers, we had to rely on a series of short documentary videos for glimpses.

Finally, we had to accept a lot of waste along the way. We had hundreds of ideas we couldn't develop. We produced dozens of casing designs to refine one that could be scaled up efficiently. A percentage of PCBs and parts failed. Devices were wasted on participants who didn't engage with them or with the filming. All these sources of waste counterbalanced the economies of scale that come with designing, building and studying a hundred devices at once.

So was it worth it? We think so.

The payoff is in the videos. Each one is only a couple of minutes long, but taken together they represent a rich and varied mix of people, settings and views. Of course it is tempting to sort these, to find ways to thematically summarise the data — and we will do that, especially for academic presentations.

But videos work well because they capture

moments that can be revisited time and time again. Moreover, along with the remarks they are edited to highlight, they give a glimpse into a person's life: their appearance, clothes, way of talking, location and the people and things that surround them.

This means videos can be viewed and reviewed, juxtaposed in different ways, looked at with different interests. In this sense, the videos keep participants' experiences alive and present, allowing the outcomes of the field trial to be accessed with far more immediacy than any analysis can convey.

Even a single video collected from a field trial is a resource that can last for years. Fifty are a gold mine. They represent a breadth and depth of information that is unprecedented in our work, and highly unusual in Research through Design more generally. They are a resource that we, and others, will be able to draw on for years.

Whether it was worth working at such a scale is not just up to us, however. In the next section, we reproduce transcripts of each of the videos. This allows the participants to speak for themselves. And they will allow you, the reader, to decide for yourself.

Voices

We sent the video soundtracks for full verbatim transcription.

Deployment — Battersea car boot sale part 1

Female: This isn't good is it? It's challenging, and I think fascinating erm bits of knowledge.

Male: Yeah.

Female: Useless bits of knowledge. Someone here previously thought this area was a rat area. Was that me?

Male: We just did that.

Female: We just did that, it's come up now. '20% of this community is obese.' Oh my goodness.

Male: Is that surprising? It's quite surprising.

Female: That's quite a lot.

Male: 20%, that's one in five.

Female: So 20% of the people here are obese.

Male: Are obese.

Female: Probably I'm one of them. 'There are more moths here in North Kensington,' oh no. 'You are closer to the sea now than nearby in West Brompton.'

Male: That's nice to know. It's always nice to be close to sea.

Female: That's nice to know, nearer to the sea. And I want to get it back to my area so I can see what's happening in my area, yeah? That was really interesting. Actually that's, why don't you get one?

—

Deployment — Battersea car boot sale part 2

Male 1: ...and stuff from Twitter, loads of different sources. Idea being, you know, to see how people interact with that data. Would you be interested in taking one?

Female 1: Thanks for explaining it.

Male 1: No probs. Sort of all sorts of stuff, erm, crime stats, local economic stats, all sorts of things. Erm, if you're interested in that kind of thing, interested in being in the know or you're just interested in being in part of a research project, erm, would you be interested in taking part?

Male 2: Probably not.

Male 1: Okay. Worth a try. Worth a try. Hello there, would you like a free data device?

Female 2: No thank you.

Male 1: That doesn't really say much, does it. It scrapes the internet for interesting information about your area, the area you happen to be in. It scrapes the internet and gives you little brilliant bits of data and information. Take it for a couple of months and play with it. It's unique. There's only 120 of them in the world. This is a Datacatcher, brand new device, brand new device. It's location aware, it gives you facts and figures about your area in London as you move around.

Male 3: Okay.

Female 3: What are they?

Male 1: These are Datacatchers, they're [...].

Female 3: Okay.

—

Deployment — Man in a red jacket

Male: That's it, yeah I've got it. I'm going to turn it on, like how do I turn it on? Little blue, oh yeah.

Interviewer: Yeah?

Male: We've turned it on, what do we do now? I've never seen such a lovely, cause if you put it in your pocket like that, straight in your pocket. What you do, put it straight in your pocket and you go, "Where are we?" I'm in Dalston Lane, so then it goes to Dalston Lane.

I find it a very fan- fantastic tool.

Interviewer: Okay, so the way it works is, it's it's loading.

Male: It's loading right now, I'm not doing anything.

Interviewer: Yeah, and then it'll bring you, bring you some information up.

Male: It's loading now so erm.

Interviewer: Yeah.

Male: Very good.

Interviewer: You see the little nozzle under there?

Male: Yeah.

Interviewer: If you move that, the yellow one.

Male: Yeah.

Interviewer: Yellow one, it'll give you different information.

Male: Right. It's giving me information about the er people down here. Do you know, it's a fantastic little tool, it's a lovely little tool. Never get lost. Don't tell me that's got my name on that. Very, very interesting. Fantastic, that's good.

—

Deployment of Datacatcher number 039

Female: I've just been given this box, is it the, which college is it? Which school is it you are from?

Interviewer: From Goldsmiths.

Female: From Goldsmiths College. Erm, I'm not too sure what it is, but I'm quite happy to use it and to gain is it information about the local area?

So yeah this is, I like the colour, I like orange. I'm not sure, I'll have to read the instructions, I've got a, I've got a brief er idea what it's about, it's to understand what sort of, what area, what the area is about, you know?

I'm not too sure, but it gives information about the area. So if, if, if it's erm where the next restaurant is or the next café. I'm a home baker so I would like to know what, what cafes have opened up so I can go and approach them and ask them if they want to buy my fruit cake for Christmas.

So yeah, that would be interesting. Is that it?

Interviewer: Yes, that's it.

Female: Okay.

—

Deployment of Datacatcher number 063

Female: Guided by you. I thought it was, it's a very interesting idea. The only thing I'm a little bit confused about is that my phone gives me, gives me a lot of information and I'm not sure about the validity of this machine, how you're going to use it, basically.

But it would be interesting to see how you correlate all the information. But I travel a lot so I'll be able, in London, so I'll be able to give you masses of data. It's fascinating.

Male: You must be [...].

Female: It's a fantastic idea, let's see if it works. I'll be most interested at the end of two months to see what we've got out of it.

Interviewer: So you think you'll actually use it for two months as well?

Female: Well I would yes, [...] on the car.

Interviewer: Yeah?

Female: Yes, I think if it's helpful I will. Is that enough?

Interviewer: Perfect, thank you.

—

Deployment of Datacatcher number 096

Female: I think it's a beautifully designed object. Erm, I love the way that you're entrusting people in the local community with this research actually, I think that's a really wonderful thing.

Erm, I do live in the area so I will be sort of randomly testing it. Erm, I just think it's brilliant, frankly. I know that's probably not what you want to hear, because like...

I'm still a little unfamiliar with what's going to happen. Okay, following the instructions. 'To select questions press the dial.' So I'm now being told how many residents are in this local area and where this is connected to, which is Creekside, Greenwich.

It's just a beautifully designed object. Yeah, well done. Well a lot of my artwork is based on traversing through areas, being on public transport and filming and dealing with the boredom erm that occurs in sort of public spaces and when commuting. So I imagine I'd quite enjoy sort of like, if it works on the train, you know like Overground, being on the Overground and sort of travelling really quickly through an area and seeing what data actually comes back and how accurate that is.

So yeah, it's one of the numerous ways to fight boredom and to also learn things.

—

Deployment of Datacatcher number 098

Male: Well I didn't stop at first 'cause I thought that I was gonna to be asked for money and then realised it was actually a project that I'd heard a little bit about that seems really interesting. And I'd seen some of their other work that kind of cultural probes and amazing to get to be a part of one of these still strange experiments.

I don't know I was thinking it would be interesting to see like have it in the house and see what my housemates make of it. Erm, 'cause I live with a pool of people I think who'll find it quite interesting thing to see if it gives different information over time or if there's a way of sort of finding out about the area. It's quite, yeah, quite interesting wandering around it and seeing what kind of information you get. I do lots of walking around London so that would be quite nice to have on those walks.

I don't know, it seems very functional but it looks like quite an appealing, simple interface.

—

Deployment of Datacatcher number 118

Female: Well I stopped because I'm having a quiet day. I'm not at school today, er, so I usually don't stop for people asking me stuff on the street.

I, I mean the thing is quite big. If you ask me to take it with me everywhere it is quite big. Obviously that might be inconvenient but then it might be fun on the bus to have all these questions asked and stuff. How is this place doing? The pits, they got them on the slide all stagnant. I don't know, I, I'll try and use it today at least. Usually I'm quite busy but today's a quiet day so I am gonna use it, yeah.

—

Living with Datacatcher number 005

Female: I don't think so, I don't think it changed any of my perceptions of an area.

Like some of the, some of things seem quite shocking actually, some of the facts I was like, 'Really,' like I almost questioned whether it was true, obviously it, it is but I was like, 'Oh,' but then I think I just, I think that's probably — I wouldn't like take it out and scroll through it and then put it back and then do it again. I would like take it out, scroll through and then be like, 'Oh okay.' Then I'd sort of like almost get a bit bored and be like, 'Oh okay, I don't really need to know anything more.'

Like sometimes it, it'll repeat facts. I think maybe that was a problem as well. Like if I was taking it work every day the same similar facts were reoccurring or similar, I might just be like 'Oh okay,' like that's enough and put it away and then not use it for the rest of the day. And I didn't really see the correlation between the, erm, questions that it asked and the information that it gave you. Like the information that it gave you is all statistics and it's all facts and it's all based on truth whereas the questions that it asked you were all opinion based.

So I didn't really see how the two sides function really, correlated. Like it might be like is this a cat or dog area, but then the answers might be cat, dog, fox or like, I don't know what the other one was, but it just, it didn't really — I don't know, I was just a bit like I didn't really understand that maybe.

Erm, I think if I was maybe moving house or like if I was moving to an area and I wanted to know a lot about it, I think it'll be really useful 'cause you could take it with you and learn, erm, I guess sort of like, what type of area it is via the device. But I think in general some of the stuff that it told me I probably, I wasn't really as interested to know about. I think if any of them facts I ever did wanna find out I could probably just google it if I needed to know.

—

Living with Datacatcher number 008

Male: When I switched it on I started looking at the erm, the little er the entries. I think the thing that really shocked me first was erm what a depressing area I live in, because all the statistics are about erm crime and, and health and how unhealthy the people are in my neighbourhood and in my community.

You know, that immediately kind of starts you thinking, 'Is this the place that I'd live in? Am I really living in a place that is erm so full of crime and,

and death and unhealthy people?'

On the Datacatcher you just kind of see something slightly, slightly different about the neighbourhoods as you pass through them, which I thought was really nice.

Immediately with, well every entry you kind of start to think, 'Well, what are the borders that are being defined here by the data, by the entry?' When they talk about neighbourhoods or boroughs or whatever, who's defined that border? And is that a border that I would sort of erm feel familiar with, living in this place?

So yeah the, I quite like the fact that the, the statistics invite sort of this questioning of of where you are and how you define the borders of where you are.

—

Living with Datacatcher number 009

Female: People around the office were kind of like, 'Wow, what's that? Is, is this like a toy? What is this device?' And so that kind of got people talking erm, so the design, the colour, the shape, that was quite, er quite a good talking point.

I liked that the questions were quite kind of a lot of socially based er, you know, the kind of how, how do you feel where you are? How is the environment where you are and and how is that kind of making you feel? Is it noisy? Is it polluted?

So it felt quite personal, it wasn't kind of data in a, a wider context, or data for businesses. It was very much personal data; how do you feel right now? Erm, can you share that with us for the project? So I, I liked that, it felt quite engaging.

I would have liked a few more, a bit more variety in some of the questions and maybe slightly broader topics erm, and if, if this is something that gets expanded or, or looked at again in the future I'd love to be involved and happy to give feedback or, or trial anything again.

—

Living with Datacatcher number 011

Female: Some of the data I was quite surprised at, erm because when I pressed it and looked at like what they said about the area that I was in, most of the areas I'd I'd visited and used the Datacatcher was areas that I'd perhaps been to before anyway.

Erm, but yeah, no. Some of the the information that it stored and then fed back to me when I looked at it was quite interesting, I found that quite interesting.

You kind of got an insight of an area and depending on how it's going to be used after, if it's going to be sort of used for public domain, it would be quite interesting for other people that don't know that area to be able to have access and look at. And go, 'A percentage of people that live in that area, or have visited that area, have said this about the area.'

Because it would be interesting to see, if ten people had the Datacatcher, what would they say about let's say Deptford? Would we all have similar views because it's the area we live in, or would we all have ten different views?

—

Living with Datacatcher number 016

Female: I think initially I was just erm turning it on when I got home and reading about, it was reading the same data over and over again, and the kind of same questions were coming up and I was answering them. Erm, and I did that a few times and then I think I just got a bit bored and turned it off. And then erm I realised that I was meant to be taking it round with me, leaving it on continuously and you know, it catching the data like a kind of net going through you know, a glasshouse full of butterflies or something, and then reading back at the end of the day.

Erm, weirdly I found the kind of time stamp at the bottom and the location more fascinating to watch. So just seeing where I'd been at different times of the day, and flicking back and kind of going, 'Oh okay, well it was connected to that cell tower then at 5 o'clock. Where was I? I was on the train, and then it kind of—' And I just found that like more interesting than the data itself, which was not not the, I'm sure not the erm, not the purpose of the Datacatcher.

—

Living with Datacatcher number 017

Female: The Datacatcher provides kind of a new layer to city with the data and information that you can't really see when you walk around. So erm it shows a layer of the city that you can't otherwise perceive erm so I think that's really fascinating. It's a new way of exploring an area or a place.

I thought the idea of using it on a tube would be really interesting, where you could see the differences across areas while you travel. Erm, that didn't work unfortunately because it didn't connect to the cell tower quickly enough, but erm the idea of exploring a city with this kind of data I find quite interesting, and I like that it's also interactive. Erm, I think that's quite key to being interested over time, that it also has some kind of way of interacting with it.

The nice thing is that it has these kind of different ways of interacting with it, and this only provides you information about your area, so it's like a dedicated tool to explore your area. Whereas an app erm, I mean your phone does pretty much everything so this this just makes you more aware of this is only for that purpose, erm and I will use this when I'm interested in exploring my area or finding out more about this neighbourhood.

I think that's really nice that it's a, it's a custom device that's really dedicated to one purpose.

—

Living with Datacatcher number 018

Female: So a lot of the facts that came up I was expecting. I suppose living in the area and working in this area, I know that it's quite deprived, I know what sort of balance of people there are.

Erm, so the ones that were quite interesting were probably the ones that you don't see very much like the, I suppose the fruit and vegetable one was quite interesting.

Interviewer: What, what was that?

Female: So it was the percentage of the people that don't have enough fruit and veg. Which I suppose I could have worked out, but it was quite nice to see it.

Erm, the other one was the sick in the bus stops, just because it was quite funny. But I don't think it's made me think differently about the areas I live and work.

One I remember was about erm the central heating; how many people have central heating or how many people have electricity, I can't remember exactly. But it was quite a large number that didn't, or you know, significant, and that does er tie with my work because we work with a lot of people in poverty. Erm, again it wasn't something that I didn't know, but having it quantified was quite useful in the local area.

Erm I suppose then what I'd quite like to be able to do is go into that and then extrapolate it and look look behind it, erm you know, look at what that means for the rest of London or erm, so yeah, that one in particular helped my work.

—

Living with Datacatcher number 019

Male: So erm, it's interesting cause it looks like a torch and er, and this is a kind of anecdotal thing really but it's almost as if, it's funny cause I'm looking into it but it does remind me of holding a torch, which is an odd thing.

Erm, but then you'd use a torch to shine light at something or to kind of get, to maybe get information in the dark of things you don't know about, so there was this weird sort of physical connection that I had with it. Erm, that when I was holding it I, it was immediately apparent.

It's really satisfying as well when you use the wheel, because you get that lovely kind of clicking feel so you really feel like you, you're doing a thing. You're doing something as opposed to just flicking through digital er just a bunch of messages.

The information did feature as a conversation piece with the people I was with, and that was really interesting. So it didn't, it kind of encouraged a sort of social interaction and it was very, it was real fun.

I had a lot of fun with it, erm I would continue to have fun with it and I, I want to keep it for a while. I want to take it er with me when I'm going on holiday. I think that's when I would get more out of it. Erm, cause it would enhance the social experience, it would give me more personal information and I, I liked the sort of, sort of you know, seemingly trivial yet quite revealing erm kind of factoids, the factoid element of it.

—

Living with Datacatcher number 020

Male: Hi. My name's Frank Akinsete, I'm a freelance stylist and fashion consultant. I was approached by Goldsmith's College about two weeks ago at Battersea car boot sale one Sunday when I was doing a stall, and they basically said that I should switch it on and it will pick up data wherever I am. So that's what I've been doing sporadically.

Personally erm you know, like I said, after the, the novelty of being able to do that with the instrument, I found a lot of the data I picked up quite inane and boring, and I wondered what the point of it is. Without knowing what the project's for, it seemed somewhat pointless and I felt that a lot of the data I picked up I could either Google or get in so many other sources.

The depth of the information was that erm, it's not really astounding and erm you know, I mean even from a novelty or you know, from a fun, fun perspective I doubt I'd be the centre of any Christmas party taking this with me, to be honest with you, with the information I've got on it.

No disrespect to those people working very hard on this project, but you did want an honest response from me and I can assure you that I'll give you that. You know, my name is Frank; I'm being frank by name and nature.

—

Living with Datacatcher number 022

Female: This really is very dodgy. Okay, come on. Don't laugh at me you. It's not even on, but never mind. Oh no, here we are. It's upside down now, there we go. Datacatcher. Spiritual.

Female Child: No.

Female: Soulless.

Female Child: No.

Female: Nonsense.

Female Child: What?

Female: Yeah, it is a bit. Meaningful. Oh my God, that is a ridiculous question.

Female Child: Nonsense, do nonsense.

Female: No it's not, it's a good question. It's interesting, I really like this. It's a good, it's good questions.

Female Child: Do nonsense.

Female: I want to say, 'Soulless.' Maybe that's me though. 'Would you like to live here?' I do live here. Yes. No. Yes, yes I like it here.

How does, how do they know this stuff? Who is it, Nanny?

Female Child: No, it's...

Female: Oh Anna?

Female Child: Yeah.

Female: Oh, I forgot she was coming. Just plonk it down. I've, has she gone?

Female Child: Yeah.

Female: Do you mind if I just quickly say hi and thank you to this woman? My aunt, with all these clothes I don't want.

[Background talk 0:01:23].

—

Living with Datacatcher number 026

Male: Er, I didn't take it out much in the street but er I went to fight a parking ticket and er the adjudicator even said, 'Oh what's that?' and er we spent five minutes looking at the, looking at the information and chatting with it. But it somehow didn't convince him to er cancel my parking ticket.

It's very simple; it's got a single control so you know it's, you can't really get it wrong. And it's so different from anything else that you see out there that it immediately gets people asking questions. Like, 'What's this bright yellow thing that looks unlike anything I've ever seen before?'

People are curious and people will start asking about it. If it was just done with the same functionality but as an app for your phone then erm immediately you would be disconnected from the people around you. Because any time you are sitting looking at an app on your phone, you are ignoring everybody else around you and everybody else around you is leaving you alone because you know, you've demonstrated that you're not interested in interacting with the people around you.

When you take this out, people want to look at it and people are wondering what it is and erm people will talk to you about it, even.

—

Living with Datacatcher number 030

Female: The tweets are really interesting. I don't know how the, I don't know how you know it filters the tweets but it always come up with, you know, quite angry peop- angry tweets as well?

Or just erm, yeah just, oh yeah there was actually one that was quite good. It said, I think it's a road not far from here, it says that er number number 48 on whatever route it said, erm it's a cause of problem, you know? It's been like you know, something is happening at number 48 on that road and I just, I just wanted to know what was happening but I didn't, I didn't dare knock on the door.

You know, it's quite erm mesmerising to just you know keep staring at the screen and see what fight's going to come next, you know?

So it was, it was kind of like it was a good party trick, yeah. But yeah I don't think it's it it's meant to be taken too, I mean the data is not meant to be taken too seriously but I think the device itself is, is very interesting, especially in, in this day and age where you know, an iPhone can do pretty much about everything, you know?

Just, you know, apart from toasting bread I mean, you know? So it's, it was quite interesting to act- to actually hold something you know? Like just the grip of it is quite interesting, it's not just like a, a black square, like a black mirror you know? Like this er Channel Four programme which is quite interesting.

I mean it is kind of a black mirror as well. Erm yeah, it's just really erm, it's, it it looks archaic and very futuristic as well at the same time.

—

Living with Datacatcher number 033

Female: So erm I'm, I'm Italian. Erm, I work er in Hammersmith, I work in a brand consultancy as a user researcher, and er I live in er I live in Shoreditch.

Like yesterday I had a very, at the end of a very busy and heavy week I, I look at the [Ermenegildo], this is how I call my Datacatcher, and er the [Ermenegildo] told me that Hackney has a very low level of happiness. So I was like, 'Okay that's, that's a great start to the day.'

But on the other side is erm like they have some information like 'Fix my street', that was telling me how in er Warner E2 which is kind of close here, er residents are are kind of worried by the fact that when big trucks pass on the road their building shakes, and that's exactly what I, I mean what I was experiencing but I, I didn't really know what was going on. And actually thanks to the Datacatcher I realised that I'm not going crazy but it's something that is an actual issue that we should, should be addressed somehow.

Interviewer: And why, can you explain a bit about the name?

Female: Well [Ermenegildo] is a very weird Italian name, that's it. And I mean it's kind of weird this thing. Like, when I brought it to work everyone was like, 'Oh, so you have to like point it out and it tells you information.' So I thought like, it's a bit of a weird thing and a weird name is perfect.

—

Living with Datacatcher number 035

Male: I used it mainly here at the office to try it out, and then a few times I took it around Shoreditch, and this was mainly when we were going for lunch or for a coffee break. I have to say, for me erm the main feature was its entertainment value.

It was, yeah it was very funny to take it along and to, to look at it and see what it tells us. And so in a group we had, you know, discussions around, 'Is this useful or is this just an interesting fact? Or what does this mini survey tell us about erm the the area?' So it was a great, I think the social value, the entertainment factor was, was great.

I mean, the data searches were quite varied and surprisingly detailed often because they are very local and what do I remember? I remember, I think there were statistics on say house prices and unemployment ones, but also some more obscure ones around health or, or yeah, life expectancy, sort of general census statistics.

But also I do remember ones that were

surprising in many ways. Like not the normal, how many, what is the average age or what is the average income?

But what I liked about the Datacatcher was not just its technical functionalities but also sort of the physical representation. It's great to have this device that's very colourful and I think it was well designed as a product.

—

Living with Datacatcher number 041

Male: My, my name is Jonathan Rowley, I'm a design director of Digits2Widgets. Erm, we were involved in some of the production of the parts that make up the Datacatcher.

I think that initially I found it fascinating. I mean, it's very interesting to have a device that can kind of pull off this kind of information. Some of the data was quite old, which you know wasn't that interesting. Erm, some of it was very funny.

But in the end you know, having looked at it and used it for a little while, I just started to find it really depressing. It was a more overall impression of, 'Oh my God, is this what life is boiled down to?' You know? 'Is this what it's about?' Erm, and an awful lot of this data, you know, you can understand why it's gathered, why it's disseminated, erm and you know unfortunately an awful lot of it is about money.

Erm, and it's all very sad. And you know, it's quite an interesting little insight into the way that, you know, I certainly feel that the world is not a great place these days. A lot of that I find, I feel is down to technology which is kind of ironic for somebody who is involved in 3D printing.

—

Living with Datacatcher number 047

Male: I began using the Datacatcher in the open day offices where I did struggle a little bit to connect, but I did eventually. So there is the local area here which is I guess Shoreditch, Aldwych, is that the local area? And then also over near Shepherds Bush, erm so east and west. A lot of the information was was very interesting definitely, definitely insightful. Erm, a lot of it kind of pointed at very negative things, I found. I wasn't sure if that was a reflection of what was happening, or maybe it was a reflection of what data was being captured. But there was, I found there was quite a lot of things about erm I guess obesity in the area, kind of erm welfare, erm poverty, erm so that that was really eye opening I felt.

Erm, and also kind of seeing people, how that contrasted then with the kind of tweets that were coming in as well which were very, they were very kind of mundane things like queuing for tickets for an event and, it was kind of, the contrast there was quite interesting I think.

One thing I would like to say is that I think a lot of the information as I said was very insightful and made you aware of your surroundings more than I would have been. I think there's definitely a call for people to have broader access to that kind of information, I think.

Erm, so that when they are walking through the neighbourhood they can, instead of just passing down the road and staring at their phone they can actually draw in some information and maybe get more involved in their surroundings, the people who are around them as well, and understand what the challenges and issues are locally and, and how maybe they can be a part of making things look better. That's, that's one thing that did strike me when I was using it.

—

Living with Datacatcher number 050

Male: Well the first thing I liked is it is, like it's very easy. I was a bit surprised actually how simple they'd made it, you know, like there's, there's one button and you just turn it left or right. It's quite a sort of eye catching design and, er, I remember the first few days I took it out and I just sort of start conversations with did you know average house price in this area is er — or there are 300 people who are registered as homeless in this, in this borough.

I think for it to be useful you'd maybe need as an app or you maybe need to be able to request the information.

If you'd asked me where do you think it's got a higher life expectancy, Islington or, you now, Bulwell in Nottingham, I would have told you, I probably would have guessed well I'm gonna guess Islington's got a higher. But I don't think I ever would have guessed like how stark those differences are. Er, and, yeah, I guess that was a main thing I took away from it was walking around different areas in London and seeing quite how stark the differences were, you know, which is the sort of thing you kind of have in the back of your head but it's never is obvious.

—

Living with Datacatcher number 051

Male: I'll point this out 'cause I wouldn't know about this otherwise, the British being very very coy about what they earn and what they own and all the rest of it, but it says here a credit agency describes people around here as bright young things. And what surprised me about this area, also Stratford and Southwark, they're quite young communities. I think it says average age in 2020 in Southwark will be between 25 and 29. In Newham, which is a very young borough, it's gonna be something like 24. So it's a, it's interesting to see how young London is.

Erm, another thing on here that surprises me is how few people claim what we call the state pension. And I start thinking to myself what does that mean, 'cause we're all too young or we don't, or we're, people don't make it. So you start thinking do people don't live long enough to, to claim this benefit depending on where you live in London, I don't know. It's hard to work out. That's the only bit of information I started to think I need to go into this deeper, 'cause I, you know, I'd like to live long enough to get my pension statistically.

—

Living with Datacatcher number 054

Female: Er, I found some really interesting information about where I live, my local area. So we moved there about a year and a half ago, we bought a house, and Eltham doesn't have a great, great reputation so we found out about it just because that was the place where we could afford, and then we decided to do a bit more research around it, and then all this like, it's a racist area and people are racist, you know. All of the sort of, the media stuff started coming up then. But we went and like spent a bit of time there and talked to locals and thought, 'Well everyone's nice so we'll buy a house there.'

But the data, and like I'm I'm I'm sort of quite erm a rigorous researcher when it comes to sort of making decisions. So I did a lot of research initially on like local police data in the area, sort of really researched well before we made the decision of buying.

And, but then when I used Datacatcher in the area it gave me loads of information that I hadn't picked up, or wasn't on my radar although I thought I was being quite thorough. What I was doing was getting these interesting facts and then What'sApping them to my friends. So I was like using both of these at the same time. Or to my husband. I'd say, 'Oh look, I discovered this thing about where we live.'

So I can share with you some of the things. Erm, bird droppings is a local issue so then that was hilarious because on my way to the station there's like a little tunnel that we pass through and then some of the pigeons just use that tunnel for shelter. And there's always bird droppings, and every time I pick up the local newspaper some resident has complained to the council about bird droppings. So it was hilarious that even Datacatcher picked that up.

But overall I think erm what I found really interesting was that it's a great way of like quickly scoping out an area. So as part of the work that I do, like we often do projects in lots of different areas and have to quickly get a sense of what the local community is like, and I felt like that's a brilliant tool to use as a research tool. So if they're thinking of buying a property or even a fronting in a new area that they're not aware of, this is just a quick way of really getting a sense of of what that area's like.

So I thought that was really interesting.

—

Living with Datacatcher number 063

Female: Some were here previous it said the dogs are family dogs, no, I shouldn't think so. Family dogs, no, I don't think so, not, not in Deptford.

They would be in Battersea that's the difference. There are a lot of family dogs and dogs dressed in — and in Greenwich, 'cause we got a dog too.

There are six post offices within a mile of this

location. No, I wouldn't think that's correct.

I found some of the questions extraordinarily strange but I gather they, they were tongue in cheek anyway. Some of the things about the dogs and the cats, but in different areas there were different response, but they were just funny questions some of them, really quirky questions. And I couldn't understand why you wanted the answers to those, but it's, it's not factual it's only surmise, isn't it. It's what you think, it's your, your view of air pollution or whether it's a cat area or a dog area. It's a personal view. It's not a factual view. So I can't see what value it will be in that.

—

Living with Datacatcher number 064

Female: I mainly used it er in Shoreditch where I was working. So I would bring it in with me every day. Er, but I live in Brighton and so I tried to use it in Brighton and it didn't work unfortunately.

The main thing I did with the Datacatcher was answer the questions er because they were just really funny, some of the questions. Like, 'What are the dogs like in your area?' and then there was like answers like you know, 'Handbag,' and kind of really random things.

Erm so mostly in terms of interacting with it I used it to actually answer questions. Once I'd seen some of the information for the area I was using it in, erm like I said I found the stuff to do with erm like businesses and prosperity, economics and everything, interesting but I also found that when I used it I got quite a lot of the same information over and over again. I found it hard to get new information.

But yeah, I think the questions were the most interesting thing, and then looking at what the answers were versus what you thought the answers were on some of them where you could do that. Er I thought that was, that was most er kind of exciting because it was kind of like quizzing yourself about your knowledge. Erm, and yeah, I thought that was interesting.

—

Living with Datacatcher number 065

Female: ...at the Future Laboratory, erm which is a trend forecasting and consumer insight erm and innovation agency. We've also been looking at the idea of how humans are now very much interacting in a different way with technology than previous erm generations, and we're kind of seeing that as a new era.

So for me it was sort of an experiment erm for, with myself to see how I personally interact with erm data. There were certain patterns in my behaviour and I think using the Datacatcher made me realise that. So I erm particularly was interested in when I was at work how I interacted with it. So it would be every so often erm having a look and having this kind of almost it became an erm, a moment of stopping in the day to interact with my surroundings beyond the office, which was quite interesting. Almost like a break in my day.

It was a good way of sharing information. So whilst it's quite a personal journey when you kind of, it's, you're taking it around with you, you're, you're checking in with the erm device. 'Households within a stone's throw of here are made up of,' I missed that one. 18 metres above sea level we are here.

But it was quite an interesting way to get other people to erm to also engage with the area. So almost like creating like kind of people erm centred around a community because you start discussing the facts and you also then, almost it brings you to bigger issues in the area that normally in your day to day life you are not really brought to the attention of.

—

Living with Datacatcher number 066

Male: I found it quite amusing kind of like thinking the difference between my own area and where I work for some of these questions.

You know, like what are the dogs like here? And I think, so in my, you know one of the options is like, 'Handbag.' So I work in Regent Street, they are definitely like a handbag. But then I kind of thought they are quite like weapons where where I live, you know? You get a lot of kind of like Staffies and stuff, you know, fighting dogs and stuff like that. So, erm.

So there was a big contrast between where I work and where I live and I, I kind of knew that anyway but it was kind of interesting to see it in the statistics. So I'm looking here where I live, four to five bed house across, £570,000 to buy. But obviously like you know, average house price was something like two and a half million quid or three million quid or something.

You've bought your house and you've got a mortgage, you're always like a bit nosey about other people's areas, do you know what I mean? So it's like you know, 'House prices are lower here than somewhere else,' and you're like, 'Oh yeah, they are, yeah,' and then you know?

So it is, that comparison thing is quite interesting. I guess I would, the only thing about the questions bit is there's kind of like, there's no real feedback. You know, once you've you've entered your question, you know? It would be kind of like, and I'm not sure exactly what feedback I would expect, but er even like I say, even at at a elementary sort of thing, like, 'Thanks for,' you know, 'We've got your, we've got your answer.'

Erm, I mean my wife, she thought it was like some sort of microphone or something for like recording music. She had no idea what it was. I don't think she does either, I've just never got round to explaining to her what it is. She's just like, 'What's that weird green thing in the bedroom?' and I was like, 'I'll tell you another time.' She, she still thinks it's like a sort of mic or something like that.

—

Living with Datacatcher number 067

Male: I found it really informative. Erm, after about the second day or third day I was using it it was, it was starting to collect tweets. So erm you know, they were coming up about somebody in this area has tweeted about — so it was collecting all that stuff, you know?

I went to London Bridge with it and then it was telling me all about that, although the reception got a bit fuzzy here and there but you know, with the, what with the buildings and what have you, but it was still giving me lots of stuff about that; what are the dogs like around there?

And I said, well I did the survey and I said, 'Well basically around, around here it's er,' in this particular area it's all you know, I saw the one that came up in the options about dogs, 'Are they a weapon?' and I thought, 'Yeah, probably around here they are.' And then they were more like handbag dogs where I was.

And then definitely, I also took it to Essex er one day where it was er giving me all the information about the local area and I was, did a little survey while I was there. Er, I know obviously it's a prototype so it's obviously a bit er, and er I was on the train coming back and people were looking at me wondering why I was reading a torch.

They all just thought I was like, they probably thought, 'You do get them,' so.

—

Living with Datacatcher number 068

Male: I have had a Datacatcher for about two weeks, but only really started using it er five days ago. You know, because it's bright and flashy, it's er, it takes a little bit of getting used to carrying it in public for, for instance.

We we mentioned some other people have had this remark as well but erm it, it pushes a lot of questions, and sometimes the questions are, are very, are very funny or interesting. So sometimes I would turn to my neighbour and say like, or my friend, someone I know, erm like, 'What do you think about this question? Like, what do you think the revolution will be like in this area?'

Erm, so it was interesting. Some questions were irrelevant, some sometimes were more far-fetched, but overall I think all the questions were sort of thought provoking. So that was interesting.

—

Living with Datacatcher number 074

Male: While I'm watching my computer I just occasionally look down and see you know, if my mind's distracted for five minutes then I'll just turn round and have a look at what's going on, you know? What's the comment on the screen?

I can't see any point in the questions. I mean they're, the erm, I'm not sure what they're there for.

What I would like is probably to use it in a commercial sense where I have it in my reception area at work. Years ago I was at a restaurant in Brixton and they had these little holes cut in the wall where you had a little TV monitor with something going on, and it was just kind of funky just to see something going on with a little, even if it's a sort of Star Trek going on or some strange video. It was just a visual thing that worked out which was quite nice.

You know, I would, I would probably, if if I was going to have this thing it would be quite nice to have it set into something in the wall so people could just go and see something and see what, and be interested in what's changing over, you know? The different things that are coming up.

—

Living with Datacatcher number 080

Female: Erm, first of all I felt I couldn't work out how to work it. Cause I thought everything, everything that came up on this screen I could answer. And then I realised that it's only local data, data, whichever way you want to say it, is all you can answer on it.

And I doubt whether I'll ever go to somewhere like Sloane Square where I could answer that the dogs were 'Handbag.' So I thought the questions were quite narrow, and I, I got a bit annoyed that I couldn't put what I would answer to the question, because I took it to Canary Wharf and all sorts of places.

I'd be very, I'm very happy fiddling with stuff like that, it's very simple for me. So I'm not sure that I did learn that much about, except that I learned who Farrow & Ball are, the new Osborne & Little people. And their paint seemed to be very bland when I looked it up on the website. Beige I suppose, that's the beige people that you're calling.

And I suppose if I was ever to answer brutal to something I'd have to be up north in an industrial town for really brutal. So I'm not sure who set the answers. That was a problem.

—

Living with Datacatcher number 084

Female: Yeah, it was really cool at first. I was like checking through and finding some facts out about Hackney, but some which I thought were maybe quite incorrect. Like it said the house prices around here were really low. I was like, 'Definitely not.' Erm, so that was a bit frustrating because I was like, 'Well I don't know where they're getting their data from but it must be really old.'

Erm and then I took it to work, erm and showed some people there. They were really interested. Erm but kind of after, after, even in different boroughs erm it started coming up with the same information so I was a bit like, 'Erm, is everyone just talking about their dogs in the same way in London?' That seemed to be a common question that came up about what people were talking about their dogs.

The next one just said, 'The government says that 1,720 people in Hackney have never worked.' Well like, well what is the population of Hackney? Like, you know, is that normal? I just, yeah. Kind of, if that, if that got into the wrong hands, like they could start, you know, like really kind of making people politicised around kind of certain issues that maybe aren't very correct.

Yeah, I enjoyed using it but I kind of got frustrated that I wasn't able to input what I thought about things. So when it was kind of talking about what people had said I wanted to kind of disagree or agree or kind of say something different, and you know, used to be able to doing that in the kind of modern world where it's more participatory and it was kind of a bit frustrating to have something where there was like no other buttons or no other kind of like ways that I could actually kind of tell it what I thought.

—

Living with Datacatcher number 086

Male: Erm I think my overall reflection is that at first, when I first received the device and I saw what it did, I thought the questions were quite funny. Erm, you know, quite memorable questions with funny answers. Erm, and they were quite good answers actually I thought, quite clever, and I would be interested to see the sort of response different Datacatchers have, have provided in all those like funny questions.

But erm the, the questions didn't seem to change. And also, if I was asked to do something where it was more obvious why information was useful, then maybe I'd be more inclined to like, I'd feel like I was providing a service that was useful. But I'm not quite sure how useful knowing whether dogs are like handbags or, although it's quite funny

I'm not sure, it didn't really push me to take the, take this, this device and find other places to go and like investigate the answer to the question.

—

Living with Datacatcher number 087

Male: Erm, at the beginning I was a bit, how can I say? Not suspicious but I didn't know if I liked it really because I, I felt like er I was getting too many information, too much information from it.

That was a, was like for me, it was an opportunity to reflect on how many information we are exposed to on a daily basis and er a couple of times I had it with me er during my commute in the morning on the Bakerloo Line, and er well a lot of people were looking at it and thinking, 'What is that?' I'm sure someone in the control room of the Bakerloo Line caught me on CCTV and was wondering, 'What is that?'

This puts you in a more active position with, with other people and er yeah, because we have to tell them what it is about and er yeah. And it's not on your phone so it's another device. I mean, in order to interact with it you have to have it with you.

—

Living with Datacatcher number 090

Female: I thought it's been interesting how it's been worded. Like sometimes there's like it doesn't quite make sense and it's quite funny. I think it's like problems within your area and it's, they're in little like speech things. And it would be like rubbish, and it would just say, 'Rubbish' in quotes, and it's stuff like that that I thought was really, it's almost funny.

I don't know whether it's informative but erm, 'Is this a cat or dog area?' and like an answer can be, 'Horse.' Things like that I thought were fun.

And yeah, I think what I've enjoyed the most are kind of the, the human kind of side to it, where it's like meant to be like this machine that just like pumps out information to you. It's kind of what, the intricacies in where it's kind of not quite right is where I've kind of liked using it the most.

—

Living with Datacatcher number 091

Female: Because [...] he does text a lot to the girls around you know? Everyone comes, because sometimes I'm bored you know? So everyone needs something to do as well, you know? Let's say that.

Male: But then you can use it in a wider scale.

Interviewer: What was the main thing that you found interesting do you think, from that time you-?

Male: They tell you interesting facts.

Interviewer: You used it.

Male: It tells you what, about [...].

Female: Stuff like this because we go to museums. It's like some information about the area makes our, you know, travelling around London really interesting, if you know what I mean.

Male: We was walking up by, where [...] is, and it was telling us there are three museums in the area.

Female: We didn't even know that Bermondsey has got five museums, so—

Male: And we didn't know. That was a good thing to know.

—

Living with Datacatcher number 101

Male: The, the person who passed it to me I opened the, in front of him and it, 'cause I was really excited and I want to show him, show him this really weird thing. And we turned it on and we were completely mesmerised. We sat there for like maybe 15 minutes and I was surprise that it was, it was very, highly look like hyper located. So I was at university it told me it's connected to the King's Cross Granary Square Tower and it was exactly where I was sitting.

So it was a bit, er, unsettling in a way that it was so specific and accurate to me.

I was, I would be sitting here and I was looking and it would say something like people, people have x amount of income, 5% of this area are pensioners and stuff like that. And I felt like, so I have this information and others don't have this information, so I feel like, like I am at a higher, you know, level of wisdom than, than others. And I would go to my friends erm, 'Guys, do you know that, blah blah, blah.' They're like, 'What, ah that's why this is this and that.'

So yeah, that was really, really interesting.

I think what's missing is the ability to judge the validity of the information. Like I think what's very misleading about datas is how you judge data and how you use data because it's, from my experience it's it can be incredibly misleading and it could really, like, actually make you believe things are completely wrong.

—

Living with Datacatcher number 102

Male: Absolutely everyone who saw it was completely intrigued by the design, the shape of it and stuff. Everyone commented on it and it is a really beautiful design, I mean the colours and stuff. I saw a picture of all the different colours lined up, and didn't realise that they weren't all blue and things.

Erm, you can't really quite put it in your pocket. I was looking at my coat over there, I've got like reasonable sized pockets but erm, I was kind of careful not to get it really cold or wet as well, it was you know the end of December.

Erm, I think if it was like, if it was just that screen and it was, looked like one of those old fashioned sort of pager type things, then you would totally just have it in any pocket. But I did erm kind of answer the poll questions each time I took it to a new place, and very occasionally I would sort of get a bit of collected data from other people. So it would say like, 'Other people in this area believe that,' I don't know, one of the things that, find the questions.

Bags of sand, that's my road. 'Bags of sand dumped on [Pellet Road] is a local issue,' and it's true. Down by the Post Office at the end there was like erm, there was loads of kind of junk on the pavement for about six months; it's just been cleared away a couple of weeks before Christmas.

—

Living with Datacatcher number 104

Male: Two, three, four, five, six, seven, eight, nine, ten, eleven, twelve, can you hear me? Mic test, mic test.

I don't know basically what the actual device would be used for. Er, its idea of giving you information on location where you go was really interesting because there was places that I went to that I didn't know certain things actually occurred.

Scrolling through it was in- was interesting and erm, maybe a colour screen would be nice because that would make it easier to obviously appreciate.

Interviewer: Cool. Er you, you mentioned earlier er like that you were really into sort of David Icke's stuff.

Male: Yeah.

Interviewer: Er and can you, can you tell me a bit more about what you said earlier about how the device sort of er, you know, relates to that in a way?

Male: Yeah, well this is it. I mean the device is good, it's a nice innovative idea to see different forms of information wherever they, wherever you're actually travelling around in the London area.

As you said, I'm a David Icke fan so I don't know what the final agenda is going to be, but collecting the information I was fascinated because I wouldn't have known that information.

I can see you.

—

Living with Datacatcher number 105

Male: It's been very interesting carrying it for the last three months. However, I have found it a little bit like a mobile phone. You always forget to charge the goddam thing before you go out.

Yeah I, I thought about it and I thought it might be more productive to have it on er an application, you know, an app for your mobile phone and android, android phones. Er people could download it, it would save you the cost of producing one of these, and I'm sure people would be more likely to carry it and have it running on their mobile phone.

I've used it around London erm mainly in Islington area. However I did travel up to Liverpool erm and along the way I stopped in Warwickshire and different areas and the difference in data that it gave me was quite interesting. Er Liverpool I would say is er one of the poorer cities in the country, erm and as it shows from the data it has collected, I got up there, I asked the locals for the questions, 'What are the dogs like around here?' In Islington they're more handbag, in Liverpool they're more pit-bull, pit-bull and tattoos.

So yeah, it was, yeah, interesting. I'd like to see other kind of data on it. Erm, more financial data like what the councils are spending their money on, erm more, more data on, the councils are accountable to the public, erm, who checks their statistics? You know, we can all pull a number, all the politicians are very good at pulling numbers out the air when it suits them.

So you know, where does this data actually come from? Is it just somebody sat in an office going click, click, click, 'We'll put this in for the data release'? You know, where's the evidence to back up this data?

But yeah, I'm lost for words now. What else would you like to know?

—

Living with Datacatcher number 109

Male 1: I found it a bit, a bit, erm, a bit awkward 'cause like the first thing you felt like when you take the object is pointing at, at something, even though like you're actually meant to, to look at the screen. So it was a bit, erm, the first interaction was a bit weird.

But it always tells me like we're on the 24th of January and we are in Covent Garden which is not really, really the case. And I haven't really been to Covent Garden so, so I'm a bit confused. Erm, I wasn't too sure if that, that was me in particular, but like on the bottom of the screen below the data you have like a location and date and the time, which for me has never really been right, but, erm, always got the, the same things. Always like Covent Garden, so, erm, it's, yeah, it's a bit of a shame I guess.

—

Living with Datacatcher number 110

Female: The first thing I did with it was take it out of the house, because it just seemed a bit pointless sitting around here going, 'Oh.' I'm interested in my local area obviously, but I know about this area quite a bit, because I live here. Or at least I think I'd know the things I know.

Erm, so that was really the more interesting thing, to kind of take it out on the bus around and take it to work and compare what's my home like with where I work and that kind of thing.

I took it to my parents over Christmas. They live on the Isle of Wight which was another great place I thought to go and try out and see what it says about this area. It kept talking about potholes on the Isle of Wight which, again, we know that the Isle of Wight is a really terrible, has a really terrible problem with potholes.

Because literally I was in the car, like we were driving around looking at, 'Oh what does it say about where we're going, this area that we're going through?' And er it would say er, 'Large dangerous pothole has been described as a big issue in this local area.' Dunk, as we go over, I was like, 'Oh, okay, well yeah.'

If it had some way of reporting that kind of thing, that would have made me use it more in that way, I think. Erm, yeah, because you could just go like, 'Pothole.' You know? And use the little, or something like that.

—

Living with Datacatcher number 111

Male: Unfortunately I didn't get to move around very much because I'm not the kind of person that moves around very much. Erm, my two jobs are around the corner from here. I say, this is one job and then I work at the University of London, and then I live in Hackney. So the Datacatcher is going to show those three areas only.

But I got to read quite a bit about what there was in these areas and then I was asked questions that I couldn't fully see the relevance of, but that doesn't mean that they're not relevant to the person doing this project.

I guess the least we know about the expected results of the project, the more honest our answers will be, otherwise we could be seen as manipulating the data in favour or against the expected results of the project. If I let my curiosity take the best part of me, I would have tried to find out what was this aimed for. I didn't, and I just answered the questions erm the best I could.

—

Living with Datacatcher number 113

Female: So erm I've been using the Datacatcher for about a week now. Erm, I was introduced to the interaction research studio recently and erm I started collaborating with them, so I wanted to find out about the device that I was working with.

When you experience the device for a few days you realise that it's not about keeping an eye constantly but more about erm having a look every now and then.

And carrying it around with you is quite important because er certainly when I went out of London I had a very different experience from my erm locations. I think it has made me reflect a bit about the areas in which I move around, and especially the kind of people that live in my surroundings as well.

I I think it's something that I would use every now and then, because I think when it becomes interesting is when you travel. So when you go, for example if I was looking for a house it would be something really good to use. To sort of like bring to other places, like it tells you things like the schools, erm or the, the amount of erm train stations or kind of like it gives you a sense of the location. But it's, I'm not sure if it would be something I would use daily for a really long term.

—

Living with Datacatcher number 114

Male: Hi. I'm Robin, erm I was part of the Datacatcher development team over the summer of 2014. Erm, I took the Datacatcher home with me for Christmas erm which led to me looking at all the messages from where I grew up and it sparked really interesting conversations between me and my family about where I erm grew up in Chester compared to where I live now in New Cross.

Erm, also the messages about sort of demographic and happiness, er where I grew up in the North West it had a very high level of happiness which is great, made me think of having a nice childhood, that sort of thing, really challenged my notions of demographic and sort of like culture in different areas which was really, really interesting.

Another little anecdote was erm I reported through erm FixMyStreet.com which is one of the data sources for the Datacatcher erm reporting that at the bottom of my road there is a erm phone box that had been smashed up and there was glass everywhere. And erm there's a primary school at the top of our road so there were all these school kids walking past the glass.

So I reported it on the website and then the er message actually came up on the Datacatcher and then it was fixed at the end of the month, so that was really interesting to see.

—

Living with Datacatcher number 118

Female 1: I used it like the first couple of days but then I forgot about it a bit. I suppose they're like pretty dry facts isn't it, like, erm, percentages of people being over and under that age or people have diseases and how long they live for, stuff like that. I don't really, they don't really stick in my head, so I can't really remember any of them but they're like, they're nice to read on the tube.

I don't think, I mean I went to Stratford for a swim not to find out what the population there is like, so it wasn't really relevant to me then. So, erm, I use it more like a fun thing and not really as a serious fact thingy to give me facts about a place.

Hmm, I mean you could use Google easily enough if you want facts about an area 'cause then you get the facts when you need them as well, 'cause I'm, I'm, I can't really take facts in unless I actually need them on the spot. So, erm, if I needed the facts then it would be useful definitely, but I just didn't when I was looking at it, sorry.

These transcripts are taken from videos that can be viewed at: http://vimeo.com/channels/datacatcher